Taste of Home

KITCHEN HACKS

AND RECIPES
THAT GO WITH THEM

TASTE OF HOME BOOKS • RDA ENTHUSIAST BRANDS, LLC • MILWAUKEE, WI

International Standard Book Number:
978-1-61765-839-6

LOCC: 2019931316

Deputy Editor: Mark Hagen
Senior Art Director: Raeann Thompson
Editor: Christine Rukavena
Designer: Arielle Jardine
Copy Editor: Amy Rabideau Silvers
Editorial Intern: Salam Fatayer
Cover Photography: Taste of Home Photo Studio

Printed in China
3 5 7 9 10 8 6 4 2

AT-A-GLANCE ICONS

Icons throughout the book indicate
freezer-friendly, slow-cooked and
good-for-you fare.

P. 47

P. 234

P. 181

(CONTENTS)

MORE WAYS TO CONNECT WITH US:

THE SMARTEST KITCHEN TRICKS
OUR BEST RECIPES & EXPERT SECRETS!

For the first time, the team at *Taste of Home* assembled the best timesaving hacks, tips and how-to's into one terrific book!

Inside, our Test Kitchen pros share tricks of the trade you simply won't believe. Learn how to save time in the kitchen, cut costs at the grocery store and entertain with ease. Enjoy light-bulb ideas for organizing your kitchen, going green and creating economical household cleaners you'll wonder how you ever lived without.

The secrets to preparing hearty in-a-hurry breakfasts, change-of-pace lunches and impressive desserts that come together in a pinch are all at your fingertips. It's never been so simple to eat seasonally, cook healthfully, and set delicious meals on the table fast.

In fact, you'll find 222 recipes that use the hacks and techniques found here. Not only will you discover new ways to cook—you'll likely start adding your own creative twists to family favorites.

So what are you waiting for? Get ready to cook like a boss with incredible timesavers, mouthwatering recipes and smart how-to's. It's easy with *Taste of Home Kitchen Hacks!*

P. 95

P. 238

P. 24

P. 177

P. 248

HOMEMADE
GUACAMOLE, P. 17

GENIUS SNACK
& PARTY HACKS

[Great hosts make it look so easy...and you can, too, with these quick tricks for simple snacks, drinks and appetizers. Let the good times roll.]

Snackers

These crispy, chewy treats are our favorite travel snack. I always make a double batch so we have some left when we reach our destination.
—*W. H. Gregory, Roanoke, VA*

- -

Takes: 20 min.
Makes: about 1½ dozen

3	cups Crispix cereal
½	cup salted peanuts
⅓	cup packed brown sugar
⅓	cup corn syrup
¼	cup peanut butter

1. In a large bowl, combine cereal and peanuts; set aside.

2. In a microwave, heat brown sugar and corn syrup for 30-60 seconds or until sugar is dissolved, stirring occasionally. Stir in peanut butter. Pour over the cereal mixture; toss to coat. Drop by rounded tablespoonfuls onto waxed paper.

2 pieces: 190 cal., 8g fat (1g sat. fat), 0 chol., 156mg sod., 28g carb. (16g sugars, 1g fiber), 5g pro.

HACK

To make natural or homemade peanut butter super easy to mix, just store the jar upside-down. Flip the jar right side up and the oil, which will have settled to the "bottom" of the jar, will rise back to the top, making it easier to incorporate.

Apple Cartwheels

Stuff apples with a yummy filling, then slice the fruit into rings to make eye-appealing after-school snacks. The filling is an irresistible combination of creamy peanut butter, sweet honey, miniature chocolate chips and raisins.
—*Miriam Miller, Thorp, WI*

- -

Prep: 20 min. + chilling
Makes: about 2 dozen

¼	cup peanut butter
1½	tsp. honey
½	cup miniature semisweet chocolate chips
2	Tbsp. raisins
4	medium unpeeled Red Delicious apples, cored

In a small bowl, combine peanut butter and honey; fold in chocolate chips and raisins. Fill hollow centers of apples with peanut butter mixture; refrigerate for at least 1 hour. Cut into ¼-in. rings.

1 piece: 50 calories, 3g fat (1g saturated fat), 0 cholesterol, 13mg sodium, 7g carbohydrate (6g sugars, 1g fiber), 1g protein.

HOMEMADE PEANUT BUTTER

Homemade Peanut Butter

By making my own peanut butter, I know exactly what goes into it— and it's a whole lot tastier!
—*Marge Austin, North Pole, AK*

- -

Takes: 15 min. • **Makes:** About 1 cup

- 2 **cups unsalted dry roasted peanuts**
- ½ **tsp. salt**
- 1 **Tbsp. honey**

Process nuts and salt in food processor until desired consistency, about 5 minutes, scraping sides as needed. Blend in honey. Refrigerate.

1 Tbsp.: 111 cal., 9g fat (1g sat. fat), 0 chol., 75mg sodium, 5g carb. (2g sugars, 2g fiber), 4g pro. **Diabetic exchanges:** 2 fat.

A Little Indulgence

Reach for the immersion blender when you need to whip up a small amount of cream. It's handy that you can whip it right in a tumbler or measuring cup.

CREAMY IRISH COFFEE

Creamy Irish Coffee

My maternal grandmother seldom drank more than a single glass of champagne at Christmas, but she couldn't resist my Creamy Irish Coffee.

—Rebecca Little, Park Ridge, IL

Takes: 10 min. • **Makes:** 4 servings

> 3 cups hot strong brewed coffee
> 4 oz. Irish cream liqueur
> Sweetened whipped cream and chocolate shavings, optional

Divide coffee and liqueur among 4 mugs; stir. If desired, top with sweetened whipped cream and chocolate shavings.

¾ cup: 118 cal., 4g fat (0 sat. fat), 0 chol., 1mg sod., 8g carb. (6g sugars, 0 fiber), 0 pro.

Heavenly Drinking Chocolate

The name says it all—sipping this beverage is like experiencing an out-of-this-world blend of dark and milk chocolate. The only thing to make it better? A dollop of whipped cream on top.

—Taste of Home Test Kitchen

Takes: 20 min. • **Makes:** 5 cups

> 4 cups half-and-half cream
> 2 bars (3½ oz. each) 70% cacao dark chocolate, chopped
> 2 oz. milk chocolate, chopped
> 1 tsp. vanilla extract
> ¼ tsp. ground nutmeg
> Dash salt
> Sweetened whipped cream

In a large saucepan, heat cream over medium heat until bubbles form around sides of pan (do not boil). Remove from the heat; whisk in the chocolates, vanilla, nutmeg and salt until smooth. Return to the heat; cook and stir until heated through. Pour into mugs; top with whipped cream.

1 cup: 489 cal., 35g fat (23g sat. fat), 105mg chol., 130mg sod., 37g carb. (33g sugars, 4g fiber), 9g pro.

Homemade Flavored Whipped Cream

What better way to chase away chills on a cold winter day than with a steamy drink? Your favorite cocoa or coffee tastes even better topped with a gourmet whipped cream.

Peppermint Kiss Cream

Beat ½ heavy whipping cream until it begins to thicken. Add 1 Tbsp. sugar and ⅛ tsp. peppermint extract; beat until cream forms stiff peaks. Garnish drinks with crushed peppermint candies. Makes: 1 cup.

Irish Whipped Cream

Beat ½ heavy whipping cream and 1 Tbsp. Irish cream liqueur until stiff peaks form. Makes: 1 cup.

Chocolate Cream

Beat ½ cup heavy whipping cream until it begins to thicken. Add 2 Tbsp. chocolate syrup; beat until stiff peaks form. Garnish drinks with grated chocolate if desired. Makes: 1 cup.

Sparkling Summer Champagne

Sipping this drink reminds me of sitting on the back porch in summer and enjoying a good conversation with friends. I use tonic water to make a nonalcoholic version.
—*Corey Carbery, Mokena, IL*

Takes: 10 min. • **Makes:** 4 servings

- 1 medium lemon, cut into wedges
- 1 bottle (750 ml) champagne or other sparkling wine, chilled
- ½ cup thawed orange juice concentrate

Squeeze the juice from the lemon into a small pitcher; drop lemon into pitcher. Stir in champagne and orange juice concentrate.
1 cup: 187 cal., 0 fat (0 sat. fat), 0 chol., 2mg sod., 17g carb. (14g sugars, 1g fiber), 1g pro.

HACK

Quick-Chill Wine

The fastest way to chill a bottle of wine is to immerse it in ice water with a small handful of salt. Turn the bottle periodically. It'll be ready in about 20 minutes!

Autumn Fizz

Champagne infuses sweet apple brandy with fun fizz in this celebratory fall cocktail. It adds a special feel to get-togethers when the weather turns crisp. Or swap the apple juice for first-of-the-season apple cider.
—Taste of Home *Test Kitchen*

Takes: 5 min. • **Makes:** 1 serving

- ½ oz. apple brandy
- 1 tsp. sugar
- 1 mint sprig
- 2 oz. unsweetened apple juice, chilled
- 2 oz. champagne or other sparkling wine, chilled

Place the brandy, sugar and mint in a champagne flute or wine glass; gently crush mint with a small spoon. Add apple juice and champagne.
1 serving: 116 cal., 0 fat (0 sat. fat), 0 chol., 2mg sod., 12g carb. (10g sugars, 0 fiber), 0 pro.

Sparkling Pom-Berry Splash

Add a splash of color to cocktail hour with this lovely red beverage. Lime slices and blueberries make pretty garnishes.
—*Shirley Warren, Thiensville, WI*

Takes: 5 min. • **Makes:** 1 serving

- 2 oz. pomegranate blueberry juice, chilled
- 1 tsp. lime juice
- ⅓ cup sparkling moscato wine, chilled

Pour pomegranate blueberry and lime juices into a champagne flute; top with wine.
1 serving: 92 cal., 0 fat (0 sat. fat), 0 chol., 11mg sod., 10g carb. (9g sugars, 0 fiber), 0 pro.

Poinsettia

Mixing festive red cranberry juice, Triple Sec and champagne creates the perfect cocktail for Christmas parties, a New Year's Eve bash or any gathering during the winter season. Garnish with a few fresh berries and enjoy.
—Taste of Home *Test Kitchen*

Takes: 5 min. • **Makes:** 1 serving

- 1 oz. cranberry juice
- ½ oz. Triple Sec, optional
- 4 oz. chilled champagne or other sparkling wine

GARNISH
- 3 fresh cranberries

Pour cranberry juice into a champagne flute or wine glass. Add Triple Sec if desired. Top with champagne. Garnish as desired.
Note: To make a batch of Poinsettias (6 servings), slowly pour 1 bottle (750 ml) chilled champagne into a pitcher. Stir in ¾ cup cranberry juice and 3 oz. Triple Sec if desired.
1 serving: 95 cal., 0 fat (0 sat. fat), 0 chol., 7mg sod., 5g carb. (4g sugars, 0 fiber), 0 pro.

SPARKLING POM-BERRY SPLASH

POINSETTIA

Lemon Mint Cooler

Here's a fizzy refresher that blends lemon sherbet, cool mint and ginger ale. It's sure to hit the spot on a hot afternoon.

—*Chavelyin Marie Karlovich, Monroe, CT*

- -

Takes: 15 min. • **Makes:** about 5 cups

- 2¼ cups water
- ½ cup coarsely chopped fresh mint
- ½ cup lemon juice
- 2 medium lemons, sliced
- ½ cup lemon sherbet, softened
- 1 liter ginger ale, chilled

For mint ice cubes, combine water, mint and lemon juice; pour into 2 ice cube trays. Freeze until set. In a pitcher, combine the lemons and sherbet; slowly stir in ginger ale. Add the mint ice cubes.

1 cup: 104 cal., 0 fat (0 sat. fat), 1mg chol., 24mg sod., 27g carb. (23g sugars, 1g fiber), 0 pro.

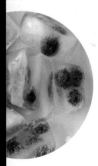

Sipping Pretty

Add colorful ice cubes to make extra-special summery drinks. Just fill an ice cube tray with water and pop in fresh herbs, citrus or berries, and then freeze.

Herbs:
Basil, mint, lavender

Citrus:
Lemon, lime, orange

Berries:
Strawberries, blueberries, raspberries

Rubies on Ice

Ginger and pomegranate are made for each other, and the color of this beverage is tantalizing. If you're looking for a nonalcoholic option, you can easily leave out the vodka for a delicious and festive drink!

—*Tara Deshpande, New York, NY*

- -

Prep: 15 min. + freezing
Makes: 4 servings

- 6 Tbsp. pomegranate seeds
- ½ cup vodka
- 4 Tbsp. pomegranate molasses
- 3 Tbsp. sweetened ginger syrup
- 2 Tbsp. lime juice
- 1 cinnamon stick (3 in.)
  Club soda, chilled
- 1 to 4 tsp. pomegranate seeds, optional
  Lime slices, optional

1. Scatter pomegranate seeds over an ice cube tray, about 1 tsp. per cube; fill with water and freeze.
2. Combine vodka, molasses, ginger syrup, lime juice and the cinnamon stick. Let mixture steep 15 minutes. Strain; discard cinnamon stick. Place 4 pomegranate ice cubes in each of 4 tall glasses. Pour molasses mixture evenly into glasses; top off with chilled club soda. Stir well. Garnish with additional pomegranate seeds and lime, if desired.

½ cup: 148 cal., 0 fat (0 sat. fat), 0 chol., 3mg sod., 21g carb. (17g sugars, 0 fiber), 0 pro.

RUBIES
ON ICE

PRO TIPS

• Monin makes a
ginger-flavored syrup.
Look for it near the
coffee syrups.

• Or make your own by
combining 1 cup sugar,
½ cup water and sliced
peeled fresh ginger (a 2-in.
piece). Bring to a boil. Cool
completely, then strain out
solids. Refrigerate up
to 2 weeks.

GARDEN-FRESH SHRIMP &
AVOCADO NACHOS

Garden-Fresh Shrimp & Avocado Nachos

Since I'm such a fan of shrimp and my family loves nachos, I combined my fresh-from-the-garden ingredients with shrimp and avocado for a cool yet satisfying take on the party snack.
—*Teri Rasey, Cadillac, MI*

Prep: 30 min. + chilling
Makes: 10 servings

- 4 plum tomatoes, chopped
- 3 tomatillos, husks removed and chopped
- 4 jalapeno peppers, seeded and finely chopped
- 1 small onion, chopped
- 2 garlic cloves, minced
- ¼ cup minced fresh cilantro
- 3 Tbsp. olive oil
- 2 Tbsp. seasoned rice vinegar
- 1 Tbsp. lime juice
- 1½ tsp. sea salt
- ½ tsp. dried oregano
- 1 lb. peeled and deveined cooked shrimp, chopped

TOPPING
- 2 medium ripe avocados, peeled and pitted, divided
- ½ cup sour cream
- 2 Tbsp. lime juice
- 8 cups tortilla chips
- 1 cup shredded lettuce

1. In a large bowl, combine the first 11 ingredients. Cover and refrigerate until chilled, at least 30 minutes. Stir in shrimp.

2. To make avocado cream, mash 1 avocado with sour cream and 1 Tbsp. lime juice until smooth. Cube remaining avocado and toss with remaining lime juice.

3. To serve, arrange chips on a large platter. Top with shrimp mixture, cubed avocado, lettuce and avocado cream. Serve immediately.

1 serving: 264 cal., 16g fat (3g sat. fat), 72mg chol., 542mg sod., 20g carb. (3g sugars, 3g fiber), 12g pro.

HACK

PDQ Avocados

- When life hands you hard, less-than-ripe avocados, here's how to ripen them ASAP. Place avocados in a paper bag with an apple or banana. Poke the bag a few times with a toothpick or scissors, and let ripen at room temperature for a day or two. The more fruits (and ethylene gas they give off), the faster the results.

- Once cut, place avocado in a container with a few pieces of raw onion, and seal. The sulfur fumes from the onions helps stop any discoloration.

Homemade Guacamole

Nothing is better than fresh guacamole when you're eating something spicy. It's easy to whip together in a matter of minutes, and it quickly tames anything that's too hot.
—*Joan Hallford, North Richland Hills, TX*

Takes: 10 min. • **Makes:** 2 cups

- 3 medium ripe avocados, peeled and cubed
- 1 garlic clove, minced
- ¼ to ½ tsp. salt
- 2 medium tomatoes, seeded and chopped, optional
- 1 small onion, finely chopped
- ¼ cup mayonnaise, optional
- 1 to 2 Tbsp. lime juice
- 1 Tbsp. minced fresh cilantro

Mash avocados with garlic and salt. Stir in remaining ingredients.

¼ cup: 90 cal., 8g fat (1g sat. fat), 0 chol., 78mg sod., 6g carb. (1g sugars, 4g fiber), 1g pro. **Diabetic exchanges:** 1½ fat.

HACK

Keep-It-Green Guacamole

Yes, you can mash that guac ahead. To keep the dip nice and green, just cover it with a little layer of water to banish browning. Here's how:

- In an airtight container, use a spoon to flatten the surface of the guacamole and remove any air pockets.

- Slowly pour in about ½ in. water to cover the surface, using the spoon to gently disperse the water.

- Refrigerate, covered, up to two days. To serve, carefully pour off water. Stir guacamole and enjoy!

HOMEMADE GUACAMOLE

Crispy Taco Wings

These wings are everything you love about chicken—a crispy, crunchy outside with a tender, juicy center.
—*Blanche Gibson, Gordon, WI*

- -

Prep: 15 min. • **Bake:** 30 min.
Makes: 2 dozen

- ½ cup all-purpose flour
- 1 envelope taco seasoning
- ½ cup butter, melted
- 1¾ cups crushed corn chips
- 2½ lbs. chicken wingettes and drummettes

1. Preheat oven to 350°. In a shallow bowl, mix flour and taco seasoning. Place melted butter and corn chips in separate shallow bowls. Dip wings in flour mixture to coat; shake off excess. Dip in butter, then in chip mixture; pat to help coating adhere.
2. Transfer to a greased 15x10x1-in. baking pan. Bake 30-40 minutes or until juices run clear.
1 piece: 164 cal., 12g fat (4g sat. fat), 45mg chol., 203mg sod., 4g carb. (0 sugars, 0 fiber), 9g pro.

HACK

To melt butter without spattering all over the microwave, repurpose that butter wrapper you'd have otherwise tossed out. Cover the cup or bowl with the wrapper before melting a stick of butter.

HOT SPINACH SPREAD WITH PITA CHIPS

Hot Spinach Spread with Pita Chips

Warm and cheesy, this spread is absolutely scrumptious served on toasted pita wedges. Its colorful appearance makes a stunning addition to any buffet.
—*Teresa Emanuel, Smithville, MO*

- -

Prep: 30 min. • **Bake:** 20 min.
Makes: 16 servings (4 cups spread)

- 2 cups shredded Monterey Jack cheese
- 1 pkg. (10 oz.) frozen chopped spinach, thawed and squeezed dry
- 1 pkg. (8 oz.) cream cheese, cubed
- 2 plum tomatoes, seeded and chopped
- ¾ cup chopped onion
- ⅓ cup half-and-half cream
- 1 Tbsp. finely chopped seeded jalapeno pepper
- 6 pita breads (6 in.)
- ½ cup butter, melted
- 2 tsp. lemon-pepper seasoning
- 2 tsp. ground cumin
- ¼ tsp. garlic salt

1. In a large bowl, combine the first 7 ingredients. Transfer to a greased 1½-qt. baking dish. Bake, uncovered, at 375° until bubbly, 20-25 minutes.
2. Meanwhile, cut each pita bread into 8 wedges. Place in two 15x10x1-in. baking pans. Combine the butter, lemon-pepper, cumin and garlic salt; brush over pita wedges.
3. Bake for 7-9 minutes or until crisp. Serve with spinach spread.
Note: Wear disposable gloves when cutting hot peppers; the oils can burn skin. Avoid touching your face.
¼ cup spread with 3 pita wedges: 231 cal., 16g fat (10g sat. fat), 46mg chol., 381mg sod., 15g carb. (1g sugars, 1g fiber), 8g pro.

Party Cheese Bread

You can't go wrong with this recipe. The cheesy, buttery bread is so simple to make, but the taste is out of this world. Plus it looks fantastic, and people just flock to it! It's better than the usual garlic bread with pasta, too.
—*Karen Grant, Tulare, CA*

- -

Prep: 25 min. • **Bake:** 30 min.
Makes: 16 servings

1	round loaf sourdough bread (1 lb.)
1	lb. Monterey Jack cheese, sliced
½	cup butter, melted
2	Tbsp. lemon juice
2	Tbsp. Dijon mustard
1½	tsp. garlic powder
½	tsp. onion powder
½	tsp. celery salt
	Minced fresh chives, optional

1. Preheat oven to 350°. Cut the sourdough bread into 1-in. slices to within ½ in. of bottom of loaf. Repeat cuts in opposite direction. Insert cheese in cuts.
2. Mix all remaining ingredients except chives; drizzle over bread. Wrap in foil; place on a baking sheet.
3. Bake for 20 minutes. Unwrap; bake until cheese is melted, about 10 minutes. If desired, sprinkle with minced chives.

1 serving: 237 cal., 15g fat (9g sat. fat), 41mg chol., 468mg sod., 15g carb. (2g sugars, 1g fiber), 10g pro.

PRO TIPS

• A sharp serrated knife works best here so you don't end up tearing the bread.

• Experiment with different flavors: Pair Brie cheese with raspberry jam, or mozzarella with pesto.

PARTY CHEESE BREAD

Crab Dip in a Bread Bowl

I whipped up this recipe for a get-together and it's been a staple ever since. One New Year's Eve, my husband and our neighbor ate the entire bread bowl.
—*Sharon Monroe, Littleton, CO*

- -

Takes: 30 min. • **Makes:** 2½ cups

- 1 loaf (1 lb.) loaf sourdough bread
- 2 cups sour cream
- 2 cans (6 oz. each) crabmeat, drained, flaked and cartilage removed, or 2 cups imitation crabmeat
- 1 can (8 oz.) water chestnuts, drained and chopped
- 1 envelope ranch salad dressing mix
  Assorted fresh vegetables

1. Cut top fourth off of the loaf of bread; carefully hollow out bottom, leaving a 1-in. shell. Cube removed bread; set aside.

2. In a small bowl, combine the sour cream, crab, water chestnuts and salad dressing mix.

3. Fill bread shell with crab dip. Serve with fresh vegetables and reserved bread cubes.

¼ cup: 147 cal., 8g fat (6g sat. fat), 62mg chol., 357mg sod., 6g carb. (2g sugars, 1g fiber), 9g pro.

HACK

Raid the Silverware Drawer

If you have a grapefruit knife, use its double-serrated blade to make quick work of carving out a bread bowl.

BREAD BOWLS

Beer Cheese in a Bread Bowl

My entire family loves this cheese dip, and my friends always request that I bring it to gatherings. It's quite attractive thanks to the bread bowl. Chopped green onions make a pretty garnish on top.
—*Julie Koch, Delaware, OH*

- -

Takes: 15 min.
Makes: 20 servings (2½ cups dip)

- 1 **round loaf (1 lb.) pumpernickel bread**
- 2 **jars (5 oz. each) sharp American cheese spread**
- 1 **pkg. (8 oz.) cream cheese, softened**
- ¼ **cup beer or nonalcoholic beer**
- ½ **cup bacon bits**

1. Cut top fourth off loaf of bread; carefully hollow out bottom, leaving a ½-in. shell. Cube removed bread; set aside.
2. In a microwave-safe bowl, combine cheese spread and cream cheese. Microwave, uncovered, on high for 2 minutes, stirring every 30 seconds. Stir in beer. Microwave, uncovered, 20 seconds longer. Stir in bacon.
3. Fill bread shell with cheese dip. Serve with reserved bread cubes.
2 Tbsp.. 147 cal., 9g fat (5g sat. fat), 26mg chol., 506mg sod., 12g carb. (0 sugars, 1g fiber), 6g pro.

Marinated Shrimp & Olives

This is my favorite appetizer to serve party guests. The flavors in this colorful dish blend beautifully, and the shrimp are tender and tasty.

—*Carol Gawronski, Lake Wales, FL*

Prep: 10 min. • **Cook:** 5 min. + chilling
Makes: 20 servings

- 1½ lbs. peeled and deveined cooked shrimp (31-40 per lb.)
- 1 can (6 oz.) pitted ripe olives, drained
- 1 jar (5¾ oz.) pimiento-stuffed olives, drained
- 2 Tbsp. olive oil
- 1½ tsp. curry powder
- ½ tsp. ground ginger
- ¼ tsp. salt
- ¼ tsp. pepper
- 2 Tbsp. lemon juice
- 1 Tbsp. minced fresh parsley or 1 tsp. dried parsley flakes

1. Combine the shrimp and olives; set aside.

2. In a small saucepan, heat olive oil over medium heat. In a small bowl, combine the curry, ginger, salt and pepper; whisk into hot oil. Cook and stir for 1 minute. Remove from heat; stir in lemon juice and parsley. Immediately drizzle over the shrimp mixture; toss gently to coat.

3. Refrigerate, covered, up to 6 hours, stirring occasionally. Serve with toothpicks.

⅓ cup: 71 cal., 4g fat (0 sat. fat), 52mg chol., 292mg sod., 2g carb. (0 sugars, 0 fiber), 7g pro. **Diabetic exchanges:** 1 lean meat, 1 fat.

MARINATED
SHRIMP & OLIVES

Shrimp Cocktail

During the '60s, shrimp cocktail was one of the most popular party foods around. And it's still a crowd favorite. It's the one appetizer that I serve for every special occasion.

—*Peggy Allen, Pasadena, CA*

- -

Prep: 30 min. + chilling
Makes: about 6 dozen
(1¼ cups sauce)

- 3 qt. water
- 1 small onion, sliced
- ½ medium lemon, sliced
- 2 sprigs fresh parsley
- 1 Tbsp. salt
- 5 whole peppercorns
- 1 bay leaf
- ¼ tsp. dried thyme
- 3 lbs. uncooked large shrimp, peeled and deveined (tails on)

SAUCE
- 1 cup chili sauce
- 2 Tbsp. lemon juice
- 2 Tbsp. prepared horseradish
- 4 tsp. Worcestershire sauce
- ½ tsp. salt
  Dash cayenne pepper

1. In a Dutch oven, combine the first 8 ingredients; bring to a boil. Add shrimp. Reduce heat; simmer, uncovered, for 4-5 minutes or until shrimp turn pink.
2. Drain shrimp and immediately rinse in cold water. Refrigerate for 2-3 hours or until cold. In a small bowl, combine sauce ingredients. Refrigerate until serving.
3. Arrange shrimp on a serving platter; serve with sauce.

3 shrimp with about 2 tsp. sauce: 59 cal., 1g fat (0 sat. fat), 66mg chol., 555mg sod., 4g carb. (2g sugars, 0 fiber), 9g pro.

Blue Cheese-Stuffed Shrimp

Jumbo shrimp becomes even more extraordinary when stuffed with creamy blue cheese. The mild flavor has mass appeal.

—*Amy Dollimount, Glace Bay, NS*

- -

Prep: 20 min. + chilling
Makes: 2 dozen

- 3 oz. cream cheese, softened
- ⅔ cup minced fresh parsley, divided
- ¼ cup crumbled blue cheese
- 1 tsp. chopped shallot
- ½ tsp. Creole mustard
- 24 cooked jumbo shrimp, peeled and deveined

1. In a small bowl, beat cream cheese until smooth. Beat in ⅓ cup parsley, blue cheese, shallot and mustard. Refrigerate at least 1 hour.
2. Make a deep slit along the back of each shrimp to within ¼-½ in. of the bottom. Stuff with cream cheese mixture; press remaining parsley onto cream cheese mixture.

1 stuffed shrimp: 43 cal., 2g fat (1g sat. fat), 54mg chol., 89mg sod., 0 carb. (0 sugars, 0 fiber), 6g pro.
Diabetic exchanges: 1 meat.

HACK

Keep Shrimp Cold on a Buffet

You can serve shrimp attractively and keep it at a safe temperature with a lettuce-lined bowl. Fill a large shallow bowl (plastic is great here because it's a natural insulator) two-thirds full with crushed ice placed in a zippered plastic bag. Disguise the ice with lettuce leaves, then place the shrimp on top. If serving a shrimp sauce, nestle the bowl down into the center.

Spicy Crab Salad Tapas

I served these at a party and everyone went wild! These delicious puff pastry tapas have a crispy, flaky outside filled with creamy, sweet crab.

—*Vanessa Mason, Summerdale, AL*

Prep: 35 min. + chilling
Bake: 20 min. + cooling
Makes: about 2 dozen

- 1   **can (16 oz.) lump crabmeat, drained**
- ¼   **cup finely chopped sweet red pepper**
- ¼   **cup finely chopped sweet yellow pepper**
- ¼   **cup finely chopped green onions**
- 1   **jalapeno pepper, seeded and finely chopped**
- 1   **Tbsp. minced fresh cilantro**
- 1   **Tbsp. lemon juice**
- 2   **garlic cloves, minced**
- 1   **tsp. ground mustard**
- ½   **cup mayonnaise**
- ½   **tsp. salt**
- ¼   **tsp. pepper**
- 1   **pkg. (17.3 oz.) frozen puff pastry, thawed**
- 1   **large egg**
- 1   **Tbsp. water**
-     **Optional: minced fresh parsley and seafood seasoning**

1. Preheat oven to 375°. Combine the first 12 ingredients. Refrigerate, covered, at least 1 hour.

2. On a lightly floured surface, unfold puff pastry. Roll each pastry piece into a 10-in. square; cut each into twenty-five 2-in. squares. Using a round 1½-in. cookie cutter, cut out the centers of half of the puff pastry squares. Whisk egg and water; brush over pastry. Place cutout squares on top of solid squares; transfer to parchment-lined baking sheets.

3. Bake until golden brown, about 18 minutes. Cool. Just before serving, spoon 1 heaping Tbsp. of crab salad into center of each. If desired, top with parsley and seasoning.

1 appetizer: 145 cal., 9g fat (2g sat. fat), 25mg chol., 240mg sod., 11g carb. (0 sugars, 2g fiber), 5g pro.

Ham Salad

Flecked with pimientos and chives, this fast, flavorful ham salad boasts crunchy pecans, tart pineapple and chewy raisins. It makes a delectable appetizer stuffed into puff pastry shells or profiteroles.

—Taste of Home *Test Kitchen*

Takes: 15 min. • **Makes:** 2 cups

- 1½   **cups diced fully cooked ham**
- ½   **cup unsweetened crushed pineapple, drained and patted dry**
- ¼   **cup golden raisins**
- ¼   **cup chopped pecans, toasted**
- 1   **Tbsp. diced pimientos, drained**
- 3   **Tbsp. mayonnaise**
- 1   **Tbsp. ranch salad dressing**
- 1   **Tbsp. sour cream**
- 1   **Tbsp. minced chives**
- ⅛   **tsp. pepper**

In a large bowl, combine the ham, pineapple, raisins, pecans and pimientos. In a small bowl, combine mayonnaise, ranch dressing, sour cream, chives and pepper. Pour over ham mixture and toss gently to coat. Refrigerate until serving. Just before serving, spoon ½ cup ham salad into each cream puff shell; replace tops.

¼ cup: 96 cal., 7g fat (0 sat. fat), 15mg chol., 246mg sod., 6g carb. (3g sugars, 2g fiber), 4g pro.

**SPICY CRAB
SALAD TAPAS**

PRO TIPS

• The puff pastry shells can be made a few hours ahead of time and filled as your guests are walking up to the door.

• If you want to boost the heat, sprinkle each appetizer with a little cayenne pepper.

Cranberry Brie Pinwheels

People will know you care when you present these crisp, flaky pinwheels ...you'll know they're easy to make. The filling is bursting with savory goodness and a touch of sweetness. They're perfect on a cheese tray.
—*Marcia Kintz, South Bend, IN*

- -

Prep: 20 min. • **Bake:** 15 min.
Makes: 1 dozen

- 1 sheet frozen puff pastry, thawed
- 2 Tbsp. Dijon mustard
- 2 Tbsp. honey
- 1 cup finely chopped fresh spinach
- ½ cup finely chopped Brie cheese
- ½ cup finely chopped walnuts
- ¼ cup dried cranberries, finely chopped

1. Unfold pastry. Combine mustard and honey; spread over pastry. Layer with spinach, cheese, walnuts and cranberries. Roll up jelly-roll style; cut into 12 slices. Place cut side down on an ungreased baking sheet.
2. Bake at 400° for 15-20 minutes or until golden brown.
1 pinwheel: 173 cal., 10g fat (3g sat. fat), 6mg chol., 167mg sod., 18g carb. (5g sugars, 2g fiber), 4g pro.

Fig Jam

I have had a love of figs ever since I had an amazing appetizer that combined them with blue cheese and prosciutto. Since then, I created this fig jam and have used it as a glaze on our Easter ham, smeared on a bagel with cream cheese and dolloped on pizza.
—*Monica Keleher, Methuen, MA*

- -

Takes: 30 min. • **Makes:** 2 cups

- 2 cups chopped dried figs
- 2 cups water
- ½ cup white wine
- 2 Tbsp. honey
- 1 tsp. grated lemon zest
- ¼ tsp. salt

1. In a large saucepan, combine figs and water; bring to a boil. Reduce heat; simmer, uncovered, stirring occasionally, until liquid is almost evaporated, 12-14 minutes. Add wine; stirring occasionally, cook for 6-8 minutes longer or until liquid is almost evaporated.
2. Remove from heat; stir in honey, lemon zest and salt. Cool slightly. Process in a food processor until blended. Transfer to covered jars; refrigerate up to 1 week.
2 Tbsp. jam: 61 cal., 0 fat (0 sat. fat), 0 chol., 39mg sod., 14g carb. (11g sugars, 2g fiber), 1g pro.

Holiday Salsa

When we offer this cream-cheesy salsa of fresh cranberries, cilantro and a little jalapeno kick, everyone hovers around the serving dish until it's scraped clean.
—*Shelly Pattison, Lubbock, TX*

- -

Prep: 20 min. + chilling
Makes: 12 servings

- 1 pkg. (12 oz.) fresh or frozen cranberries
- 1 cup sugar
- 6 green onions, chopped
- ½ cup fresh cilantro leaves, chopped
- 1 jalapeno pepper, seeded and finely chopped
- 1 pkg. (8 oz.) cream cheese, softened
   Assorted crackers or tortilla chips

1. Pulse cranberries and sugar in a food processor until coarsely chopped. Stir together with onions, cilantro and jalapeno. Cover and refrigerate several hours or overnight.
2. To serve, place cream cheese on a serving plate. Drain salsa; spoon over cream cheese. Serve with crackers or tortilla chips.
1 serving: 146 cal., 7g fat (4g sat. fat), 21mg chol., 71mg sod., 22g carb. (19g sugars, 2g fiber), 1g pro.

Build a Perfect Cheese Platter

Make a beautiful, bountiful cheese board the centerpiece of your next celebration. Follow these steps to build the perfect cheese tray.

1. Determine how much

If you want to plan for just enough, you'll need 3-4 oz. of cheese per guest (2 lbs. for 8 guests).

2. Pick an assortment

For a variety of tastes and textures, choose at least one cheese from each category—soft, firm, blue and aged. Try to include at least one familiar type of cheese in the mix. When in doubt, you can't go wrong with cheddar.

3. Add accoutrements

- The base: crackers, baguette slices, digestive biscuits and other cheese vehicles

- Fresh and dried fruits: apples or pears, grapes, berries, figs and dried apricots

- Salty, savory components: thinly sliced prosciutto or sausage, olives, oven-roasted peppers or tomatoes

- Crunch: roasted almonds, pistachios, walnut halves

- Sweet surprises: jam, chutney, granola clusters, candied pecans

4. Let stand

Let the cheese platter stand at room temperature for 30 minutes before guests arrive. It tastes better and soft cheeses spread more easily at room temperature.

Meet the cheeses

ASIAGO Mild in flavor, Asiago gets harder and more crumbly as it ages. The taste is similar to Parmesan.

CAMEMBERT This soft, earthy variety usually comes in a small wheel, making it a good focal point for a cheese board. And, yes, you can (and should) eat the rind.

SHARP CHEDDAR As cheddar ages, the flavor grows tangier and more intense. The texture of a 5-year cheddar is firm and rather flaky, with tiny saltlike crystals throughout.

MOZZARELLA So versatile—feel free to include a few varieties. Try fresh mozzarella balls or string cheese wrapped in prosciutto. Both types are mild in flavor and fun to eat.

BLUE CHEESE Blue is a pungent, semi-soft cheese that tastes sharp and salty. Its characteristic blue veins make it a colorful and delicious option.

GOAT CHEESE Creamy, light and mild in flavor, fresh goat cheese makes an excellent choice for a brunch board. Give it a little extra flavor and color by rolling the log in minced parsley.

VEGETARIAN
LINGUINE, P. 47

EVERYDAY COOKING TRICKS

[Prep like a pro, take genius shortcuts and have fun cooking with these easy, everyday hacks. You'll do more, faster, and get tastier results!]

Turkey Meatballs in Garlic Sauce

Garlic and meatballs pair beautifully, especially over hot rice or noodles.

—Audrey Thibodeau, Gilbert, AZ

Prep: 10 min. • **Bake:** 30 min.
Makes: 2 servings

2   Tbsp. whole milk
½   tsp. Worcestershire sauce
2   to 3 drops hot pepper sauce
½   cup finely crushed Ritz crackers (about 10 crackers)
1   Tbsp. minced fresh parsley
¼   tsp. salt
⅛   tsp. pepper
½   lb. lean ground turkey
1   cup V8 juice
¼   cup chicken broth
2   garlic cloves, minced
    Hot cooked rice

1. In a large bowl, combine the first 7 ingredients. Crumble turkey over mixture and mix well. Shape into 6 meatballs. Place in a greased 9-in. pie plate. Bake, uncovered, at 400° for 10 minutes.
2. Meanwhile, in a small bowl, combine the V8 juice, broth and garlic. Turn meatballs; spoon sauce over top. Reduce heat to 350°. Bake 20 minutes longer, basting every 5 minutes. Serve over rice.
3 meatballs: 330 cal., 15g fat (4g sat. fat), 92mg chol., 1038mg sod., 23g carb. (7g sugars, 1g fiber), 23g pro.

Split-Second Shrimp

I use my microwave to hurry along the prep of this super fast shrimp scampi. It's deliciously buttery and full of garlic flavor. We love it as a main dish, but it makes an excellent appetizer, too.

—Jalayne Luckett, Marion, IL

Takes: 10 min. • **MAKES:** 4 servings.

2   Tbsp. butter
1   large garlic clove, minced
⅛   to ¼ tsp. cayenne pepper
2   Tbsp. white wine or chicken broth
5   tsp. lemon juice
1   Tbsp. minced fresh parsley
½   tsp. salt
1   lb. uncooked shrimp (26-30 per lb.), peeled and deveined

1. Place butter, garlic and cayenne in a 9-in. microwave-safe pie plate. Microwave, covered, on high until butter is melted, about 1 minute. Stir in wine, lemon juice, parsley and salt. Add shrimp; toss to coat.
2. Microwave, covered, on high until shrimp turns pink, 2½-3½ minutes. Stir before serving.
3 oz. cooked shrimp: 157 cal., 7g fat (4g sat. fat), 153mg chol., 476mg sodium, 2g carb. (0 sugars, 0 fiber), 19g pro. **Diabetic exchanges:** 3 lean meat, 1½ fat.

Tomato-Basil Baked Fish

This recipe can be made with different kinds of fish as desired, and I usually have the rest of the ingredients on hand. Baked fish is wonderful, and I fix this healthy dish often.

—Annie Hicks, Zephyrhills, FL

Takes: 15 min. • **Makes:** 2 servings

1   Tbsp. lemon juice
1   tsp. olive oil
8   oz. red snapper, cod or haddock fillets
¼   tsp. dried basil
⅛   tsp. salt
⅛   tsp. pepper
2   plum tomatoes, thinly sliced
2   tsp. grated Parmesan cheese

1. In a shallow bowl, combine the lemon juice and oil. Add fish fillets; turn to coat. Place in a greased 9-in. pie plate. Sprinkle with half of the basil, salt and pepper. Arrange tomatoes over top; sprinkle with cheese and remaining seasonings.
2. Cover and bake fish at 400° for 10-12 minutes or until fish flakes easily with a fork.
1 serving: 121 cal., 4g fat (1g sat. fat), 24mg chol., 256mg sod., 4g carb. (2g sugars, 1g fiber), 18g pro. **Diabetic exchanges:** 3 lean meat, 1 vegetable, ½ fat.

HACK

Dinner in a Pie Plate

If you have a tiny kitchen, it's smart to maximize space wherever you can. One way is to own just a few pieces of bakeware. A really useful piece is a deep-dish pie plate. It works perfectly for many tasks, such as roasting veggies, making apple crisp, holding quiche and baking a small batch of brownies or bars. If you're usually cooking for one or two, you'll appreciate the small yield, too. And because you can also use it for pie, the dish is more versatile than a typical 8x8 casserole dish.

SPLIT-SECOND
SHRIMP

CITRUS SALMON EN PAPILLOTE

Citrus Salmon en Papillote

This salmon dish is so simple, nutritious and easy to make yet so delicious, elegant and impressive.
—*Dahlia Abrams, Detroit, MI*

Prep: 20 min. • **Bake:** 15 min.
Makes: 6 servings

- 6   orange slices
- 6   lime slices
- 6   salmon fillets (4 oz. each)
- 1   lb. fresh asparagus, trimmed and halved
      Olive oil-flavored cooking spray
- ½   tsp. salt
- ¼   tsp. pepper
- 2   Tbsp. minced fresh parsley
- 3   Tbsp. lemon juice

1. Preheat the oven to 425°. Cut parchment or heavy-duty foil into six 15x10-in. pieces; fold in half. Arrange citrus slices on 1 side of each piece. Top with fish and asparagus. Spritz with cooking spray. Sprinkle with salt, pepper and parsley. Drizzle with lemon juice.
2. Fold parchment over the fish; draw edges together and crimp with fingers to form tightly sealed packets. Place in baking pans.
3. Bake until fish flakes easily with a fork, 12-15 minutes. Open packets carefully to allow steam to escape.

1 packet: 224 cal., 13g fat (2g sat. fat), 57mg chol., 261mg sod., 6g carb. (3g sugars, 1g fiber), 20g pro. **Diabetic exchanges:** 3 lean meat, 1 vegetable.

PRO TIP

Cooking fish in parchment is a healthy, mess-free technique that seals in vitamins. It delicately infuses the fish with citrus and herb flavors.

ORANGE TILAPIA IN PARCHMENT

Orange Tilapia in Parchment

Sweet orange juice and spicy cayenne pepper give this no-fuss dish fabulous flavor. A bonus? Cleanup is a breeze!
—Tiffany Diebold, Nashville, TN

Takes: 30 min. • **Makes:** 4 servings

- ¼ **cup orange juice**
- 4 **tsp. grated orange zest**
- ¼ **tsp. salt**
- ¼ **tsp. cayenne pepper**
- ¼ **tsp. pepper**
- 4 **tilapia fillets (6 oz. each)**
- ½ **cup julienned carrot**
- ½ **cup julienned zucchini**

1. Preheat oven to 450°. In a small bowl, combine first 5 ingredients; set aside. Cut parchment or heavy-duty foil into four 18x12-in. lengths; place a fish fillet on each. Top with carrot and zucchini; drizzle with the orange juice mixture.

2. Fold parchment over fish. Working from bottom inside corner, fold up about ¾ in. of the paper and crimp both layers to seal. Repeat, folding the edges up and crimping, until a half-moon-shaped packet is formed. Repeat for remaining packets. Place on baking sheets.

3. Bake until fish flakes easily with a fork, 12-15 minutes. Open packets carefully to allow steam to escape.

1 packet: 158 cal., 2g fat (1g sat. fat), 83mg chol., 220mg sod., 4g carb. (2g sugars, 1g fiber), 32g pro. **Diabetic exchanges:** 5 lean meat.

Keep Fish Fresh

Fish stays freshest when stored on ice. To keep it ice-cold without mess or damaging the fish's texture, place frozen gel packs or blue ice blocks in a container, then top with the wrapped fish. Place in the meat drawer. Use within a few days. Wash the ice packs with hot soapy water before re-use.

**SAUCY GRILLED
PORK CHOPS**

Saucy Grilled Pork Chops

My mamaw in Kentucky used this dip (as she called it) on many grilled meats, including chicken and steak.
—*Misty Schneider, Bayport, MN*

- -

Prep: 5 min. • **Grill:** 10 min.
Makes: 8 servings

- ½ cup butter, cubed
- ½ cup packed light brown sugar
- ½ cup lemon juice
- 8 bone-in pork loin chops (¾ in. thick)
  Lemon wedges, optional

1. In a microwave-safe dish, microwave cubed butter, covered, until melted; add brown sugar and lemon juice, stirring to dissolve sugar. Reserve ⅔ cup for drizzling.
2. Brush pork chops with remaining sauce. Grill, covered, on an oiled rack over medium heat or broil 4 in. from heat for 4-5 minutes on each side or until a thermometer reads 145°. Let stand for 5 minutes before serving.
3. Stir sauce to combine and gently reheat if necessary; drizzle over pork chops. Serve with lemon if desired.
1 pork chop: 476 cal., 30g fat (14g sat. fat), 141mg chol., 162mg sod., 15g carb. (14g sugars, 0 fiber), 36g pro.

EDAMAME SALAD
WITH SESAME GINGER
DRESSING

Edamame Salad with Sesame Ginger Dressing

This bright baby kale salad is packed with a little bit of everything—hearty greens, a nutty crunch, a zip of citrusy goodness and a protein punch. It's pure bliss in a bowl.
—*Darla Andrews, Schertz, TX*

- -

Takes: 15 min. • **Makes:** 6 servings

- 6 cups baby kale salad blend (about 5 oz.)
- 1 can (15 oz.) garbanzo beans or chickpeas, rinsed and drained
- 2 cups frozen shelled edamame (about 10 oz.), thawed
- 3 clementines, peeled and segmented
- 1 cup fresh bean sprouts
- ½ cup salted peanuts
- 2 green onions, diagonally sliced
- ½ cup sesame ginger salad dressing

Divide the salad blend among 6 bowls. Top with all remaining ingredients except salad dressing. Serve with dressing.
1 serving: 317 cal., 17g fat (2g sat. fat), 0 chol., 355mg sod., 32g carb. (14g sugars, 8g fiber), 13g pro.

HACK

Easy Artistry

Cutting green onions thinly on the diagonal is an easy way to give them a delicate look, especially in Asian dishes.

Pesto Grilled Salmon

Using just a few ingredients, this fresh and easy summertime dish is sure to become a family favorite.
—*Sonya Labbe, West Hollywood, CA*

- -

Takes: 30 min. • **Makes:** 12 servings

- 1   **salmon fillet (3 lbs.)**
- ½   **cup prepared pesto**
- 2   **green onions, finely chopped**
- ¼   **cup lemon juice**
- 2   **garlic cloves, minced**

1. Lightly oil grill rack. Place salmon skin side down on grill rack. Grill, covered, over medium heat or broil 4 in. from the heat for 5 minutes.
2. In a small bowl, combine pesto, chopped onions, lemon juice and garlic. Carefully spoon some of the pesto mixture over salmon. Grill for 15-20 minutes longer or until fish flakes easily with a fork, basting occasionally with the remaining pesto mixture.

3 oz. cooked salmon: 262 cal., 17g fat (4g sat. fat), 70mg chol., 147mg sod., 1g carb. (0 sugars, 0 fiber), 25g pro.
Diabetic exchanges: 3 lean meat, 3 fat.
» **Glazed Asian Salmon:** Replace the basting ingredients with ½ cup reduced-sodium soy sauce, ¼ cup brown sugar, ½ tsp. each crushed red pepper flakes and ground ginger, and ¼ tsp. sesame oil. Grill and baste salmon as directed.
» **Herbed Salmon:** Place salmon on double thickness of heavy-duty foil. Mix ½ cup softened butter with ¼ cup each minced fresh chives, tarragon and thyme; spread over salmon. Top with ⅓ cup finely chopped red onion, ¼ tsp. each salt and pepper, and 1 thinly sliced lemon. Seal foil and grill 20-25 minutes. Open carefully to allow steam to escape.

Plank-Grilled Ginger-Herb Trout

After tinkering with the herbs and spices of my go-to fish recipe, I decided to grill the fish on a plank and what a world of difference it made! Hands down, this is now one of our favorite ways to cook fish.
—*Judy Castranova, New Bern, NC*

- -

Prep: 15 min. + soaking • **Grill:** 15 min.
Makes: 4 servings

- 2   **grilling planks**
- 2   **Tbsp. butter, softened**
- 2   **Tbsp. minced fresh gingerroot**
- 4   **tsp. each minced fresh basil, cilantro and parsley**
- 1   **Tbsp. honey**
- 2   **tsp. grated lemon zest**
- ¼   **tsp. kosher salt**
- ⅛   **tsp. pepper**
- 4   **trout fillets (6 oz. each)**

1. Soak grilling planks in water at least 1 hour. Combine butter, ginger, herbs, honey, lemon zest, salt and pepper in a small bowl.
2. Place planks on grill over direct medium heat. Cover and heat for 3 minutes or until light to medium smoke comes from the plank and the wood begins to char. (This indicates the plank is ready.) Turn plank over and place on indirect heat.
3. Spread herb mixture over flesh side of fillets. Place fish on planks, skin side down. Grill, covered, over medium heat for 10-15 minutes or until fish flakes easily with a fork.
1 fillet: 305 cal., 15g fat (6g sat. fat), 115mg chol., 219mg sod., 5g carb. (4g sugars, 0 fiber), 36g pro.

HOW-TO

Grill a Whole Salmon Fillet

- Prepare the salmon according to the recipe, leaving the skin on (this makes it easier to remove the fish from the grill). Lightly oil the hot grill to prevent sticking, then place the whole fillet, skin side down, onto the grill. Cover and cook until done. There is no need to turn the fillet during cooking.

- With a spatula, gently remove the salmon to a serving platter. The cooked fish easily separates from the skin, which makes serving up portions of the fillet quite simple.

**PLANK-GRILLED
GINGER-HERB TROUT**

GARLIC BREAD PIZZA SANDWICHES

Chicken Thai Pizza

This is a recipe I make for my friends on a girl's night filled with fun and laughter. It is simple to make but is full of flavor.

*—Kimberly Knuppenburg,
Menomonee Falls, WI*

Takes: 25 min. • **Makes:** 6 servings

- 1 prebaked 12-in. pizza crust
- ⅔ cup Thai peanut sauce
- 2 Tbsp. reduced-sodium soy sauce
- 2 Tbsp. creamy peanut butter
- 1 cup shredded cooked chicken breast
- 1 cup shredded part-skim mozzarella cheese
- 3 green onions, chopped
- ½ cup bean sprouts
- ½ cup shredded carrot

1. Preheat oven to 400°. Place crust on an ungreased 12-in. pizza pan or baking sheet. In a small bowl, combine peanut sauce, soy sauce and peanut butter. Add chicken; toss to coat. Spread over crust; sprinkle with cheese and onions.

2. Bake 10-12 minutes or until cheese is melted. Top with bean sprouts and shredded carrot.

1 slice: 361 cal., 15g fat (4g sat. fat), 29mg chol., 1183mg sod., 35g carb. (4g sugars, 3g fiber), 23g pro.

HACK

Not Just for Slicing Pizza

- The continuously turning wheel of a pizza cutter works in both directions, making it the ideal tool for chopping herbs. Simply bunch up the herbs and run the pizza cutter back and forth until they're chopped as finely as desired.

- To easily slice Garlic Bread Pizza Sandwiches cleanly without making a mess of the gooey melted cheese, use a pizza cutter instead of a knife.

Garlic Bread Pizza Sandwiches

I love inventing new ways to make grilled cheese sandwiches for my kids. This version tastes like pizza. Using frozen garlic bread is a timesaver.

—Courtney Stultz, Weir, KS

Takes: 20 min. • **Makes:** 4 servings

- 1 pkg. (11¼ oz.) frozen garlic Texas toast
- ¼ cup pasta sauce
- 4 slices provolone cheese
- 16 slices pepperoni
- 8 slices thinly sliced hard salami
  Additional pasta sauce, warmed, optional

1. Preheat griddle over medium-low heat. Add garlic toast; cook until lightly browned, 3-4 minutes per side.

2. Spoon 1 Tbsp. sauce over each of 4 toasts. Top with cheese, pepperoni, salami and remaining toasts. Cook until crisp and cheese is melted, 3-5 minutes, turning as necessary. If desired, serve with additional sauce.

1 sandwich: 456 cal., 28g fat (10g sat. fat), 50mg chol., 1177mg sod., 36g carb. (4g sugars, 2g fiber), 19g pro.

Garlic Salmon Linguine

This garlicky pasta is so nice to make on busy weeknights because I usually have everything I need already on hand. I serve mine with asparagus, rolls and fruit.

—*Theresa Hagan, Glendale, AZ*

Takes: 20 min. • **Makes:** 6 servings

- 1   pkg. (16 oz.) linguine
- ⅓   cup olive oil
- 3   garlic cloves, minced
- 1   can (14¾ oz.) salmon, drained, bones and skin removed
- ¾   cup chicken broth
- ¼   cup minced fresh parsley
- ½   tsp. salt
- ⅛   tsp. cayenne pepper

1. Cook linguine according to package directions; drain.
2. Meanwhile, in a large skillet, heat oil over medium heat. Add garlic; cook and stir until tender, about 1 minute (do not allow to brown). Stir in the remaining ingredients; heat through. Add linguine; toss gently to combine.
1 serving: 489 cal., 19g fat (3g sat. fat), 31mg chol., 693mg sod., 56g carb. (3g sugars, 3g fiber), 25g pro.

GARLIC SALMON LINGUINE

HACK

Long-Lasting Herb Bunch

To keep parsley fresh for up to a month, trim the stems and place the bunch in a tumbler with an inch of water. Be sure no leaves are in the water. Tie a produce bag around the tumbler to trap humidity; store in the refrigerator. Each time you use the parsley, change the water and turn the produce bag inside out so any moisture that has built up inside the bag can escape.

Skillet Hasselback Sweet Potatoes

Sweet potatoes dressed with buttery, herby, garlicky goodness make for a stunning and delicious side dish.
—*Lauren Knoelke, Des Moines, IA*

Prep: 25 min. • **Bake:** 45 min.
Makes: 8 servings

- 8 small sweet potatoes (about 7 oz. each)
- ½ cup butter, melted
- 3 Tbsp. finely chopped shallot
- 3 garlic cloves, minced
- 1½ tsp. salt
- ½ tsp. fresh ground pepper
- 2 tsp. minced fresh parsley
- 2 tsp. minced fresh thyme
- 2 tsp. minced fresh sage
- ½ cup soft whole wheat bread crumbs
- ¼ cup grated Parmesan cheese
- ½ cup chopped toasted nuts, optional

1. Preheat oven to 425°. Cut thin slices lengthwise from bottom of sweet potatoes to allow them to lie flat; discard slices. Place potatoes flat side down; cut crosswise into ⅛-in. slices, leaving them intact at the bottom. Arrange sweet potatoes in a 12-in. cast-iron skillet.

2. Stir together next 5 ingredients. Spoon half of butter mixture over sweet potatoes. Bake 35 minutes.

3. Meanwhile, add herbs to remaining butter mixture. Toss bread crumbs with Parmesan. Remove skillet from oven. Spoon the remaining butter mixture over potatoes; top with bread crumb mixture. Return to oven until potatoes are tender and topping is golden brown, 10-12 minutes. If desired, top with toasted nuts.

1 sweet potato: 333 cal., 13g fat (8g sat. fat), 33mg chol., 620mg sod., 52g carb. (20g sugars, 6g fiber), 5g pro.

SKILLET HASSELBACK SWEET POTATOES

Cheese & Herb Potato Fans

It's downright fun to make and serve these potatoes—and they taste incredible, too. The fresh herbs, butter and cheeses are just what a good potato needs.
—*Susan Curry, West Hills, CA*

- -

Prep: 20 min. • **Bake:** 55 min.
Makes: 8 servings

  8 **medium potatoes**
  ½ **cup butter, melted**
  2 **tsp. salt**
  ½ **tsp. pepper**
  ⅔ **cup shredded cheddar cheese**
  ⅓ **cup shredded Parmesan cheese**
  2 **Tbsp. each minced fresh chives, sage and thyme**

1. Preheat oven to 425°. With a sharp knife, cut each potato crosswise into ⅛-in. slices, leaving slices attached at the bottom; fan potatoes slightly and place in a greased 13x9-in. baking dish. In a small bowl, mix butter, salt and pepper; drizzle over potatoes.
2. Bake, uncovered, 50-55 minutes or until potatoes are tender. Toss cheeses with minced herbs; sprinkle over potatoes. Bake 5 minutes longer or until cheese is melted.
1 potato: 318 cal., 15g fat (10g sat. fat), 43mg chol., 797mg sod., 39g carb. (3g sugars, 4g fiber), 8g pro.

PRO TIPS

• A wooden spoon can help you avoid cutting through the bottoms of Hasselback potatoes.

• Position the spoon alongside the potato, then cut carefully until the blade hits the handle.

• For a crispier potato, use olive oil instead of butter.

HACK

Simple and Sensational

To make stacking easier, set the baking dish on its side; fill with squash slices. When dish is full, return to original position. Try the technique with scalloped potatoes or sweet potatoes.

Crunchy Honey-Glazed Butternut Squash

I'm now required to bring this to every family gathering during the holidays because it's so awesome! Why not start a new tradition for your family?
—*Sarah Farmer, Waukesha, WI*

- -

Prep: 20 min. • **Bake:** 45 min.
Makes: 10 servings

½ cup honey
1 tsp. dried thyme, divided
1 large butternut squash (about 5 lbs.), peeled, halved, seeded and thinly sliced
3 Tbsp. water
¼ cup plus 2 Tbsp. olive oil, divided
1½ tsp. salt, divided
1½ tsp. pepper, divided
½ cup panko (Japanese) bread crumbs

1. Preheat oven to 375°. In a large saucepan, heat honey and ½ tsp. thyme, stirring occasionally, over low heat until fragrant, 3-4 minutes.
2. Meanwhile, in a microwave-safe dish, combine squash and water; microwave, covered, on high until squash is tender, 6-8 minutes. Drain. Add ¼ cup olive oil, 1 tsp. salt and 1 tsp. pepper; toss to coat.
3. On a flat surface, stack squash slices. Arrange stacks on their sides in a greased 9-in. square baking dish. Drizzle with 3 Tbsp. honey mixture.
4. Bake until the squash is tender, 45-50 minutes. In a small skillet, heat remaining oil over medium heat. Add bread crumbs; toss with remaining thyme and remaining salt and pepper. Cook and stir until golden brown, about 5 minutes. Sprinkle over baked squash; if desired, drizzle with additional honey mixture.
1 serving: 237 cal., 8g fat (1g sat. fat), 0 chol., 373mg sod., 43g carb. (20g sugars, 8g fiber), 3g pro.

CRUNCHY HONEY-GLAZED BUTTERNUT SQUASH

Oven Fries

I jazz up my fries with paprika and garlic powder. Something about the combination of spices packs a heck of a punch. We've discovered that the leftovers are even good nibbled cold!
—*Heather Byers, Pittsburgh, PA*

- -

Prep: 10 min. • **Bake:** 40 min.
Makes: 4 servings

- 4 medium potatoes
- 1 Tbsp. olive oil
- 2½ tsp. paprika
- ¾ tsp. salt
- ¾ tsp. garlic powder

1. Preheat oven to 400°. Cut each potato into 12 wedges. In a large bowl, combine oil, paprika, salt and garlic powder. Add potatoes; toss to coat.
2. Transfer to a 15x10x1 in. baking pan coated with cooking spray. Bake for 40-45 minutes or until tender, turning once.
12 pieces: 204 cal., 4g fat (1g sat. fat), 0 chol., 456mg sod., 39g carb. (3g sugars, 4g fiber), 5g pro.

SPICY SWEET POTATO FRIES

HACK

Apple Slicer Makes Steak Fries

Cut one end off the potato for stability. Stand the potato upright, place the apple slicer on top and gently push down. Presto!

Spicy Sweet Potato Fries

Better pile these sweet and spicy fries high on the plate! Served with a thick dipping sauce, they instill a craving for more.
—*Mary Jones, Athens, OH*

- -

Prep: 25 min. • **Bake:** 30 min.
Makes: 5 servings

- 1 tsp. coriander seeds
- ½ tsp. fennel seed
- ½ tsp. dried oregano
- ½ tsp. crushed red pepper flakes
- ½ tsp. salt
- 2 lbs. sweet potatoes (about 4 medium), peeled and cut into wedges
- 2 Tbsp. canola oil

SPICY MAYONNAISE DIP
- 1¼ cups mayonnaise
- 2 Tbsp. lime juice
- 2 Tbsp. minced fresh cilantro
- 2 garlic cloves, minced
- 1 tsp. ground mustard
- ¼ tsp. cayenne pepper
- ⅛ tsp. salt

1. In a spice grinder or with a mortar and pestle, combine the coriander, fennel, oregano and pepper flakes; grind until mixture becomes a fine powder. Stir in salt.
2. In a large bowl, combine potatoes, oil and ground spices; toss to coat. Transfer to a greased 15x10x1-in. baking pan.
3. Bake sweet potatoes, uncovered, at 400° for 30-35 minutes or until crisp and golden brown, turning occasionally. Meanwhile, in a small bowl, combine the dip ingredients; chill until serving. Serve with fries.
¾ cup fries with ¼ cup sauce: 573 cal., 50g fat (6g sat. fat), 20mg chol., 607mg sod., 28g carb. (11g sugars, 4g fiber), 2g pro.

Safely Venting Your Pressure Cooker

Just pick up a pair of tongs for safe, easy venting of your electric pressure cooker. Use the tongs to carefully turn the release valve—and keep your hands and face clear of the steam vent.

25-Minute Turkey Chili

This is a nice change of pace from traditional beef chili, offering a whole new set of flavors to enjoy. It's also ready fast, too. I like cheddar cheese bread on the side or try over rice.

—*Traci Wynne, Denver, PA*

Takes: 25 min. + releasing
Makes: 8 servings (2 qt.)

- 1 can (16 oz.) kidney beans, rinsed and drained
- 1 can (15 oz.) black beans, rinsed and drained
- 1 can (14½ oz.) Mexican stewed tomatoes, undrained
- 1 can (8 oz.) tomato sauce
- 1 small sweet red pepper, finely chopped
- 1 small onion, chopped
- 1 cup beef broth
- 1 jalapeno pepper, seeded and minced
- 2 Tbsp. chili powder
- ½ tsp. salt
- ¼ tsp. pepper
- 1¼ lbs. ground turkey
  Optional: sour cream and sliced jalapeno

1. Combine the first 11 ingredients in a 6-qt. electric pressure cooker. Crumble turkey over top; stir to combine. Lock lid; make sure vent is closed. Select manual setting; adjust the pressure to high and set time for 5 minutes.

2. When finished cooking, allow pressure to naturally release for 10 minutes, then quick-release any remaining pressure according to manufacturer's directions. Stir chili. If desired, serve with sour cream and additional jalapeno.

Note: Wear disposable gloves when cutting hot peppers; the oils can burn skin. Avoid touching your face.

1 cup: 268 cal., 11g fat (3g sat. fat), 48mg chol., 781mg sod., 25g carb. (6g sugars, 7g fiber), 19g pro.

Diabetic exchanges: 2 medium-fat meat, 1 starch, 1 vegetable.

25-MINUTE
TURKEY CHILI

Chicken Corn Soup with Rivels

Traditional chicken soup is rich with a dumplinglike soup-stretcher called rivels. This healthy recipe is brimming with chicken, vegetables and herbs. You won't be able to resist it.

—*Elissa Armbruster, Medford, NJ*

- -

Takes: 25 min. • **Makes:** 7 servings

- 1 cup chopped carrots
- 1 celery rib, chopped
- 1 medium onion, chopped
- 2 tsp. canola oil
- 2 cans (14½ oz. each) reduced-sodium chicken broth
- 2 cups fresh or frozen corn
- 2 cups cubed cooked chicken breast
- ½ tsp. minced fresh parsley
- ¼ tsp. salt
- ¼ tsp. dried tarragon
- ¼ tsp. pepper
- ¾ cup all-purpose flour
- 1 large egg, beaten

1. In a large saucepan, saute the carrots, celery and onion in oil until tender. Add the broth, corn, chicken, parsley, salt, tarragon and pepper. Bring to a boil.

2. Meanwhile, for rivels, place the flour in a bowl; mix in egg with a fork just until blended. Drop dough by teaspoonfuls into boiling soup, stirring constantly. Cook and stir for 1-2 minutes or until rivels are cooked through.

1 cup: 191 cal., 4g fat (1g sat. fat), 57mg chol., 482mg sod., 22g carb. (5g sugars, 2g fiber), 17g pro. **Diabetic exchanges:** 1½ starch, 2 lean meat.

HACK

De-Salt That Soup

Next time you accidentally oversalt your soup, toss in a few wedges of raw apple or potato. Simmer for 10 minutes, then discard the wedges—along with the excess salt.

VEGETARIAN
LINGUINE

STOVETOP MACARONI & CHEESE

🍎 Vegetarian Linguine

Looking for a tasty alternative to meat-and-potatoes meals? Try this colorful pasta dish. My oldest son came up with the stick-to-the-ribs supper that takes advantage of fresh mushrooms, zucchini and other vegetables as well as basil and provolone cheese.
—*Jane Bone, Cape Coral, FL*

- -

Takes: 30 min. • **Makes:** 6 servings

6	oz. uncooked linguine
2	Tbsp. butter
1	Tbsp. olive oil
2	medium zucchini, thinly sliced
½	lb. fresh mushrooms, sliced
1	large tomato, chopped
2	green onions, chopped
1	garlic clove, minced
½	tsp. salt
¼	tsp. pepper
1	cup shredded provolone cheese
3	Tbsp. shredded Parmesan cheese
2	tsp. minced fresh basil

Cook linguine according to package directions. Meanwhile, in a large skillet, heat butter and oil over medium heat. Add zucchini and mushrooms; saute 3-5 minutes. Add tomato, onions, garlic and seasonings. Reduce heat; simmer, covered, about 3 minutes. Drain linguine; add to vegetable mixture. Sprinkle with cheeses and basil. Toss to coat.

1½ cups: 260 cal., 13g fat (7g sat. fat), 25mg chol., 444mg sod., 26g carb. (3g sugars, 2g fiber), 12g pro. **Diabetic exchanges:** 1½ starch, 1½ fat, 1 medium-fat meat, 1 vegetable.

Stovetop Macaroni & Cheese

When I was a girl, Mama used Texas longhorn cheese in this recipe. After it melted all over the macaroni, I loved to dig in and see how many strings of cheese would follow my spoonful.
—*Imogene Hutton, Brownwood, TX*

- -

Takes: 25 min. • **Makes:** 6 servings

1	pkg. (7 oz.) elbow macaroni
¼	cup butter, cubed
¼	cup all-purpose flour
½	tsp. salt
	Dash pepper
2	cups whole milk
8	oz. sharp cheddar cheese, shredded
	Paprika, optional

1. Cook macaroni according to package directions. Meanwhile, in a large saucepan, melt butter over medium heat. Stir in the flour, salt and pepper until smooth; gradually whisk in milk. Bring to a boil, stirring constantly; cook and stir 1-2 minutes longer or until thickened.

2. Stir in cheese until melted. Drain macaroni; add to cheese sauce and stir to coat. If desired, sprinkle the top with paprika.

1 cup: 388 cal., 22g fat (15g sat. fat), 72mg chol., 542mg sod., 33g carb. (5g sugars, 1g fiber), 16g pro.

» **Swiss Mac & Cheese:** Saute ⅓ cup chopped onion in ¼ cup melted butter; add flour and proceed as directed. Substitute Swiss cheese for cheddar and add ⅛ tsp. nutmeg.

HACK

No-Stick Grated Cheese

A quick spritz of cooking spray will keep cheese from sticking to the grater. Cleanup is a lot easier.

Honey Garlic Green Beans

Green beans are great, but they can seem ordinary on their own. Just a few extra ingredients give them sweet and salty attitude.

—*Shannon Dobos, Calgary, AB*

- -

Takes: 20 min. • **Makes:** 8 servings

- 4 **Tbsp. honey**
- 2 **Tbsp. reduced-sodium soy sauce**
- 4 **garlic cloves, minced**
- ¼ **tsp. salt**
- ¼ **tsp. crushed red pepper flakes**
- 2 **lbs. fresh green beans, trimmed**

1. Whisk together first 5 ingredients; set aside. In a 6-qt. stockpot, bring 10 cups water to a boil. Add beans in batches; cook, uncovered, just until crisp-tender, 2-3 minutes. Remove beans and immediately drop into ice water. Drain and pat dry.

2. Coat stockpot with cooking spray. Add beans; cook, stirring constantly, over high heat until slightly blistered, 2-3 minutes. Add sauce; continue stirring until beans are coated and sauce starts to evaporate slightly, 2-3 minutes. Remove from heat.

¾ cup: 72 cal., 0 fat (0 sat. fat), 0 chol., 225mg sod., 18g carb. (12g sugars, 4g fiber), 2g pro. **Diabetic exchanges:** 1 vegetable, ½ starch.

**HONEY GARLIC
GREEN BEANS**

Quickly Separate and Peel Garlic Cloves

• Place the head of garlic in one bowl and smash with the bottom of a similar-sized bowl. You can also smash between two cutting boards.

• Put the whole crushed bulb in a hard-sided bowl with a similar-sized bowl over the top. Metal is best, but you can use glass or even a firm plastic food storage container with a lid. A jar works, too, but it takes longer to shake. Shake vigorously for 10-15 seconds to separate the papery outer layer from the garlic clove.

• The cloves are peeled and the skins can be easily discarded.

• The more finely you mince garlic, the stronger and more pungent it will be. More coarsely chopped garlic will have a milder impact.

• To remove the smell of garlic from your hands, scrub them with a mixture of baking soda and salt, then rinse with warm water. Alternatively, you can wash your hands with soap and water, and then rub them over a stainless steel surface (such as the sink faucet, an appliance or a pot).

Quickly De-Stem Fresh Herbs

- Getting all the small leaves off a sprig of thyme can be tricky, so try our Test Kitchen's simple hack. Simply thread a stem through a hole in a colander. This will remove every tiny bit of thyme while collecting it in the basin of the strainer.

- To remove cilantro and parsley leaves quickly and easily, run a fork along the stem. This will gently remove the leaves. You can then use the leaves whole for a more rustic presentation or give them a rough chop for sprinkling on top of your favorite dish.

Potato Kielbasa Skillet

Smoky kielbasa steals the show in this hearty home-style meal. It's especially good on chilly nights in late fall and early winter.
—Taste of Home *Test Kitchen*

Takes: 30 min. • **Makes:** 4 servings

- 1 lb. red potatoes (3-4 medium), cut into 1-in. pieces
- 3 Tbsp. water
- 2 Tbsp. brown sugar
- 2 Tbsp. cider vinegar
- 1 Tbsp. Dijon mustard
- 1½ tsp. minced fresh thyme or ½ tsp. dried thyme
- ¼ tsp. pepper
- 1 Tbsp. olive oil
- ½ cup chopped onion
- ¾ lb. smoked kielbasa or Polish sausage, cut into ¼-in. slices
- 4 cups fresh baby spinach
- 5 bacon strips, cooked and crumbled

1. Place potatoes and water in a microwave-safe dish. Microwave, covered, on high until potatoes are tender, 3-4 minutes; drain.
2. Meanwhile, mix the brown sugar, vinegar, mustard, thyme and pepper. In a large skillet, heat olive oil over medium-high heat; saute onion and kielbasa until onion is tender.
3. Add potatoes; cook and stir until lightly browned, 3-5 minutes. Stir in brown sugar mixture; bring to a boil. Reduce heat; simmer, uncovered, 2 minutes, stirring occasionally. Stir in spinach until wilted. Stir in bacon.
1½ cups: 472 cal., 31g fat (10g sat. fat), 66mg chol., 873mg sod., 31g carb. (10g sugars, 3g fiber), 17g pro.

Enchilada Casser-Ole!

My husband loves this casserole, and it never lasts long. Packed with black beans, cheese, tomatoes and plenty of Southwest flavor, it's an impressive-looking entree that's as simple as it is simply delicious.
—Marsha Wills, Homosassa, FL

Prep: 25 min. • **Bake:** 30 min.
Makes: 8 servings

- 1 lb. lean ground beef (90% lean)
- 1 large onion, chopped
- 2 cups salsa
- 1 can (15 oz.) black beans, rinsed and drained
- ¼ cup reduced-fat Italian salad dressing
- 2 Tbsp. reduced-sodium taco seasoning
- ¼ tsp. ground cumin
- 6 flour tortillas (8 in.)
- ¾ cup reduced-fat sour cream
- 1 cup shredded reduced-fat Mexican cheese blend
- 1 cup shredded lettuce
- 1 medium tomato, chopped
- ¼ cup minced fresh cilantro

1. In a large skillet, cook beef and onion over medium heat until meat is no longer pink; drain. Stir in the salsa, beans, dressing, taco seasoning and cumin. Place 3 flour tortillas in an 11x7-in. baking dish coated with cooking spray. Layer with half of the meat mixture, sour cream and cheese. Repeat layers.
2. Cover and bake at 400° for 25 minutes. Uncover; bake until heated through, 5-10 minutes longer. Let stand for 5 minutes; top with lettuce, tomato and cilantro.
1 piece: 357 cal., 12g fat (5g sat. fat), 45mg chol., 864mg sod., 37g carb. (6g sugars, 3g fiber), 23g pro. **Diabetic exchanges:** 3 lean meat, 2 starch, 1 vegetable, 1 fat.

ENCHILADA
CASSER-OLE!

MATTHEW'S
BEST EVER
MEAT LOAF

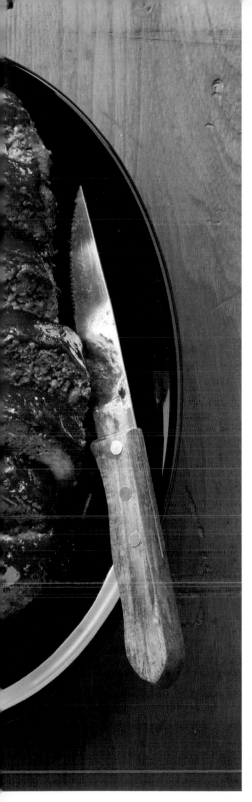

❄

Matthew's Best Ever Meat Loaf

This is comfort food at its best. Mushrooms, beef stock, tomato paste, Worcestershire and soy sauce help boost the meaty flavor of this classic diner staple.

—*Matthew Hass, Ellison Bay, WI*

Prep: 30 min.
Bake: 1¼ hours + standing
Makes: 8 servings

- 3 slices white bread, torn into small pieces
- ½ cup beef stock
- 2 large portobello mushrooms (about 6 oz.), cut into chunks
- 1 medium onion, cut into wedges
- 1 medium carrot, cut into chunks
- 1 celery rib, cut into chunks
- 3 garlic cloves, halved
- 1 Tbsp. olive oil
- 2 Tbsp. tomato paste
- 2 large eggs, lightly beaten
- 1¼ lbs. ground beef
- ¾ lb. ground pork
- 1 Tbsp. Worcestershire sauce
- 1 Tbsp. reduced-sodium soy sauce
- 1¼ tsp. salt
- ¾ tsp. pepper

GLAZE
- ½ cup ketchup
- 2 Tbsp. tomato paste
- 2 Tbsp. brown sugar
- 1 tsp. ground mustard

1. Preheat oven to 350°. Combine bread and stock; let stand until liquid is absorbed.

2. Meanwhile, pulse mushrooms, onion, carrot, celery and garlic in a food processor until finely chopped. In a large skillet, heat oil over medium heat. Add mushroom mixture; cook and stir until tender and liquid is evaporated, 5-6 minutes. Stir in tomato paste; cook 1 minute longer. Cool slightly.

3. Add next 7 ingredients and cooked vegetables to bread mixture; mix thoroughly. Place a 12x7-in. piece of foil on a rack in a foil-lined rimmed baking pan. Transfer meat mixture to the foil and shape into a 10x6-in. loaf.

4. Bake 1 hour. Mix together glaze ingredients; spread over loaf. Bake until a thermometer reads 160°, about 15-25 minutes longer. Let stand 10 minutes before slicing.

Freeze option: Shape meat loaf on a plastic wrap-lined baking sheet; wrap and freeze until firm. Remove from pan and wrap securely in foil; return to freezer. To use, unwrap the meat loaf and bake as directed, increasing initial baking time to 2 hours. Mix the glaze ingredients; spread over loaf. Bake until a thermometer inserted in center reads 160°, 15-25 minutes longer. Let stand 10 minutes before slicing.

1 slice: 341 cal., 18g fat (6g sat. fat), 119mg chol., 832mg sod., 19g carb. (11g sugars, 2g fiber), 25g pro.

HACK

Before cooking, place a cooling rack in a foil-lined baking pan; top the rack with a piece of foil slightly larger than the formed meat loaf. Set the loaf on the foil. This keeps the loaf from sinking into the rack and allows the grease to drip down into the pan.

Sneaky Turkey Meatballs

Like most kids, mine refuse to eat certain veggies. In order to feed them healthy foods, I have to be sneaky sometimes. The veggies in this recipe keep the meatballs moist while providing nutrients—and I'm happy to say my kids love 'em.
—*Courtney Stultz, Weir, KS*

Prep: 15 min. • **Bake:** 20 min.
Makes: 6 servings

¼ head fresh cauliflowerets
½ cup finely shredded cabbage
1 Tbsp. potato starch
 or cornstarch
1 Tbsp. balsamic vinegar
1 tsp. sea salt
1 tsp. dried basil
½ tsp. pepper
1 lb. ground turkey
 Optional: barbecue sauce
 and chopped fresh basil leaves

1. Preheat oven to 400°. Place the cauliflower in a food processor; pulse until finely chopped. Transfer to a large bowl. Add the cabbage, potato starch, vinegar, salt, basil and pepper.
2. Add the turkey; mix lightly but thoroughly. With ice cream scoop or with wet hands, shape into 1½-in. balls. Place meatballs on a greased rack in a 15x10x1-in. baking pan. Bake 20-24 minutes or until cooked through. If desired, toss with barbecue sauce and top with basil.
2 meatballs: 125 cal., 6g fat (1g sat. fat), 50mg chol., 370mg sod., 4g carb. (1g sugars, 1g fiber), 15g pro. **Diabetic exchanges:** 2 medium-fat meat.

Quick Work of Healthy Meatballs

• Speed up prep time by pulsing the veggies for meatballs in a food processor.

• The finer the veggies are chopped, the better they'll be distributed throughout. This makes for a smoother texture.

SNEAKY TURKEY
MEATBALLS

DENVER OMELET FRITTATA

Denver Omelet Frittata

This frittata is filled with the classic ingredients of a Denver omelet —pepper, onion and ham—along with potatoes to make it hearty. It's the perfect dish for after church.

—*Connie Eaton, Pittsburgh, PA*

Prep: 25 min. • **Cook:** 3 hours
Makes: 6 servings

- 1 cup water
- 1 Tbsp. olive oil
- 1 medium Yukon Gold potato, peeled and sliced
- 1 small onion, thinly sliced
- 12 large eggs
- 1 tsp. hot pepper sauce
- ½ tsp. salt
- ¼ tsp. pepper
- ½ lb. deli ham, chopped
- ½ cup chopped sweet green pepper
- 1 cup shredded cheddar cheese, divided

1. Layer two 24-in. pieces of foil; starting with a long side, fold foil to create a 1-in.-wide strip. Shape strip into a coil to make a rack for bottom of a 6-qt. oval slow cooker. Add water to slow cooker; set foil rack in water.
2. In a large skillet, heat olive oil over medium-high heat. Add potato and onion; cook and stir 4-6 minutes or until potato is lightly browned. Transfer to a greased 1½-qt. baking dish (dish must fit in slow cooker).
3. Whisk eggs, pepper sauce, salt and pepper; stir in ham, green pepper and ½ cup cheese. Pour over potato mixture. Top with remaining cheese. Place dish on foil rack.
4. Cook, covered, on low 3-4 hours or until eggs are set and a knife inserted in the center comes out clean.
1 serving: 314 cal., 19g fat (7g sat. fat), 407mg chol., 726mg sod., 10g carb. (3g sugars, 1g fiber), 25g pro.

HACK

Ramekins Extend Cook Times, Range of Foods You Can Slow-Cook

- Both of the recipes shown here cook in a ramekin placed inside the crock of a slow cooker. This creates extra-gentle heat for tender (not rubbery, scorched or tough) results.
- The same technique works with small ramekins or jars. Place them on a homemade foil coil to slow-cook a small batch of creme brulee or custard. Try Slow Cooker Chocolate Pots de Creme (p. 144).
- Oatmeal lovers, here's the best way to wake up to perfectly cooked hot oatmeal. Use the ramekin technique for all your steel-cut oats stovetop recipes, or for Overnight Flax Oatmeal (p. 119). Cook the oats on low in a ramekin for 10 hours.

GOOEY OLD-FASHIONED STEAMED MOLASSES BREAD

Gooey Old-Fashioned Steamed Molasses Bread

When I was growing up, the smell of this bread greeted me after school. I thought everyone baked bread in a slow cooker. Like my grandmother and mother, my daughters and I now bake this glorious comfort food.
—*Bonnie Geavaras, Chandler, AZ*

- -

Prep: 20 min.
Cook: 3 hours + cooling
Makes: 16 servings

- 2   cups All-Bran
- 1   cup all-purpose flour
- 1   cup whole wheat flour
- 1   cup dried cranberries
- 1½ tsp. baking powder
- 1   tsp. baking soda
- 1   tsp. salt
- ½   tsp. ground cinnamon
- 1   large egg
- 1¾ cups buttermilk
- ½   cup molasses
- 2   Tbsp. honey

1. Layer two 24-in. pieces of foil. Starting with a long side, roll up foil to make a 1-in.-wide strip; shape into a coil. Place on bottom of a 5-qt. slow cooker to make a rack.

2. Combine bran, flours, cranberries, baking powder, baking soda, salt and cinnamon. In another bowl, beat egg, buttermilk, molasses and honey. Stir into flour mixture just until blended (do not overbeat). Pour into a greased and floured 2-qt. baking dish. Tightly cover with lightly greased foil. Place in prepared slow cooker. Cook, covered, on high until a thermometer reads 190-200°, about 3 hours.

3. Remove dish to a wire rack; cool 10 minutes before inverting loaf onto the rack. Serve warm or cold.

1 wedge: 157 cal., 1g fat (0 sat. fat), 13mg chol., 351mg sod., 36g carb. (19g sugars, 4g fiber), 4g pro.

SPICY LENTIL &
CHICKPEA STEW, P. 67

FLAVOR SECRETS

[The best cooks build layers of flavor, and you'll learn how with these tricks. Discover our favorite ways to make the taste pop.]

Chili-Lime Mushroom Tacos

I used to make this dish with beef, but substituting portobello mushrooms turned it into my family's favorite vegetarian meal. It's quick, nutritious, low in fat and tasty.

—*Greg Fontenot, The Woodlands, TX*

- -

Takes: 25 min. • **Makes:** 4 servings

- 4 **large portobello mushrooms (about ¾ lb.)**
- 1 **Tbsp. olive oil**
- 1 **medium sweet red pepper, cut into strips**
- 1 **medium onion, halved and thinly sliced**
- 2 **garlic cloves, minced**
- 1½ **tsp. chili powder**
- ½ **tsp. salt**
- ½ **tsp. ground cumin**
- ¼ **tsp. crushed red pepper flakes**
- 1 **tsp. grated lime zest**
- 2 **Tbsp. lime juice**
- 8 **corn tortillas (6 in.), warmed**
- 1 **cup shredded pepper jack cheese**

1. Remove stems from mushrooms; if desired, remove gills using a spoon. Cut mushrooms into ½-in. slices.
2. In a large skillet, heat oil over medium-high heat; saute the sliced mushrooms, red pepper and onion until mushrooms are tender, cooking 5-7 minutes. Stir in garlic, seasonings, lime zest and juice; cook and stir for 1 minute. Serve in tortillas; top with cheese.

2 tacos: 300 cal., 14g fat (6g sat. fat), 30mg chol., 524mg sod., 33g carb. (5g sugars, 6g fiber), 13g pro. **Diabetic exchanges:** 2 vegetable, 1½ starch, 1 medium-fat meat, ½ fat.

> **PRO TIP**
>
> Preparing these same tacos with lean ground beef adds almost 4 grams saturated fat per serving. That's a good reason to make it a meatless Taco Tuesday!

CHILI-LIME MUSHROOM TACOS

HOW-TO

Julienne Peppers Like a Pro

- Trim stem from pepper so it sits flat on its top.

- Cut one side off the pepper, being careful to leave the seeds and core intact.

- Rotate pepper and cut off another side. Continue turning and cutting until only the core remains; trim or discard core.

- Cut each pepper fillet into thin strips.

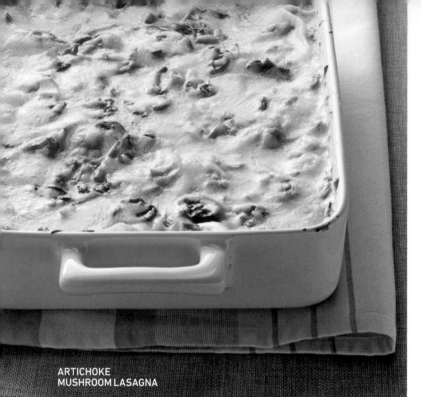

**ARTICHOKE
MUSHROOM LASAGNA**

Artichoke Mushroom Lasagna

Artichokes and baby portobellos add delightful flavor and depth to this impressive dish.
—*Bonnie Jost, Manitowoc, WI*

- -

Prep: 30 min.
Bake: 1 hour + standing
Makes: 12 servings

- 1   lb. sliced baby portobello mushrooms
- 2   Tbsp. butter
- 3   garlic cloves, minced
- 2   cans (14 oz. each) water-packed artichoke hearts, rinsed, drained and chopped
- 1   cup chardonnay or other white wine
- ¼   tsp. salt
- ¼   tsp. pepper
- SAUCE
- ¼   cup butter, cubed
- ¼   cup all-purpose flour
- 3½ cups 2% milk
- 2½ cups shredded Parmesan cheese
- 1   cup chardonnay or other white wine
- ASSEMBLY
- 9   no-cook lasagna noodles
- 4   cups shredded part-skim mozzarella cheese, divided

1. Preheat oven to 350°. In a large skillet, saute mushrooms in butter until tender. Add garlic; cook for 1 minute. Add artichokes, wine, salt and pepper; cook over medium heat until liquid is evaporated.
2. For sauce, in a large saucepan over medium heat, melt butter. Stir in flour until smooth; gradually add milk. Bring to a boil; cook and stir until thickened, about 1 minute. Stir in the Parmesan cheese and wine.
3. Spread 1 cup sauce into a greased 13x9-in. dish. Layer with 3 noodles, 1⅔ cups sauce, 1 cup mozzarella and 1⅓ cups artichoke mixture. Repeat layers twice.
4. Cover and bake for 45 minutes. Sprinkle with remaining mozzarella cheese. Bake, uncovered, until cheese is melted, 15-20 minutes. Let stand for 15 minutes before cutting.
1 piece: 383 cal., 18g fat (11g sat. fat), 54mg chol., 751mg sod., 29g carb. (6g sugars, 1g fiber), 24g pro.

Philly Cheese Fakes

Mushrooms are the key to this twist on popular Philly steak sandwiches— a nice meatless meal option that's tangy and tasty.
—*Veronica Vichit-Vadakan, Portland, OR*

- -

Prep: 30 min. • **Broil:** 5 min.
Makes: 4 servings

- ¼   cup lemon juice
- 3   garlic cloves, minced
- 1   Tbsp. olive oil
- ½   tsp. smoked paprika
- ¼   tsp. salt
- ¼   tsp. pepper
- 1   lb. sliced fresh shiitake mushrooms
- 2   medium green peppers, sliced
- 1   small onion, thinly sliced
- 4   hoagie buns, split
- 4   slices reduced-fat provolone cheese

1. Preheat oven to 450°. In a small bowl, whisk the first 6 ingredients. In a large bowl, combine mushrooms, green peppers and onion. Pour the dressing over vegetables; toss to coat.
2. Transfer to two 15x10x1-in. baking pans coated with cooking spray. Bake 15-20 minutes or until crisp-tender, stirring once.
3. Divide mushroom mixture among buns and top with cheese. Broil 3-4 in. from heat 2-3 minutes or until cheese is melted. Replace tops.
1 serving: 344 cal., 12g fat (4g sat. fat), 10mg chol., 681mg sod., 47g carb. (9g sugars, 4g fiber), 17g pro.

Mushrooms Add Meaty Flavor to Meatless Dishes

- With their rich taste and meaty texture, mushrooms make vegetarian meals that are wonderfully satisfying.

- Portobellos are fully grown cremini mushrooms, a cousin of the familiar button mushrooms found in most stores.

- Portobello stems are tough and woody. Discard them, or use well-rinsed and coarsely chopped stems in broth.

PHILLY CHEESE FAKES

Smoky Spices Enhance Vegetarian Dishes

• Ground chipotle pepper is a delicious accent to sweet potatoes and acorn squash, as featured in the recipes at right. It adds sweetness, heat and smoky notes, letting you enjoy a satisfying bacony taste without unwanted calories and fat (and no meat).

• Smoked paprika (used on p. 67) tastes similar but with less heat. It gives rich, hearty taste to bean and lentil dishes. You can use it in recipes that call for ground chipotle pepper. Just add a little cayenne or chili powder to boost the heat if desired.

SOUTHWEST HASH WITH ADOBO-LIME CREMA

Southwest Hash with Adobo-Lime Crema

Adobo sauce adds so much extra flavor that you won't even miss butter or meat in this smoky hash.

—Brooke Keller, Lexington, KY

- -

Prep: 20 min. • **Bake:** 25 min.
Makes: 4 servings

- 3 medium sweet potatoes (about 1½ lbs.), cubed
- 1 medium onion, chopped
- 1 medium sweet red pepper, chopped
- 1 Tbsp. canola oil
- 1 tsp. garlic powder
- 1 tsp. smoked paprika
- ¾ tsp. ground chipotle pepper
- ½ tsp. salt
- ¼ tsp. pepper
- ⅔ cup canned black beans
- 4 large eggs
- ½ cup reduced-fat sour cream
- 2 Tbsp. lime juice
- 2 tsp. adobo sauce
- ½ medium ripe avocado, peeled and sliced, optional
- 2 Tbsp. minced fresh cilantro

1. Preheat oven to 400°. Place sweet potatoes, onion and red pepper in a 15x10x1-in. baking pan coated with cooking spray. Drizzle with oil; sprinkle with seasonings. Toss to coat. Roast 25-30 minutes or until potatoes are tender, adding beans during the last 10 minutes of cooking time.

2. Place 2-3 in. of water in a large saucepan or skillet with high sides. Bring to boil; adjust heat to maintain a gentle simmer. Break cold eggs, 1 at a time, into a small bowl; holding bowl close to surface of water, slip egg into water.

3. Cook, uncovered, 3-5 minutes or until whites are completely set and yolks begin to thicken but are not hard. Using a slotted spoon, lift eggs out of water.

4. In a small bowl, mix sour cream, lime juice and adobo sauce. Serve sweet potato mixture with egg, sour cream mixture and, if desired, avocado. Sprinkle with cilantro.

1 serving: 304 cal., 12g fat (3g sat. fat), 222mg chol., 520mg sod., 37g carb. (15g sugars, 6g fiber), 13g pro. **Diabetic exchanges:** 2 starch, 1½ fat, 1 medium-fat meat.

Waffle-Iron Acorn Squash

I love to get the kids involved in cooking, and this squash is so simple even a small child can cook it with minimal adult supervision. The recipe is fun, fast and no-fuss, and it doesn't use up valuable oven space.

—Donna Kelly, Draper, UT

- -

Prep: 10 min. • **Bake:** 5 min./batch
Makes: 4 servings

- 3 Tbsp. maple syrup
- ¾ tsp. ground chipotle pepper
- ½ tsp. salt
- 1 small acorn squash

1. Preheat a greased waffle maker. Mix syrup, chipotle pepper and salt.

2. Cut acorn squash crosswise into ½-in.-thick slices. Using round cookie cutters, cut out centers to remove squash strings and seeds. If necessary, halve slices to fit waffle maker.

3. Bake slices just until tender and lightly browned, 3-4 minutes. Serve with syrup mixture.

1 serving: 98 cal., 0 fat (0 sat. fat), 0 chol., 463mg sod., 25g carb. (12g sugars, 2g fiber), 1g pro. **Diabetic exchanges:** 1½ starch.

HOW-TO

Easily Pit an Avocado

- Cut ripe avocado top to bottom until you hit the seed. Turn avocado and cut again to make quarters.

- Gently twist the halves to separate.

- Pull out the seed.

- Pull the skin back like a banana peel. Slice as you like.

MUSHROOM-BEAN
BOURGUIGNON

HOW-TO

Fake a Meaty Flavor with Fond

• Browning tomato paste (as in the Mushroom-Bean Bourguignon recipe) is a classic way to create a rich brown sauce.

• After browning, deglaze with wine or broth and scrape up any browned bits, (that's the fond) from the pan.

• Did you know? You can repeat the browning and deglazing steps as often as you like. Brown the tomato paste, deglaze with a little liquid, let liquid evaporate, and then brown the tomato paste again. Repeat over and over to create a dark vegetarian sauce that looks and tastes like it was made with meat!

Mushroom-Bean Bourguignon

In our family, boeuf bourguignon has been a staple for generations. I wanted a meatless alternative. All this dish needs is a French baguette.
—*Sonya Labbe, West Hollywood, CA*

Prep: 15 min. • **Cook:** 1¼ hours
Makes: 10 servings (2½ qt.)

- 4 Tbsp. olive oil, divided
- 5 medium carrots, cut into 1-in. pieces
- 2 medium onions, halved and sliced
- 2 garlic cloves, minced
- 8 large portobello mushrooms, cut into 1-in. pieces
- 1 Tbsp. tomato paste
- 1 bottle (750 ml) dry red wine
- 2 cups mushroom broth or vegetable broth, divided
- 1 tsp. salt
- 1 tsp. minced fresh thyme or ½ tsp. dried thyme
- ½ tsp. pepper
- 2 cans (15½ oz. each) navy beans, rinsed and drained
- 1 pkg. (14.4 oz.) frozen pearl onions
- 3 Tbsp. all-purpose flour

1. In a Dutch oven, heat 2 Tbsp. olive oil over medium-high heat. Add the carrots and onions; cook and stir until onions are tender, 8-10 minutes. Add garlic; cook 1 minute longer. Remove from pan.
2. In same pan, heat 1 Tbsp. oil over medium-high heat. Add half of the mushrooms; cook and stir until lightly browned. Remove from pan; repeat with remaining oil and mushrooms.
3. Return mushrooms to pan. Add tomato paste; cook and stir 1 minute. Stir in wine, 1½ cups broth, salt, thyme, pepper and carrot mixture; bring to a boil. Reduce heat; simmer, covered, 25 minutes.
4. Add beans and pearl onions; cook 30 minutes longer. In a small bowl, whisk flour and remaining broth until smooth; stir into pan. Bring to a boil; cook and stir 2 minutes or until slightly thickened.

1 cup: 234 cal., 6g fat (1g sat. fat), 0 chol., 613mg sod., 33g carb. (6g sugars, 7g fiber), 9g pro. **Diabetic exchanges:** 2 starch, 2 vegetable, 1 lean meat, 1 fat.

Spicy Lentil & Chickpea Stew

This recipe came to me from a previous co-worker at a health food store. I changed a few things until I found a version that my family loves. My son doesn't like things too spicy, so I make the stew milder for him and add a sprinkle of extra spice in mine. My husband works outdoors for long hours at a time and finds this soup hearty enough to keep him satisfied.
—*Melanie MacFarlane, Bedeque, PE*

- -

Prep: 25 min. • **Cook:** 8 hours
Makes: 8 servings (2¾ qt.)

- 2 tsp. olive oil
- 1 medium onion, thinly sliced
- 1 tsp. dried oregano
- ½ tsp. crushed red pepper flakes
- 2 cans (15 oz. each) chickpeas or garbanzo beans, rinsed and drained
- 1 cup dried lentils, rinsed
- 1 can (2¼ oz.) sliced ripe olives, drained
- 3 tsp. smoked paprika
- 4 cups vegetable broth
- 4 cans (8 oz. each) no-salt-added tomato sauce
- 4 cups fresh baby spinach
- ¾ cup fat-free plain yogurt

1. In a small skillet, heat oil over medium-high heat. Add onion, oregano and pepper flakes; cook and stir 8-10 minutes or until onion is tender. Transfer to a 5- or 6-qt. slow cooker.

2. Add chickpeas, lentils, olives and paprika; stir in broth and tomato sauce. Cook, covered, on low until lentils are tender, 8-10 hours. Stir in spinach. Top servings with yogurt.

1⅓ cups: 266 cal., 4g fat (0 sat. fat), 0 chol., 712mg sod., 45g carb. (11g sugars, 10g fiber), 14g pro. **Diabetic exchanges:** 2 starch, 2 vegetable, 1 lean meat.

SPICY LENTIL & CHICKPEA STEW

Vegetable Broth

The flavor of celery and mushrooms comes through in this homemade vegetable broth. It makes a fine substitute for chicken broth.
—Taste of Home *Test Kitchen*

- -

Prep: 45 min. • **Cook:** 1¾ hours
Makes: 5½ cups

- 2   Tbsp. olive oil
- 2   medium onions, cut into wedges
- 2   celery ribs, cut into 1-in. pieces
- 1   whole garlic bulb, separated into cloves and peeled
- 3   medium leeks, white and light green parts only, cleaned and cut into 1-in. pieces
- 3   medium carrots, cut into 1-in. pieces
- 8   cups water
- ½   lb. fresh mushrooms, quartered
- 1   cup packed fresh parsley sprigs
- 4   sprigs fresh thyme
- 1   tsp. salt
- ½   tsp. whole peppercorns
- 1   bay leaf

1. Heat oil in a stockpot over medium heat until hot. Add onions, celery and garlic. Cook and stir 5 minutes or until tender. Add the leeks and carrots; cook and stir 5 minutes. Add water, mushrooms, parsley, thyme, salt, peppercorns and bay leaf; bring to a boil. Reduce heat; simmer, uncovered, for 1 hour.

2. Remove from heat. Strain through a cheesecloth-lined colander; discard vegetables. If using immediately, skim fat. Or refrigerate 8 hours or overnight; remove fat from surface. Broth can be refrigerated up to 3 days or frozen up to 6 months.

1 cup: 148 cal., 6g fat (1g sat. fat), 0 chol., 521mg sod., 22g carb. (9g sugars, 5g fiber), 4g pro.

Make Homemade Broth

Making vegetable broth is as easy as cook, strain and serve! Follow along with our step-by-step guide.

• Sweat the vegetables. The recipe for vegetable broth aptly begins by cooking vegetables. Heat oil in a stockpot over medium heat until hot; you should start to see it shimmer. Add onions, celery and garlic. Then cook and stir for 5 minutes or until tender. Take a whiff—the pot should smell wonderful. Next, add in the leeks and carrots. Cook and stir 5 minutes longer.

• Add water and simmer. Time to add more to the pot. Carefully pour in water and add the mushrooms, parsley, thyme, salt, peppercorns and bay leaf. Bring the mixture to a boil. Reduce heat and simmer, uncovered, for 1 hour

• Strain and enjoy (or store for later). Remove the stockpot from the heat. Line a colander with cheesecloth (or use a fine mesh sieve or a coffee filter) and strain. Compost or discard the vegetables.

Savory Accent

To make a vegetable broth
that's rich and flavorful,
add cinnamon sticks and
star aniseed. The aroma of
the simmering broth is
amazing—and this savory
base is perfect for pho,
curry and noodle soups.

Coconut Curry Cauliflower Soup

When I'm in need of comfort food, I stir up a big velvety batch of this Asian-inspired soup. Then I finish it with a sprinkle of fresh cilantro over the top.

—*Elizabeth DeHart, West Jordan, UT*

- -

Prep: 10 min. • **Cook:** 25 min.
Makes: 10 servings (2½ qt.)

- 2 Tbsp. olive oil
- 1 medium onion, finely chopped
- 3 Tbsp. yellow curry paste
- 2 medium heads cauliflower, broken into florets
- 1 carton (32 oz.) vegetable broth
- 1 cup coconut milk
   Minced fresh cilantro, optional

1. In a large saucepan, heat oil over medium heat. Add onion; cook and stir until softened, 2-3 minutes. Add curry paste and cook until fragrant, 1-2 minutes. Add cauliflower and broth. Increase heat to high; bring to a boil. Reduce heat to medium-low; cook, covered, about 20 minutes.
2. Stir in coconut milk; cook an additional minute. Remove from heat; cool slightly. Puree in batches in a blender or food processor. If desired, top with minced fresh cilantro.
1 cup: 111 cal., 8g fat (5g sat. fat), 0 chol., 532mg sod., 10g carb. (4g sugars, 3g fiber), 3g pro.

CHRISTMAS TORTELLINI & SPINACH SOUP

Christmas Tortellini & Spinach Soup

I made this soup for the first time in the summer, but when I saw its bright red and green colors, my first thought was that it would make a perfect first course for Christmas dinner.

—*Marietta Slater, Justin, TX*

- -

Takes: 25 min. • **Makes:** 6 servings

- 2 cans (14½ oz. each) vegetable broth
- 1 pkg. (9 oz.) refrigerated cheese tortellini or tortellini of your choice
- 1 can (15 oz.) cannellini beans, rinsed and drained
- 1 can (14½ oz.) Italian diced tomatoes, undrained
- ¼ tsp. salt
- ⅛ tsp. pepper
- 3 cups fresh baby spinach
- 3 Tbsp. minced fresh basil
- ¼ cup shredded Asiago cheese

1. In a large saucepan, bring broth to a boil. Add tortellini; reduce heat. Simmer, uncovered, 5 minutes. Stir in beans, tomatoes, salt and pepper; return to a simmer. Cook 4-5 minutes longer or until tortellini are tender.
2. Stir in spinach and basil; cook until wilted. Top servings with cheese.
1 cup: 239 cal., 5g fat (3g sat. fat), 23mg chol., 1135mg sod., 38g carb. (7g sugars, 5g fiber), 11g pro.

PRO TIP

Hold the Salt

To reduce the sodium in this recipe, use homemade broth (for 165 milligrams less sodium per serving). Substitute no-salt-added diced tomatoes and skip the ¼ tsp. salt to reduce total sodium to 767 milligrams per serving.

Create Your Perfect Pasta Salad

Start with a shape. Toss with mix-ins. Add dressing and flavorful accents.
Here is the simplest, most delicious equation. The result? Potluck perfection.

Pasta		Mix-ins		Dressing		Accents
Asian Noodle Whole wheat spaghetti	+	Cubed chicken, coleslaw mix, mandarin oranges	+	Sesame-ginger vinaigrette	+	Chow mein noodles
California Waldorf Orecchiette	+	Smoked turkey, apples, celery, strawberries	+	2:1 mix of plain yogurt and mayo	+	Walnuts, Dijon mustard
Garden Ranch Tricolor rotini	+	Broccoli, cucumbers, tomatoes	+	Ranch dressing	+	Crumbled bacon
Taco Beef Rotini	+	Taco meat, cheddar, tomatoes, peppers	+	Catalina dressing	+	Tortilla chips, black olives
Classic Mac Macaroni	+	Ham, cheddar, peas, green onions	+	Mayo thinned with vinegar	+	Pickle relish
Tortellini Time Cheese tortellini	+	Broccoli, red peppers	+	Red wine vinaigrette	+	Prosciutto, green olives
Under the Sea Shells	+	Imitation crab, peas	+	Mayonnaise	+	Dill
Spinach Bow Ties Farfalle	+	Baby spinach, yellow pepper, dried apricots	+	Balsamic vinaigrette	+	Sliced almonds

CUCUMBER SHELL SALAD

Cucumber Shell Salad

Ranch dressing is the mild coating for this pleasant pasta salad alive with the fresh flavors of crunchy cucumber, onion and green peas. Someone always seems to want the recipe!

—Paula Ishii, Ralston, NE

- -

Prep: 20 min. + chilling
Makes: 16 servings

- 1 pkg. (16 oz.) medium pasta shells
- 1 pkg. (16 oz.) frozen peas, thawed
- 1 medium cucumber, halved and sliced
- 1 small red onion, chopped
- 1 cup ranch salad dressing

Cook pasta according to package directions; drain and rinse in cold water. In a large bowl, combine the pasta, peas, cucumber and onion. Add dressing; toss to coat. Cover and chill at least 2 hours before serving.
¾ cup: 165 cal., 1g fat (0 sat. fat), 0 chol., 210mg sod., 33g carb. (0 sugars, 3g fiber), 6g pro. **Diabetic exchanges:** 2 starch.

HOW-TO

Make Any Pasta Salad

Boil a pound of pasta in salted water according to package directions for al dente; drain.

• Rinse pasta well in cold water to stop the cooking. Drain well.

• Add your favorite mix-ins. Go for a variety of flavors, colors and textures.

• Add a cup or more of dressing and stir well to combine. (Pasta salad will absorb dressing as it sits.)

• Add some bold flavor accents such as crisp bacon, spicy curry powder, crunchy nuts or tangy lemon.

• Refrigerate until serving.

Tzatziki Chicken

I like to make classic chicken recipes for my family but the real fun is trying a fresh new twist.

—*Kristen Heigl, Staten Island, NY*

Takes: 30 min. • **Makes:** 4 servings

- 1½ **cups finely chopped peeled English cucumber**
- 1 **cup plain Greek yogurt**
- 2 **garlic cloves, minced**
- 1½ **tsp. chopped fresh dill**
- 1½ **tsp. olive oil**
- ⅛ **tsp. salt**

CHICKEN
- ⅔ **cup all-purpose flour**
- 1 **tsp. pepper**
- 1 **tsp. salt**
- ¼ **tsp. baking powder**
- 1 **large egg**
- ⅓ **cup 2% milk**
- 4 **boneless skinless chicken breast halves (6 oz. each)**
- ¼ **cup canola oil**
- ¼ **cup crumbled feta cheese Lemon wedges, optional**

1. For sauce, mix first 6 ingredients; refrigerate until serving.

2. In a shallow bowl, whisk together flour, salt, pepper and baking powder. In another bowl, whisk together egg and milk. Pound chicken breasts with a meat mallet to ½-in. thickness. Dip in flour mixture to coat both sides; shake off excess. Dip in egg mixture, then again in flour mixture.

3. In a large skillet, heat oil over medium heat. Cook chicken until golden brown and chicken is no longer pink, 5-7 minutes per side. Top with cheese. Serve with sauce and, if desired, lemon wedges.

1 chicken breast half with ⅓ cup sauce: 482 cal., 27g fat (7g sat. fat), 133mg chol., 737mg sod., 17g carb. (4g sugars, 1g fiber), 41g pro.

Lamb Pitas with Yogurt Sauce

The spiced lamb in these stuffed pita pockets goes perfectly with cool cucumber and yogurt. It's like having your own Greek gyro stand in the kitchen!
—*Angela Leinenbach, Mechanicsville, VA*

- -

Prep: 35 min. • **Cook:** 6 hours
Makes: 8 servings

TZATZIKI
CHICKEN

2	Tbsp. olive oil
2	lbs. lamb stew meat (¾-in. pieces)
1	large onion, chopped
1	garlic clove, minced
⅓	cup tomato paste
½	cup dry red wine
1¼	tsp. salt, divided
1	tsp. dried oregano
½	tsp. dried basil
1	medium cucumber
1	cup plain yogurt
16	pita pocket halves, warmed
4	plum tomatoes, sliced

1. In a large skillet, heat oil over medium-high heat; brown lamb in batches. Transfer lamb to a 3- or 4-qt. slow cooker, reserving the drippings in skillet.

2. In the drippings, saute onion over medium heat until tender, 4-6 minutes. Add garlic and tomato paste; cook and stir 2 minutes. Stir in wine, 1 tsp. salt, oregano and basil. Add to lamb. Cook, covered, on low until lamb is tender, 6-8 hours.

3. To serve, dice enough cucumber to measure 1 cup; thinly slice remaining cucumber. Combine diced cucumber with yogurt and remaining salt. Fill pitas with lamb mixture, tomatoes, sliced cucumbers and yogurt mixture.

Freeze option: Freeze cooled lamb mixture in freezer containers. To use, partially thaw in refrigerator overnight. Heat through in a saucepan, stirring occasionally and adding a little broth or water if necessary.

2 filled pita halves: 383 cal., 11g fat (3g sat. fat), 78mg chol., 766mg sod., 39g carb. (5g sugars, 3g fiber), 31g pro. **Diabetic exchanges:** 3 lean meat, 2½ starch, 1 fat.

PRO TIP

Cool-as-a-Cucumber Sauce

- Cool, creamy cucumber-yogurt sauce is a popular condiment in both the Middle East and India (where it's called tzatziki sauce and raita, respectively).

- Add fresh herbs (especially mint) for an even cooler, more refreshing counterpoint to very spicy dishes.

- In a pinch, thin down some sour cream with milk or lemon juice and season it with mint, dill or basil (dried works OK for this).

GREAT-GRANDMA'S
ITALIAN MEATBALLS

Old-Fashioned Flavor with Less Fat

• Baking on a rack ensures a crisp and browned exterior, and helps to drain away any excess fat.

• Using a combination of lean ground turkey and beef boosts flavor and saves nearly 10 percent calories compared to using only lean ground beef.

Great-Grandma's Italian Meatballs

A classic Italian dish isn't complete without homemade meatballs. This versatile recipe can be used in other dishes starring meatballs, too.
—*Audrey Colantino, Winchester, MA*

Prep: 30 min. • **Bake:** 20 min.
Makes: 8 servings

- 2 tsp. olive oil
- 1 medium onion, chopped
- 3 garlic cloves, minced
- ¾ cup seasoned bread crumbs
- ½ cup grated Parmesan cheese
- 2 large eggs, lightly beaten
- 1 tsp. each dried basil, oregano and parsley flakes
- ¾ tsp. salt
- 1 lb. lean ground turkey
- 1 lb. lean ground beef (90% lean)
  Hot cooked pasta and pasta sauce, optional

1. Preheat oven to 375°. In a small skillet, heat oil over medium-high heat. Add onion; cook and stir until tender, 3-4 minutes. Add garlic; cook 1 minute longer. Cool slightly.
2. In a large bowl, combine bread crumbs, cheese, eggs, seasonings and onion mixture. Add the turkey and beef; mix lightly but thoroughly. Shape into 1½-in. balls.
3. Place meatballs on a rack coated with cooking spray in a 15x10x1-in. baking pan. Bake until lightly browned and cooked through, 18-22 minutes. If desired, serve with hot pasta and pasta sauce.
1 serving: 271 cal., 13g fat (5g sat. fat), 125mg chol., 569mg sod., 10g carb. (1g sugars, 1g fiber), 27g pro.
Diabetic exchanges: 4 lean meat, 1 fat, ½ starch.

Zucchini-Crusted Pizza

Flavorful, nutritious and versatile, this pizza is easy to prep and fun to make with the kids. It also quadruples nicely. What's not to like?
—*Ruth Hartunian-Alumbaugh, Willimantic, CT*

Prep: 20 min. • **Bake:** 25 min.
Makes: 6 servings

- 2 large eggs, lightly beaten
- 2 cups shredded zucchini (about 1½ medium), squeezed dry
- ½ cup shredded part-skim mozzarella cheese
- ½ cup grated Parmesan cheese
- ¼ cup all-purpose flour
- 1 Tbsp. olive oil
- 1 Tbsp. minced fresh basil
- 1 tsp. minced fresh thyme

TOPPINGS
- 1 jar (12 oz.) roasted sweet red peppers, julienned
- 1 cup shredded part-skim mozzarella cheese
- ½ cup sliced turkey pepperoni

1. Preheat oven to 450°. Mix first 8 ingredients; transfer to a 12-in. pizza pan coated generously with cooking spray. Spread mixture to an 11-in. circle.
2. Bake pizza until light golden brown, 13-16 minutes. Reduce oven setting to 400°. Add toppings. Bake until cheese is melted, 10-12 minutes longer.
1 slice: 219 cal., 12g fat (5g sat. fat), 95mg chol., 680mg sod., 10g carb. (4g sugars, 1g fiber), 14g pro.
Diabetic exchanges: 2 medium-fat meat, ½ starch, ½ fat.

> **PRO TIP**
>
> Using a zucchini crust saves about 20 grams carbohydrates and 40 calories per serving compared to a regular pizza crust.

ZUCCHINI-CRUSTED PIZZA

SLOW-COOKED
CARIBBEAN POT ROAST

Slow-Cooked Caribbean Pot Roast

This dish is definitely a year-round recipe. Sweet potatoes, orange zest and baking cocoa are my surprise ingredients.

—*Jenn Tidwell, Fair Oaks, CA*

Prep: 30 min. • **Cook:** 6 hours
Makes: 10 servings

- 2 **medium sweet potatoes, cubed**
- 2 **large carrots, sliced**
- ¼ **cup chopped celery**
- 1 **boneless beef chuck roast (2½ lbs.)**
- 1 **Tbsp. canola oil**
- 1 **large onion, chopped**
- 2 **garlic cloves, minced**
- 1 **Tbsp. all-purpose flour**
- 1 **Tbsp. sugar**
- 1 **Tbsp. brown sugar**
- 1 **tsp. ground cumin**
- ¾ **tsp. salt**
- ¾ **tsp. ground coriander**
- ¾ **tsp. chili powder**
- ½ **tsp. dried oregano**
- ⅛ **tsp. ground cinnamon**
- ¾ **tsp. grated orange zest**
- ¾ **tsp. baking cocoa**
- 1 **can (15 oz.) tomato sauce**

1. Place potatoes, carrots and celery in a 5-qt. slow cooker. In a large skillet, brown meat in oil on all sides. Transfer meat to slow cooker.

2. In the same skillet, saute onion in drippings until tender. Add garlic; cook 1 minute longer. Combine the flour, sugar, brown sugar, seasonings, orange zest and cocoa. Stir in tomato sauce; add to skillet and heat through. Pour over beef.

3. Cover and cook on low until beef and vegetables are tender, 6-8 hours.

3 oz. cooked beef with ½ cup vegetable mixture: 278 cal., 12g fat (4g sat. fat), 74mg chol., 453mg sod., 16g carb. (8g sugars, 3g fiber), 25g pro. **Diabetic exchanges:** 3 lean meat, 1 starch, 1 vegetable, ½ fat.

Cauliflower & Tofu Curry

Cauliflower, garbanzo beans and tofu are subtle on their own, but together they make an awesome base for curry. We have this recipe weekly because one of us is always craving it.

—*Patrick McGilvray, Cincinnati, OH*

Takes: 30 min. • **Makes:** 6 servings

- 1   **Tbsp. olive oil**
- 2   **medium carrots, sliced**
- 1   **medium onion, chopped**
- 3   **tsp. curry powder**
- ¼   **tsp. salt**
- ¼   **tsp. pepper**
- 1   **small head cauliflower, broken into florets (about 3 cups)**
- 1   **can (14½ oz.) fire-roasted crushed tomatoes**
- 1   **pkg. (14 oz.) extra-firm tofu, drained and cut into ½-in. cubes**
- 1   **cup vegetable broth**
- 1   **can (15 oz.) garbanzo beans or chickpeas, rinsed and drained**
- 1   **can (13.66 oz.) coconut milk**
- 1   **cup frozen peas**
       Hot cooked rice
       Chopped fresh cilantro

1. In a 6-qt. stockpot, heat olive oil over medium-high heat. Add carrots and onion; cook and stir until onion is tender, 4-5 minutes. Stir in the seasonings.

2. Add cauliflower, tomatoes, tofu and broth; bring to a boil. Reduce heat; simmer, covered, 10 minutes. Stir in garbanzo beans, coconut milk and peas; return to a boil. Reduce heat to medium; cook, uncovered, stirring occasionally, until slightly thickened and cauliflower is tender, 5-7 minutes.

3. Serve with hot rice. Sprinkle with fresh cilantro.

1⅓ cups: 338 cal., 21g fat (13g sat. fat), 0 chol., 528mg sod., 29g carb. (9g sugars, 7g fiber), 13g pro.

CAULIFLOWER
& TOFU CURRY

Big Daddy's BBQ Ribs

There's nothing left on the platter when I cook these for my co-workers.
—*Eric Brzostek, East Islip, NY*

- -

Prep: 30 min. + chilling
Bake: 1½ hours • **Makes:** 8 servings

- ¾ cup packed brown sugar
- 2 Tbsp. mesquite seasoning
- 4½ tsp. garlic powder
- 4½ tsp. paprika
- 1 Tbsp. dried minced onion
- 1 Tbsp. seasoned salt
- 1 Tbsp. ground cinnamon
- 1 Tbsp. ground cumin
- 1 Tbsp. pepper
- 1 tsp. salt
- 8 lbs. pork spareribs, cut into serving-size pieces
- 3½ cups barbecue sauce

1. Combine first 10 ingredients. Rub over ribs; refrigerate overnight.
2. Place ribs on a rack in a shallow roasting pan. Cover and bake at 350° for 1 hour; drain. Brush some of the barbecue sauce over ribs. Bake, uncovered, 30-45 minutes or until tender, basting with the remaining barbecue sauce.

1 serving: 1027 cal., 67g fat (24g sat. fat), 255mg chol., 2071mg sod., 40g carb. (35g sugars, 3g fiber), 64g pro.

BIG DADDY'S
BBQ RIBS

Island Pork Roast

This fork-tender pork roast is a tempting mixture of sweet and tang, especially good when served over rice. Any leftovers, should you be so lucky, make wonderful sandwiches.
—*Heather Campbell, Lawrence, KS*

- -

Prep: 25 min. • **Cook:** 5 hours
Makes: 10 servings

- 1 boneless pork loin roast (about 4 lbs.)
- 1 large onion, sliced
- 2 cans (8 oz. each) unsweetened pineapple chunks, undrained
- ½ cup sugar
- ½ cup lime juice
- ½ cup soy sauce
- ¼ cup packed brown sugar
- 2 Tbsp. teriyaki sauce
- 2 garlic cloves, minced
- 1 tsp. ground ginger
- 1 tsp. curry powder
- ¼ tsp. salt
- ¼ tsp. pepper
- 1 bay leaf
- ¼ cup cornstarch
- ½ cup cold water

1. Cut roast in half. Place onion in a 4- or 5-qt. slow cooker. Add pork. Drain pineapple, reserving juice; set pineapple aside. In a small bowl, combine the sugar, lime juice, soy sauce, brown sugar, teriyaki sauce, garlic, ginger, curry, salt, pepper, bay leaf and reserved juice. Pour over the pork roast.
2. Cover and cook on low for 5-6 hours or until a thermometer reads 160°. Add pineapple during the last hour of cooking.
3. Remove the meat, onion and pineapple to a serving platter; keep warm. Discard bay leaf. Skim fat from cooking juices; transfer juice to a small saucepan and bring to a boil. Combine cornstarch and water until smooth; gradually stir into the pan. Bring to a boil; cook and stir for 2 minutes or until thickened. Serve with pork.

4 oz. cooked pork with ¼ cup pineapple mixture and ⅓ cup sauce: 341 cal., 8g fat (3g sat. fat), 90mg chol., 976mg sod., 27g carb. (22g sugars, 1g fiber), 37g pro.

All-Day Apple Butter

I make several batches of this luscious apple butter to freeze in jars. Gauge how sweet the apples are and adjust the sugar to taste.
—*Betty Ruenholl, Syracuse, NE*

- -

Prep: 20 min. • **Cook:** 11 hours
Makes: 4 pints

5½ lbs. apples, peeled, cored
   and finely chopped
4 cups sugar
2 to 3 tsp. ground cinnamon
¼ tsp. ground cloves
¼ tsp. salt

1. Place apples in a 3-qt. slow cooker. Combine sugar, cinnamon, cloves and salt; pour over apples and mix well. Cover and cook on high for 1 hour.
2. Reduce heat to low; cover and cook for 9-11 hours or until thickened and dark brown, stirring occasionally (stir more frequently as it thickens to prevent sticking).
3. Uncover and cook on low 1 hour longer. If desired, stir with a wire whisk until smooth. Spoon into freezer containers, leaving ½-in. headspace. Cover and refrigerate or freeze.

2 Tbsp.: 68 cal., 0 fat (0 sat. fat), 0 chol., 9mg sod., 17g carb. (16g sugars, 1g fiber), 0 pro.

Spinach Salad with Apple Dressing

Apple butter gives a delightful sweetness to this spinach salad. Pecans and Swiss cheese add to the flavor and are a great pairing, too.
—Taste of Home *Test Kitchen*

- -

Takes: 10 min. • **Makes:** 4 servings

½ cup apple butter
3 Tbsp. olive oil
1 Tbsp. cider vinegar
⅛ tsp. pepper
6 cups fresh baby spinach
½ cup pecan halves
¼ cup shredded Swiss cheese

For dressing, in a jar with a tight-fitting lid, combine the apple butter, oil, vinegar and pepper; shake well. Divide spinach among 4 plates; sprinkle with pecans and cheese. Drizzle with the salad dressing.
1 serving: 272 cal., 21g fat (3g sat. fat), 6mg chol., 54mg sod., 18g carb. (13g sugars, 3g fiber), 4g pro.

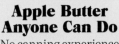

Apple Butter Anyone Can Do

No canning experience needed to make the simple, hands-free All-Day Apple Butter. Use it as a flavorful starter for salads, pork dishes and the recipes on p. 83. It's a perfect excuse to go apple-picking!

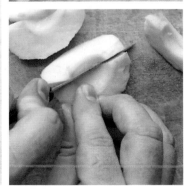

ALL-DAY APPLE BUTTER

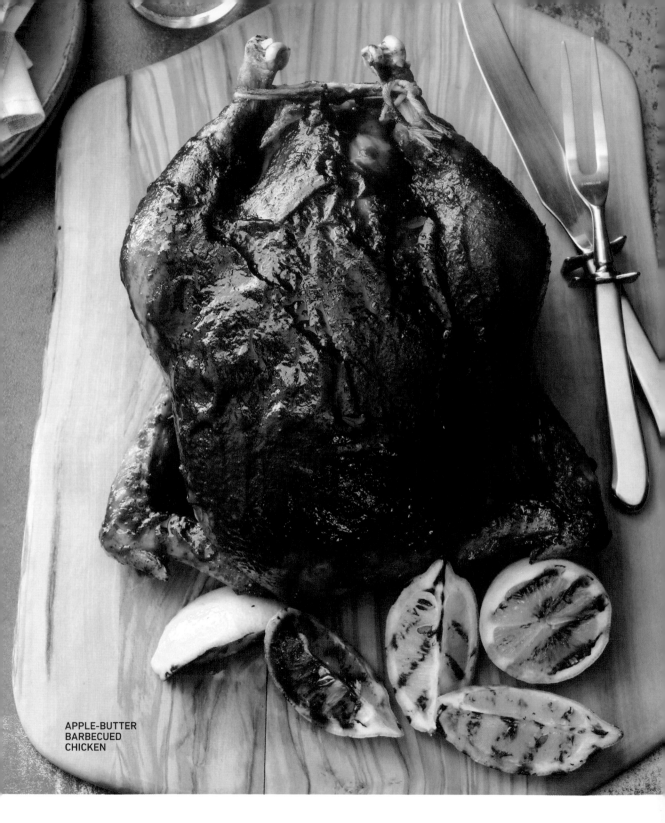

APPLE-BUTTER
BARBECUED
CHICKEN

Apple-Butter Barbecued Chicken

I love cooking so much I sometimes think of recipes in my sleep and wake up to write them down! This dream-inspired dish is my family's most-requested chicken recipe.

—Holly Kilbel, Akron, OH

- -

Prep: 15 min.
Grill: 1½ hours + standing
Makes: 8 servings

- 1   tsp. salt
- ¾   tsp. garlic powder
- ¼   tsp. pepper
- ⅛   tsp. cayenne pepper
- 1   roasting chicken (6 to 7 lbs.)
- 1   can (11½ oz.) unsweetened apple juice
- ½   cup apple butter
- ¼   cup barbecue sauce

1. Combine the salt, garlic powder, pepper and cayenne; sprinkle over roasting chicken.
2. Prepare grill for indirect heat, using a drip pan. Pour half of the apple juice into another container and save for another use. With a can opener, poke additional holes in the top of the can. Holding the chicken with legs pointed down, lower chicken over the can so it fills the body cavity. Place chicken on grill rack over drip pan.
3. Grill, covered, over indirect medium heat 1½-2 hours or until a thermometer reads 180°. Combine apple butter and barbecue sauce; baste chicken occasionally during the last 30 minutes. Remove chicken from grill; cover and let stand for 10 minutes. Remove chicken from can before carving.
6 oz. cooked chicken: 441 cal., 24g fat (7g sat. fat), 134mg chol., 489mg sod., 11g carb. (10g sugars, 0 fiber), 43g pro.

Breakfast Meatballs in Apple Butter

Apple butter and maple syrup make these meatballs irresistible on a breakfast spread. They're unique and delicious.

—Joan Reesman, Franklin, TN

- -

Prep: 5 min. + marinating
Makes: 8 meatballs

- ¼   lb. bulk pork sausage
- 2   Tbsp. apple butter
- 1   tsp. maple syrup

1. Roll sausage into 1-in. balls. Place on a microwave-safe plate. Cover and microwave on high for 1-2 minutes or until a thermometer reads 160°. Cool.
2. Transfer to a microwave-safe serving dish. In a small dish, combine apple butter and syrup; pour over meatballs and gently stir to coat. Cover and refrigerate overnight.
3. Microwave, covered, on high for 1 minute or until heated through.
1 meatball: 44 cal., 3g fat (1g sat. fat), 8mg chol., 87mg sod., 3g carb. (2g sugars, 0 fiber), 2g pro.

Nutty Caramel Apple Dip

Looking for a standout appetizer that could double as a dessert? Try this fast, no-fuss favorite that whips up easily for family and friends. It's a fun and an easy way to get folks to snack on apples instead of junk food.

—Darlene Brenden, Salem, OR

- -

Takes: 15 min. • **Makes:** 2 cups

- 1   pkg. (8 oz.) cream cheese, softened
- ½   cup apple butter
- ¼   cup packed brown sugar
- ½   tsp. vanilla extract
- ½   cup chopped salted peanuts
    Sliced apples

In a small bowl, beat the cream cheese, apple butter, brown sugar and vanilla until combined. Stir in the peanuts. Serve with apple slices. Refrigerate leftovers.
¼ cup: 210 cal., 14g fat (6g sat. fat), 29mg chol., 131mg sod., 18g carb. (14g sugars, 1g fiber), 4g pro.

PRO TIP

Dip on the Go

- Pop ¼-cup servings of this dip into small containers for a healthy-ish snack or dessert while on the go. Just grab an apple!

- Also try the dip with graham crackers, pretzels, mini bagels or even celery and carrot sticks.

Beer Can Chicken

You'll be proud to serve this chicken at any gathering. Treated with a savory rub and then roasted over a can of beer, it's so tasty you'll want to call dibs on the leftovers!
—*Shirley Warren, Thiensville, WI*

- -

Prep: 20 min.
Grill: 1¼ hours + standing
Makes: 4 servings

- 4 tsp. chicken seasoning
- 2 tsp. sugar
- 2 tsp. chili powder
- 1½ tsp. paprika
- 1¼ tsp. dried basil
- ¼ tsp. pepper
- 1 broiler/fryer chicken (3 to 4 lbs.)
- 1 Tbsp. canola oil
- 2 lemon slices
- 1 can (12 oz.) beer or nonalcoholic beer

1. Combine the first 6 ingredients. Gently loosen skin from chicken. Brush chicken with oil. Sprinkle 1 tsp. spice mixture into cavity. Rub remaining spice mixture over and under the skin. Place lemon in neck cavity. Tuck wing tips behind the back.

2. Prepare grill for indirect heat, using a drip pan. Pour out half the beer, reserving for another use. Poke additional holes in top of the can with a can opener. Holding the chicken with legs pointed down, lower chicken over the can so it fills the body cavity.

3. Place the chicken over drip pan; grill, covered, over indirect medium heat until a thermometer reads 180°, 1¼-1½ hours. Remove chicken from grill; cover and let stand 10 minutes. Remove chicken from beer can before carving.

7 oz. cooked chicken: 415 cal., 25g fat (6g sat. fat), 131mg chol., 366mg sod., 3g carb. (2g sugars, 1g fiber), 42g pro.

PRO TIP

Grill over Cans

Grilling chicken over a can of beer or apple juice is just the beginning. Try this technique with Caribbean spices and Dr Pepper, lemon-pepper and Sprite, or barbecue seasoning and root beer or cola.

BEER CAN CHICKEN

SMOKED HONEY-PEPPERCORN SALMON

Smoked Honey-Peppercorn Salmon

I found this recipe in an Alaska fishing guide. Now it's the only way we do salmon. The brine gives it a sweet, caramelized coating, and the hickory chips give the fish a smoky flavor.

—*Judy Ashby, Jamestown, TN*

Prep: 20 min. + marinating
Grill: 45 min. • **Makes:** 4 servings

- 1   cup packed brown sugar
- 1   cup water
- ⅓   cup salt
- 1   Tbsp. minced fresh gingerroot
- 2   bay leaves
- 1   tsp. ground allspice
- ½   cup cold water
- 1   salmon fillet (1 lb.)
- ¼   cup honey
- 1   Tbsp. whole peppercorns, crushed
- 2   cups soaked hickory wood chips

1. In a small saucepan, bring first 6 ingredients to a boil. Cook and stir until sugar and salt are dissolved. Remove from heat. Add cold water to cool brine to room temperature.

2. Place salmon in a large resealable plastic bag; carefully pour cooled brine into bag. Squeeze out air; seal bag and turn to coat. Chill 4 hours, turning occasionally.

3. Drain and discard brine; rinse salmon and pat dry. Spread honey over fillet; sprinkle with peppercorns.

4. Add wood chips to grill according to manufacturer's directions. Place salmon on greased grill rack, skin side down. Grill, covered, over indirect medium heat until fish flakes easily with a fork, 45-50 minutes.

1 serving: 244 cal., 10g fat (2g sat. fat), 57mg chol., 143mg sod., 18g carb. (18g sugars, 0 fiber), 19g pro.
Diabetic exchanges: 3 lean meat, 1 starch.

Get Real Jamaican Flavor

Don't skip the applewood chips or allspice berries on the grill. It's as close to the flavor of Jamaican pimento wood as you can get.

MATT'S JERK CHICKEN

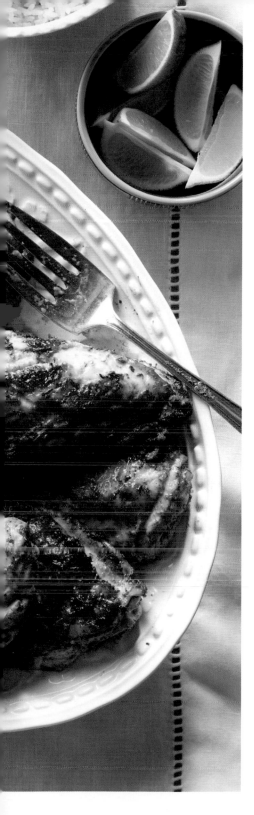

❄

Matt's Jerk Chicken

Get ready for a trip to the Islands. You may think jerk chicken is complicated, but really, all it takes is time. Throw on some tunes, grab an icy drink and prepare to be transported. Have a smoker? You can smoke the chicken first and then finish it on the grill.
—*Jenn Hall, Collingswood, NJ*

Prep: 25 min. + marinating
Grill: 50 minutes • **Makes:** 16 servings

- 1 large onion, chopped
- 3 green onions, chopped
- ¾ cup white vinegar
- ½ cup orange juice
- ¼ cup dark rum
- ¼ cup olive oil
- ¼ cup soy sauce
- 2 Tbsp. lime juice
- 1 habanero or Scotch bonnet pepper, seeded and minced
- 2 Tbsp. garlic powder
- 1 Tbsp. sugar
- 1 Tbsp. ground allspice
- 1 Tbsp. dried thyme
- 1½ tsp. cayenne pepper
- 1½ tsp. rubbed sage
- 1½ tsp. pepper
- ¾ tsp. ground nutmeg
- ¾ tsp. ground cinnamon
- 8 lbs. bone-in chicken breast halves and thighs
- ½ cup whole allspice berries
- 1 cup applewood chips
- ½ cup ketchup

1. Process the first 18 ingredients, covered, in a blender until smooth. Divide chicken into 2 large resealable plastic bags; pour half the onion mixture in each. Seal bags; turn to coat. Refrigerate overnight.

2. Soak allspice berries in water for 30 minutes. Drain chicken, reserving 1½ cups marinade. Preheat grill and prepare for indirect heat. On a piece of heavy-duty foil (12 in. square), place soaked allspice berries; fold foil around berries to form a packet, crimping edges to seal. Using a small skewer, poke holes in packet. Repeat process for the applewood chips. Place packets over heat on grate of gas grill or in coals of charcoal grill.

3. Place the chicken pieces on a greased grill rack, skin side down. Grill, covered, over indirect medium heat until a thermometer reads 165° when inserted into breasts and 170°-175° when inserted into thighs, 50-60 minutes.

4. Meanwhile, in a small saucepan over high heat, bring reserved marinade to a full rolling boil for at least 1 minute. Add ketchup; cook and stir until heated through. Remove from heat.

5. To serve Jamaican-style, remove meat from bones and chop with a cleaver. Toss chicken with sauce.

Freeze option: Arrange grilled chicken pieces in a greased 13x9-in. baking dish; add sauce. Cool; cover and freeze. To use, partially thaw in refrigerator overnight. Remove from refrigerator 30 minutes before baking. Preheat oven to 350°. Reheat chicken, covered, until a thermometer reads 165°, for 40-50 minutes.

1 serving: 346 cal., 18g fat (5g sat. fat), 109mg chol., 419mg sod., 7g carb. (4g sugars, 1g fiber), 36g pro.

BASIL & PARSLEY
PESTO, P. 95

FEED YOUR FREEZER

[Rest easy knowing you have great food on ice! Find microwave burritos, ready-to-bake cookie dough, pan pizzas and more freezer faves here.]

Mojito Slush

Whether you're splashing poolside or watching the kids inside, this slushy beverage has just the right balance of minty crispness and limey tartness that's sure to tingle your taste buds.
—*Jessica Ring, Chicago, IL*

- -

Prep: 30 min. + freezing
Makes: 13 servings
(about 2 qt. slush mix)

- 1 pkg. (3 oz.) lime gelatin
- 2 Tbsp. sugar
- 1 cup boiling water
- 1 cup fresh mint leaves
- 2 cans (12 oz. each) frozen limeade concentrate, thawed
- 2 cups cold water
- 1 cup grapefruit soda
- 1 cup rum or additional grapefruit soda

EACH SERVING
- ⅔ cup grapefruit soda
GARNISH
  Lime wedge and/or fresh mint leaves

1. In a small bowl, dissolve gelatin and sugar in boiling water; add mint leaves. Cover and steep for 20 minutes. Press through a sieve; discard mint. Stir in the limeade concentrate, cold water, soda and rum. Pour into a 2½-qt. freezer container. Freeze overnight or until set.
2. For each serving, scoop ⅔ cup slush into a glass. Pour soda into the glass; garnish as desired.
1 serving: 278 cal., 0 fat (0 sat. fat), 0 chol., 28mg sod., 61g carb. (59g sugars, 0 fiber), 1g pro.

Brandy Slush

This slush with a hint of citrus keeps you cool on hot summer days. Even if you're not a tea lover, you'll likely find the mix of flavors pleasing.
—Taste of Home *Test Kitchen*

- -

Prep: 15 min. + freezing
Makes: 21 servings
(about 4 qt. slush mix)

- 4 green or black tea bags
- 9 cups water, divided
- 2 cups brandy
- 1 can (12 oz.) frozen lemonade concentrate, thawed
- 1 can (12 oz.) frozen orange juice concentrate, thawed

EACH SERVING
- ¼ cup lemon-lime soda, chilled
GARNISH
  Lime wedge, optional

1. Place tea bags in a small bowl. Bring 2 cups water to a boil; pour over tea bags. Cover and steep for 5 minutes. Discard tea bags. Transfer the tea to a large pitcher; stir in the brandy, lemonade concentrate, juice concentrate and remaining water. Pour into a 4-qt. freezer container. Freeze overnight or until set.
2. For each serving, scoop ¾ cup slush into a rocks glass. Pour lemon-lime soda into the glass; if desired, serve with lime wedge.
1 serving: 129 cal., 0 fat (0 sat. fat), 0 chol., 8mg sod., 20g carb. (19g sugars, 0 fiber), 0 pro.

MOJITO SLUSH

PRO TIP

Fizzy & Fancy

Offer a cocktail slush when company drops by. Keep lime La Croix instead of soda pop on hand if you prefer your slushes a bit less sweet.

More Frosty, Fun Slush Mixes

You'll always have time for cocktails when you keep slush mix in the freezer. Store some cans of soda, ginger ale or mineral water in the pantry and you'll be ready to go.

Old-Fashioned Slush

Combine 9 cups water, 2 cups bourbon, 2 cans orange juice concentrate and 2 Tbsp. bitters. Pour into a 4-qt. freezer container. Freeze mixture overnight or until set.
For each serving, scoop ¾ cup slush into a rocks glass; top slush with lemon-lime soda.

Cranberry Bog Slush

Combine 9 cups water, 2 cups vodka, 1 can cranberry juice concentrate and 1 can limeade concentrate. Pour into a 4-qt. freezer container. Freeze overnight or until set.
For each serving, scoop ¾ cup slush into a rocks glass; top with ginger ale.

Southern Sweet Tea Slush

Combine 9 cups water, 2 cups sweet tea vodka and 2 cans lemonade concentrate. Pour into a 4-qt. freezer container. Freeze overnight or until set. For each serving, scoop ¾ cup slush into a rocks glass; top with lemon-lime soda.

Negroni Slush

Combine 9 cups water, 1½ cups gin, ½ cup Campari, 1 can limeade concentrate, 1 can cranberry juice concentrate and 2 Tbsp. sweet vermouth. Pour into a 4-qt. freezer container. Freeze overnight or until set. For each serving, scoop ¾ cup slush into a rocks glass; top slush with lemon-lime soda.

BRANDY
SLUSH

On-the-Go Breakfast Muffins

My family often requests these muffins. I usually prepare them on Sunday night, so when we're running late on weekday mornings, the kids can grab these to eat on the bus.
—Irene Wayman, Grantsville, UT

Prep: 30 min. • **Bake:** 15 min.
Makes: 1½ dozen

- 1 lb. bulk Italian sausage
- 7 large eggs, divided use
- 2 cups all-purpose flour
- ⅓ cup sugar
- 3 tsp. baking powder
- ½ tsp. salt
- ½ cup 2% milk
- ½ cup canola oil
- 1 cup shredded cheddar cheese, divided

1. Preheat oven to 400°. In a large nonstick skillet, cook sausage over medium heat 6-8 minutes or until no longer pink, breaking into crumbles. Remove; drain on paper towels. Wipe skillet clean.

2. In a small bowl, whisk 5 eggs. Pour into same skillet; cook and stir over medium heat until thickened and no liquid egg remains. Remove from the heat.

3. In a large bowl, whisk flour, sugar, baking powder and salt. In another bowl, whisk remaining eggs, milk and oil until blended. Add to flour mixture; stir just until moistened. Fold in ⅔ cup shredded cheese, cooked sausage and scrambled eggs.

4. Fill greased or paper-lined muffin cups three-fourths full. Sprinkle tops with remaining cheese. Bake until a toothpick inserted in center comes out clean, 12-15 minutes. Cool for 5 minutes before removing from pans to wire racks. Serve warm.

Freeze option: Freeze cooled muffins in an airtight freezer container. To use, microwave each muffin on high for 45-60 seconds or until heated through.

1 muffin: 238 cal., 16g fat (4g sat. fat), 93mg chol., 357mg sod., 15g carb. (4g sugars, 0 fiber), 8g pro.

HACK

A ⅓-cup spring-release ice cream scoop makes it quick work to portion muffins.

ON-THE-GO
BREAKFAST
MUFFINS

BIG-BATCH
DINNER ROLLS

Big-Batch Dinner Rolls

Because homemade rolls are always in demand, I like to make them ahead, partially bake and freeze them. The rolls zoom from freezer to oven when guests are on the way.

—Mary Jane Henderson, Salem, NJ

Prep: 25 min. + rising • **Bake:** 15 min.
Makes: 4 dozen

- 2 pkg. (¼ oz. each) active dry yeast
- 1 cup warm water (110° to 115°)
- 2 cups warm 2% milk (110° to 115°)
- ½ cup shortening
- ¼ cup sugar
- 3 tsp. salt
- 10 cups all-purpose flour

1. Dissolve yeast in warm water; set aside. In a large bowl, combine milk, shortening, sugar, salt, yeast mixture and 2½ cups flour; beat on medium speed until smooth. Stir in enough remaining flour to form a stiff dough.

2. Turn dough onto a floured surface; knead until smooth and elastic, about 6-8 minutes. Place in a greased bowl, turning once to grease the top. Cover and let rise in a warm place until doubled, about 1½ hours.

3. Punch down dough. Turn onto a lightly floured surface; divide and shape into 48 balls. Place 2 in. apart on greased baking sheets. Cover with kitchen towels; let rise in a warm place until doubled, about 20 minutes.

4. Preheat oven to 375°. Bake until golden brown, 12-15 minutes.

Freeze option: Partially bake rolls at 325° for 10 minutes. Freeze cooled partially baked rolls in an airtight container. To use, bake frozen rolls on greased baking sheets at 375° for 12-15 minutes or until golden brown.

1 roll: 124 cal., 3g fat (1g sat. fat), 1mg chol., 251mg sod., 22g carb. (2g sugars, 1g fiber), 3g pro.

HACK

Dress Up Frozen Dinner Rolls

To give any roll a quick upgrade, thaw rolls until softened. Brush tops with egg wash and dip in a blend of ⅓ cup shelled pumpkin seeds, 1 tsp. Italian seasoning and ⅓ cup grated Parmesan. Bake according to recipe or package directions.

BASIL &
PARSLEY PESTO

HACK

Upcycle Egg Cartons

Washed plastic egg cartons
are a perfect stand-in if you
don't have or don't want to
store ice trays in your
kitchen. Portion homemade
sauces, leftover wine or other
foods into the cartons and
freeze. Store cubes in the
carton or pop them out
to store in a freezer container
for a more compact option.

❄ Basil & Parsley Pesto

Toss this herby pesto with pasta, spread it over sandwiches or stir it into an Italian-style soup, such as minestrone.

—Lorraine Stevenski, Land O' Lakes, FL

- -

Takes: 15 min. • **Makes:** 1¼ cups

- 2 cups loosely packed basil leaves
- 1 cup loosely packed Italian parsley
- ¼ cup slivered almonds, toasted
- 2 garlic cloves
- 4 tsp. grated lemon zest
- ⅓ cup lemon juice
- 2 Tbsp. honey
- ½ tsp. salt
- ½ cup olive oil
- ½ cup grated Parmesan cheese

Place basil, parsley, almonds and garlic in a small food processor; pulse until chopped. Add lemon zest, juice, honey and salt; process until blended. Continue processing while gradually adding oil in a steady stream. Add cheese; pulse just until blended. Store in an airtight container in the refrigerator for up to 1 week.

Freeze option: Transfer pesto to ice cube trays; cover and freeze pesto until firm. Remove from trays and transfer to a resealable plastic freezer bag; return to freezer. To use, thaw cubes in refrigerator 2 hours.

2 Tbsp: 148 cal. 13g fat (2g sat. fat), 3mg chol., 195mg sod., 6g carb. (4g sugars, 1g fiber), 2g pro.

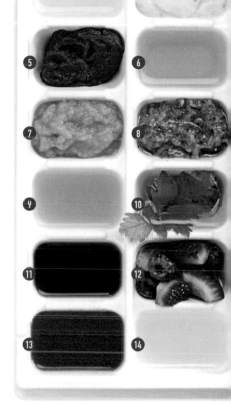

Clever Cubes

Don't ditch those last dabs and dribbles! They're culinary gold right from the deep freeze.

1. Onions Save the day when you need dinner on the table fast. Simply freeze chopped onions in water; before cooking, thaw, drain and stir them into just about anything.

2. Chipotle peppers in adobo sauce Thaw, then puree or chop and toss a cube or two into chili, salsa and marinades for a hint of smoky heat.

3. Lemon and lime juice Freeze leftover fresh juice so it's ready when you need a touch of tart.

4. Yogurt Blend 3-4 frozen cubes into juice for dynamite smoothies. Or insert a toothpick into each cube when it's partially frozen, and you'll have mini frozen pops in hardly any time.

5. Tomato paste Pop leftovers in the freezer so you'll always have that ounce or two you need for a savory sauce.

6. Tea Ice cubes made from water always dilute pitchers of iced tea as they melt. Use frozen tea cubes instead. Or try them in lemonade and juices for a new layer of flavor.

7. Pureed butternut squash Stir it into soups, stews and sauces to enhance nutrition, flavor and texture. You can also sneak a cube or two into smoothies.

8. Pesto Speed up prep time of pasta, crostini and other delights. Simply thaw the cubes in the refrigerator first.

9. Chicken broth Avoid last-minute dashes to the store by keeping this kitchen essential on hand in the freezer.

10. Chopped herbs Savor their fresh flavors all year long. Freeze herbs in water (to make them easy to remove), then thaw and drain before using.

11. Coffee Brew up a full-flavored iced coffee drink, or add a kick to desserts, gravy and more.

12. Berries Add a few to smoothies, or thaw and sprinkle on yogurt for a healthful breakfast.

13. Tomato juice Keep these on hand for chili, stew and so much more—including Bloody Marys.

14. Wine Punch up a meal by simmering a cube or two in many kinds of sauces.

Prep Your Own
Soup Starter

• Freeze abundant garden zucchini and yellow squash in resealable bags to savor the tastes of summer once it has passed. It's a quick start for a cold-weather reprisal of this healthy soup.

• In separate bags, freeze a blend of chopped celery, carrot and onion for this and other batches of soup.

• A classic ratio of these soup ingredients (called mirepoix) is 2 parts onion to 1 part each celery and carrots.

Garden Minestrone

In Italian restaurants, I always order the minestrone. After doing many trial-and-error batches, I developed a hearty veggie soup my whole family craves—kids and all.

—*Hillery Martin, Fort Leavenworth, KS*

Prep: 20 min. **Cook:** 30 min.
Makes: 10 servings (about 4 qt.)

- 2 **Tbsp. olive oil**
- 7 **medium carrots, chopped**
- 7 **celery ribs, chopped**
- 1 **medium onion, chopped**
- 3 **medium zucchini, chopped**
- 2 **yellow summer squash (about 3 cups), chopped**
- 2 **bay leaves**
- ½ **tsp. salt**
- ¼ **tsp. pepper**
- ¼ **tsp. dried thyme**
- ¼ **tsp. dried sage leaves**
- ⅛ **tsp. crushed red pepper flakes, optional**
- 3 **garlic cloves, finely chopped**
- 2 **cans (15-½ oz. each) great northern beans, rinsed and drained, divided**
- 1 **can (15 oz.) crushed tomatoes**
- 2 **cartons (32 oz. each) reduced-sodium chicken broth**
- 1 **cup uncooked ditalini or other small pasta**
- 12 **cups chopped fresh spinach (12 oz.)**

1. In a 6-quart stockpot, heat oil over medium heat. Add carrots, celery and onion; cook until tender, 6-8 minutes. Add zucchini, yellow squash and seasonings; cook and stir until squashes are crisp-tender, 4-6 minutes. Add the garlic; cook 1 minute longer.

2. Mash ½ cup beans with a fork. Stir mashed beans and tomatoes into vegetables. Add the broth; bring to a boil. Reduce heat; simmer, covered, 10-12 minutes.

3. Stir in pasta and remaining beans; return to a boil. Cook, uncovered, 7-9 minutes or just until pasta is tender. Discard bay leaves. Stir in spinach; cook until spinach is wilted.

Freeze option: Add remaining beans, but not pasta and spinach. Cool soup; freeze in freezer containers for up to 3 months. To use, partially thaw in refrigerator overnight. Place in a Dutch oven. Bring to a boil. Stir in pasta; return to a boil. Reduce heat; cook, uncovered, for 7-9 minutes or until pasta is tender. Discard bay leaves. Add spinach and cook until wilted.

1½ cups: 209 cal., 4g fat (1g sat. fat), 0 chol. 929mg sod., 35g carb. (10g sugars, 9g fiber), 12g pro.

GARDEN MINESTRONE

❄ Freezer Sweet Corn

I love having sweet corn to enjoy any time of the year. I got this recipe from my daughter's mother-in-law in Iowa.
—*Judy Oudekerk, St. Michael, MN*

Prep: 30 min. • **Cook:** 15 min.
Makes: 3 qt.

4 qt. fresh corn (about 20 ears)
1 qt. hot water
⅔ cup sugar
½ cup butter, cubed
2 tsp. salt

In a stockpot, bring all ingredients to a boil. Reduce heat; simmer, uncovered, 5-7 minutes, stirring occasionally. Transfer to large shallow containers to cool quickly, stirring occasionally. Freeze in airtight containers, allowing headspace for expansion.

½ cup: 113 cal., 5g fat (2g sat. fat), 10mg chol., 245mg sod., 18g carb. (9g sugars, 2g fiber), 2g pro.

HACK

Clean Corn Prep

A Bundt cake pan is a well-known tool for catching kernels and milk from fresh-cut corn. If you don't have one—or you don't want to risk nicking its finish—use a small bowl inverted inside a larger one.

Slow-Cooker Marinated Mushrooms

Here's a welcome and healthy addition to any spread. Mushrooms and pearl onions seasoned with herbs, balsamic and red wine are terrific on their own or alongside a tenderloin roast.

—*Courtney Wilson, Fresno, CA*

- -

Prep: 15 min. • **Cook:** 6 hours
Makes: 5 cups

- 2 **lbs. medium fresh mushrooms**
- 1 **pkg. (14.4 oz.) frozen pearl onions, thawed**
- 4 **garlic cloves, minced**
- 2 **cups reduced-sodium beef broth**
- ½ **cup dry red wine**
- 3 **Tbsp. balsamic vinegar**
- 3 **Tbsp. olive oil**
- 1 **tsp. salt**
- 1 **tsp. dried basil**
- ½ **tsp. dried thyme**
- ½ **tsp. pepper**
- ¼ **tsp. crushed red pepper flakes**

Place mushrooms, onions and garlic in a 5- or 6-qt. slow cooker. In a small bowl, whisk remaining ingredients; pour over the mushrooms. Cook, covered, on low until mushrooms are tender, 6-8 hours.

Freeze option: Freeze cooled mushrooms and juices in freezer containers. To use, partially thaw in refrigerator overnight. Microwave, covered, on high in a microwave-safe dish until heated through, stirring gently and adding a little broth or water if necessary.

¼ cup: 42 cal., 2g fat (0 sat. fat), 1mg chol., 165mg sod., 4g carb. (2g sugars, 0 fiber), 1g pro.

PRO TIP

Freeze these irresistible mushrooms in small containers to serve with a steak dinner or to add to an impromptu munchie spread.

FREEZER
SWEET CORN

SLOW-COOKER
MARINATED
MUSHROOMS

Barbecue-Glazed Meatballs

Stock your freezer with these meatballs and you'll always have a tasty snack on hand for the unexpected. We also like these as a main dish with rice or noodles on busy weeknights.

—Anna Finley, Columbia, MO

- -

Prep: 30 min. • **Bake:** 15 min./batch
Makes: 8 dozen

- 2 cups quick-cooking oats
- 1 can (12 oz.) fat-free evaporated milk
- 1 small onion, finely chopped
- 2 tsp. garlic powder
- 2 tsp. chili powder
- 3 lbs. lean ground beef (90% lean)

SAUCE
- 2½ cups ketchup
- 1 small onion, finely chopped
- ⅓ cup packed brown sugar
- 2 tsp. liquid smoke, optional
- 1¼ tsp. chili powder
- ¾ tsp. garlic powder

1. Preheat oven to 400°. In a large bowl, combine the first 5 ingredients. Add beef; mix lightly but thoroughly. Shape into 1-in. balls.
2. Place meatballs on greased racks in shallow baking pans. Bake until cooked through, 15-20 minutes. Drain on paper towels.
3. In a Dutch oven, combine sauce ingredients. Bring to a boil over medium heat, stirring constantly. Reduce heat; simmer, uncovered for 2-3 minutes or until slightly thickened. Gently stir in meatballs; heat through.
Freeze option: Freeze cooled meatball mixture in freezer containers. To use, partially thaw in refrigerator overnight. Microwave, covered, on high in a microwave-safe dish until heated through, gently stirring and adding a little water if necessary.

1 meatball: 42 cal., 1g fat (0 sat. fat), 9mg chol., 93mg sod., 4g carb. (3g sugars, 0 fiber), 3g pro.

Mini Phyllo Tacos

Crispy phyllo cups are the secret to creating an appetizer with all the flavor and appeal of a taco—and much easier to eat! The two-bite treats of spicy ground beef and zesty shredded cheese will be a surefire hit with your hungry crowd.

—Roseann Weston, Philipsburg, PA

- -

Prep: 30 min. • **Bake:** 10 min.
Makes: 2½ dozen

- 1 lb. lean ground beef (90% lean)
- ½ cup finely chopped onion
- 1 envelope taco seasoning
- ¾ cup water
- 1¼ cups shredded Mexican cheese blend, divided
- 2 pkg. (1.9 oz. each) frozen miniature phyllo tart shells

1. Preheat oven to 350°. In a small skillet, cook beef and onion over medium heat until meat is no longer pink; drain. Stir in taco seasoning and water. Bring to a boil. Reduce heat; simmer, uncovered, 5 minutes. Remove from heat; stir in ½ cup cheese blend.
2. Place tart shells in an ungreased 15x10x1-in. baking pan. Fill with the taco mixture.
3. Bake 6 minutes. Sprinkle with remaining cheese blend; bake until melted, 2-3 minutes longer.
Freeze option: Freeze cooled taco cups in a freezer container, separating layers with waxed paper. To use, reheat on a baking sheet in a preheated 350° oven until crisp and heated through.

1 appetizer: 63 cal., 3g fat (1g sat. fat), 11mg chol., 156mg sod., 4g carb. (0 sugars, 0 fiber), 4g pro.

MINI PHYLLO TACOS

Freezer Burritos

These burritos go from freezer to plate in minutes without the extra salt and chemicals of store-bought. Make a batch for quick dinners or late-night snacks—or even breakfast!
—*Laura Winemiller, Delta, PA*

Prep: 35 min. • **Cook:** 15 min.
Makes: 12 servings

- 1¼ lbs. lean ground beef (90% lean)
- ¼ cup finely chopped onion
- 1¼ cups salsa
- 2 Tbsp. reduced-sodium taco seasoning
- 2 cans (15 oz. each) pinto beans, rinsed and drained
- ½ cup water
- 2 cups shredded reduced-fat cheddar cheese
- 12 flour tortillas (8 in.), warmed

1. In a large skillet, cook beef and onion over medium heat until meat is no longer pink; drain. Stir in salsa and taco seasoning. Simmer, uncovered, 2-3 minutes. Transfer to a large bowl; set aside.

2. In a food processor, combine pinto beans and water. Cover and process until almost smooth. Add to beef mixture. Stir in cheese.

3. Spoon ½ cup mixture down center of each tortilla. Fold ends and sides over filling; roll up. Wrap each burrito in waxed paper and foil. Freeze for up to 1 month.

To use frozen burritos: Remove foil and waxed paper. Place one burrito on a microwave-safe plate. Microwave on high for 2½-2¾ minutes or until a thermometer reads 165°, flipping burrito once. Let stand 20 seconds.

1 burrito: 345 cal., 11g fat (4g sat. fat), 36mg chol., 677mg sod., 40g carb. (3g sugars, 3g fiber), 22g pro. **Diabetic exchanges:** 2½ starch, 2 lean meat, ½ fat.

PEPPERONI
PAN PIZZAS

Pepperoni Pan Pizzas

I've spent years trying to come up with the perfect pizza crust and sauce, and now they're paired up in this recipe. I often fix this crispy pizza, and it really satisfies my husband and three sons.
—*Susan Lindahl, Alford, FL*

- -

Prep: 30 min. • **Bake:** 10 min.
Makes: 2 pizzas (4 servings each)

2¾ to 3 cups all-purpose flour
  1   pkg. (¼ oz.) active dry yeast
  ¼   tsp. salt
  1   cup warm water
      (120° to 130°)
  1   Tbsp. canola oil

SAUCE
  1   can (14½ oz.) diced
      tomatoes, undrained
  1   can (6 oz.) tomato paste
  1   Tbsp. canola oil
  1   tsp. salt
  ½   tsp. each dried basil, oregano,
      marjoram and thyme
  ¼   tsp. garlic powder
  ¼   tsp. pepper

PIZZAS
  1   pkg. (3½ oz.) sliced pepperoni
  5   cups shredded part-skim
      mozzarella cheese
  ¼   cup grated Parmesan cheese
  ¼   cup grated Romano cheese

1. In a large bowl, combine 2 cups flour, yeast and salt. Add water and oil; beat until smooth. Add enough remaining flour to form a soft dough.
2. Turn onto a floured surface; knead until smooth and elastic, 5-7 minutes. Cover and let stand for 10 minutes. Meanwhile, in a small bowl, combine the tomatoes, tomato paste, oil and seasonings.
3. Divide dough in half; press into two 15x10x1-in. baking pans coated with cooking spray. Prick generously with a fork. Bake at 425° for 12-16 minutes or until lightly browned.

4. Spread sauce over crusts; top with pepperoni and cheeses. Bake until cheese is melted, 8-10 minutes.

Freeze option: Bake crusts and assemble pizzas as directed. Securely wrap and freeze unbaked pizzas. To use, unwrap pizzas; bake as directed, increasing time as necessary.

1 serving: 517 cal., 26g fat (12g sat. fat), 60mg chol., 1233mg sod., 44g carb. (5g sugars, 3g fiber), 28g pro.

❄️

Sausage Bread Sandwiches

I make these sandwiches in my spare time and freeze them so they're ready when needed, including tailgating parties when we attend Kansas State football games.

—Donna Roberts, Manhattan, KS

Prep: 30 min. • **Bake:** 20 min.
Makes: 4 sandwich loaves
(3 pieces each)

- 1 pkg. (16 oz.) hot roll mix
- 2 lbs. reduced-fat bulk pork sausage
- 2 Tbsp. dried parsley flakes
- 2 tsp. garlic powder
- 1 tsp. onion powder
- ½ tsp. dried oregano
- 2 cups shredded part-skim mozzarella cheese
- ½ cup grated Parmesan cheese
- 1 large egg
- 1 Tbsp. water

1. Preheat oven to 350°. Prepare hot roll mix dough according to the package directions.

2. Meanwhile, in a large skillet, cook pork sausage over medium heat 8-10 minutes or until no longer pink, breaking into crumbles; drain. Stir in seasonings.

3. Divide dough into 4 portions. On a lightly floured surface, roll each into a 14x8-in. rectangle. Top each with 1¼ cups sausage mixture to within 1 in. of edges; sprinkle with ½ cup mozzarella cheese and 2 Tbsp. Parmesan cheese. Roll up jelly-roll style, starting with a long side; pinch seams and ends to seal.

4. Transfer to greased baking sheets, seam side down. In a small bowl, whisk egg with water; brush over loaves. Bake 20-25 minutes or until golden brown and heated through. Cool 5 minutes before slicing.

Freeze option: Cool the cooked sandwiches 1 hour on wire racks. Cut each into thirds; wrap each securely in foil. Freeze until serving. To reheat sandwiches in the oven, place wrapped frozen sandwiches on a baking sheet. In a preheated 375° oven, heat until warmed through, 20-25 minutes.

1 piece: 432 cal., 25g fat (10g sat. fat), 103mg chol., 926mg sod., 27g carb. (5g sugars, 1g fiber), 24g pro.

❄️ 🍎

Easy Marinated Flank Steak

I got this recipe from a friend many years ago. It's how my family makes steak on the grill and a must when we're having company.

Debbie Bonczek, Tariffville, CT

Prep: 10 min. + marinating
Grill: 15 min. • **Makes:** 8 servings

- 3 Tbsp. ketchup
- 1 Tbsp. chopped onion
- 1 Tbsp. canola oil
- 1 tsp. brown sugar
- 1 tsp. Worcestershire sauce
- 1 garlic clove, minced
- ⅛ tsp. pepper
- 1 beef flank steak (about 2 lbs.)

1. In a shallow dish, combine the first 7 ingredients. Add beef; turn to coat. Refrigerate 8 hours or overnight.

2. Drain beef, discarding marinade. Grill flank steak, covered, on an oiled

rack over medium heat or broil 4 in. from heat 6-8 minutes on each side until meat reaches desired doneness (for medium-rare, a thermometer should read 135°; medium, 140°; medium-well, 145°). To serve, thinly slice steak across the grain.

Freeze option: Freeze flank steak with marinade in an airtight freezer container. To use, thaw in refrigerator overnight. Drain beef, discarding marinade. Grill as directed.

3 oz. cooked beef: 192 cal., 10g fat (4g sat. fat), 54mg chol., 145mg sod., 2g carb. (2g sugars, 0 fiber), 22g pro. **Diabetic exchanges:** 3 lean meat.

PRO TIPS

• Stock up when meat is on sale and prep additional flank steaks for the freezer.

• Or prep extra marinade and freeze in an ice tray for future use. You'll need about ¼ cup, or 2 cubes, of marinade per batch of meat.

❄ Barbecue Chicken Sliders

Thanks to rotisserie chicken, these cheesy, smoky sliders are a snap to make on a busy day. The special barbecue sauce really takes it up a notch.

—*Nancy Heishman, Las Vegas, NV*

- -

Takes: 25 min. • **Makes:** 4 servings

- ¾ cup beer
  or reduced-sodium
  chicken broth
- ½ cup barbecue sauce
- 1 Tbsp. bourbon
- 1 tsp. hot pepper sauce
- ¼ tsp. seasoned salt
- ¼ tsp. ground mustard
- 2 cups shredded
  rotisserie chicken
- 8 slider buns, split
- 1½ cups shredded smoked
  cheddar cheese

1. Preheat broiler. In a large saucepan, mix first 6 ingredients; bring to a boil. Reduce heat; simmer, uncovered, until slightly thickened, 8-10 minutes, stirring occasionally. Stir in chicken; heat through.

2. Place buns on a baking sheet, cut side up. Broil 3-4 in. from heat until lightly toasted, 30-60 seconds.

3. Remove tops of buns from baking sheet. Top bottoms with chicken mixture; sprinkle with cheese. Broil 3-4 in. from heat until cheese is melted, 1-2 minutes. Add bun tops.

Freeze option: Freeze cooled chicken mixture in freezer containers. To use, partially thaw in refrigerator overnight. Heat through in a saucepan, stirring occasionally and adding a little water if necessary.

2 sliders: 529 cal., 23g fat (10g sat. fat), 106mg chol., 1023mg sod., 42g carb. (15g sugars, 1g fiber), 36g pro.

✳ Simple Creamy Chicken Enchiladas

This is one of the first recipes that I created and cooked for my husband right after we got married. He was so impressed! Now we regularly fix these enchiladas for friends.

—Melissa Rogers, Tuscaloosa, AL

Prep: 30 min. • **Bake:** 30 min.
Makes: 2 casseroles (5 servings each)

- 2 cans (14½ oz. each) diced tomatoes with mild green chiles, undrained
- 2 cans (10½ oz. each) condensed cream of chicken soup, undiluted
- 1 can (10¾ oz.) condensed cheddar cheese soup, undiluted
- ¼ cup 2% milk
- 1 Tbsp. ground cumin
- 1 Tbsp. chili powder
- 2 tsp. garlic powder
- 2 tsp. dried oregano
- 5 cups shredded rotisserie chicken
- 1 pkg. (8 oz.) cream cheese, cubed and softened
- 20 flour tortillas (8 in.), warmed
- 4 cups shredded Mexican cheese blend

1. Preheat oven to 350°. For sauce, mix first 8 ingredients. For filling, in a large bowl, mix the chicken and cream cheese until blended; stir in 3½ cups sauce.

2. Spread ¼ cup sauce into each of 2 greased 13x9-in. baking dishes. Place ⅓ cup filling down the center of each tortilla; roll up and place seam side down in baking dishes. Pour remaining sauce over tops; sprinkle with cheese.

3. Bake, uncovered, 30-35 minutes or until heated through.

Freeze option: Cover and freeze unbaked casseroles up to 3 months. To use, partially thaw in refrigerator overnight. Remove from refrigerator 30 minutes before baking. Preheat oven to 350°. Cover casserole with greased foil; bake until heated through and a thermometer inserted in center reads 165°, about 45 minutes. Uncover; bake until the cheese is melted, 5-10 minutes longer.

2 enchiladas: 828 cal., 40g fat (17g sat. fat), 132mg chol., 1738mg sod., 72g carb. (5g sugars, 7g fiber), 42g pro.

HACK

Rotisserie Chicken Stock-Up

- Many grocery stores offer specials on rotisserie chicken. If yours does, go ahead and stock up! The meat is convenient for freezer dishes like you'll find here and on the next two pages.

- When you get the chickens home, uncover them and allow to cool for 15 minutes. Then shred by hand in a large bowl or using your mixer, as shown on p. 106.

- Use the shredded chicken in the desired recipes, then divide the leftovers among airtight containers and freeze. Consider freezing the chicken in different quantities, so it's easy to pull just the right amount for a quick lunch or a favorite recipe.

BARBECUE CHICKEN SLIDERS

Green Enchilada Bake

Good thing the recipe makes a lot, because your family won't want to stop eating this cheesy southwestern casserole. The green enchilada sauce brightens it right up.

—*Melanie Burns, Pueblo West, CO*

Prep: 20 min.
Bake: 50 min. + standing
Makes: 10 servings

- 4½ cups shredded rotisserie chicken
- 1 can (28 oz.) green enchilada sauce
- 1¼ cups sour cream
- 9 corn tortillas (6 in.), cut into 1½-in. pieces
- 4 cups shredded Monterey Jack cheese

1. Preheat oven to 375°. In a greased 13x9-in. baking dish, layer half of each of the following: chicken, enchilada sauce, sour cream, tortillas and cheese. Repeat layers.
2. Bake, covered, 40 minutes. Uncover; bake until bubbly, about 10 minutes. Let stand 15 minutes before serving.

Freeze option: Cover and freeze unbaked casserole. To use, partially thaw in refrigerator overnight. Remove from refrigerator 30 minutes before baking. Preheat oven to 375°. Bake casserole as directed, increasing time as necessary to heat through and for a thermometer inserted in center to read 165°.
1 cup: 469 cal., 29g fat (14g sat. fat), 113mg chol., 1077mg sod., 16g carb. (3g sugars, 1g fiber), 34g pro.

Slow-Cooker Chicken Bog

Chicken Bog is a South Carolina tradition with lots of variations (think herbs, spices and fresh veggies), but the standard ingredients remain sausage, chicken and rice. This slow-cooked rendition is so simple.

—*Anna Hanson, Spanish Fork, UT*

Prep: 20 min. • **Cook:** 4 hours
Makes: 6 servings

- 1 Tbsp. canola oil
- 1 medium onion, chopped
- 8 oz. smoked sausage, halved and sliced ½-in. thick
- 3 garlic cloves, minced
- 5 cups chicken broth, divided
- 2 cups uncooked converted rice
- 1 tsp. salt
- 1 tsp. pepper
- 1 rotisserie chicken (about 3 lbs.), meat removed and shredded
  Thinly sliced green onions, optional
  Hot sauce

1. In a large skillet, heat oil over medium heat. Add onion and sausage; cook until sausage is lightly browned. Add garlic and cook 1 minute more; transfer to a 5-qt. slow cooker.
2. Stir in 4 cups broth, rice, salt and pepper. Cook, covered, on low until rice is tender, 4-5 hours. Stir in the chicken and remaining broth. Cook, covered, on low until chicken is heated through, about 30 minutes. If desired, sprinkle with green onions. Serve with hot sauce.

Freeze option: Omitting green onions and hot sauce, freeze cooled meat mixture, juices and rice in freezer containers. To use, partially thaw in refrigerator overnight. Microwave, covered, on high until heated through, stirring gently and adding a little broth or water if necessary.
1⅓ cups: 681 cal., 30g fat (9g sat. fat), 134mg chol., 1728mg sod., 54g carb. (3g sugars, 0 fiber), 45g pro.

HACK

Shred Chicken Fast

- Make fast work of shredding chicken with your mixer's paddle attachment.

- One of our favorite hacks: After cooking boneless skinless chicken breasts in the pressure cooker, use a hand mixer right in the pot to quickly shred the meat for recipes.

SLOW-COOKER
CHICKEN BOG

ASIAN-STYLE
MEAT LOAF

Asian-Style Meat Loaf

Here's a family-friendly meat loaf with just a hint of Asian flair. Serve it with pea pods or steamed baby bok choy.
—Taste of Home *Test Kitchen*

Prep: 25 min.
Bake: 50 min. + standing
Makes: 2 loaves (8 servings each)

1⅓ cups panko (Japanese) bread crumbs
1 small onion, finely chopped
2 large eggs, lightly beaten
⅓ cup 2% milk
¼ cup hoisin sauce
1 Tbsp. reduced-sodium soy sauce
2 garlic cloves, minced
2 tsp. prepared mustard
1¼ tsp. ground ginger
1 tsp. salt
2 lbs. extra-lean ground turkey
1 lb. Italian turkey sausage links, casings removed
TOPPING
1 cup ketchup
½ cup packed brown sugar
2 tsp. prepared mustard

1. Preheat oven to 350°. In a large bowl, combine first 10 ingredients. Add turkey and sausage; mix lightly but thoroughly. Transfer mixture to 2 greased 9x5-in. loaf pans. Mix topping ingredients; spread over tops.
2. Bake until a thermometer reads 165°, 50-55 minutes. Let stand for 10 minutes before slicing.
Freeze option: Shape meat loaves in plastic wrap-lined loaf pans; cover and freeze until firm. Remove from pans and wrap securely in foil; return to freezer. To use, unwrap and bake meat loaves as directed, increasing time to 1¼-1½ hours or until a thermometer inserted in center reads 165°.

1 slice: 187 cal., 6g fat (1g sat. fat), 67mg chol., 636mg sod., 17g carb. (12g sugars, trace fiber), 16g pro.
Diabetic exchanges: 2 lean meat, 1 starch.

All-American Meat Loaf

There are many variations on meat loaf, but my family loves this classic stick-to-your-ribs version.
—*Margie Williams, Mount Juliet, TN*

Prep: 30 min.
Bake: 50 min. + standing
Makes: 2 loaves (8 servings each)

1 large green pepper, chopped
1 large onion, chopped
2 tsp. olive oil
4 garlic cloves, minced
2 large eggs, lightly beaten
1 cup 2% milk
6 slices bread, cubed
1½ cups shredded cheddar cheese
2¼ tsp. dried rosemary, crushed
2 tsp. salt
1 tsp. pepper
2 lbs. lean ground beef (90% lean)
1 lb. ground pork
1½ cups ketchup
¼ cup packed brown sugar
2 tsp. cider vinegar

1. Saute green pepper and onion in oil in a large skillet until tender. Add garlic; cook 1 minute longer. Transfer sauteed vegetables to a large bowl; cool to room temperature.
2. Preheat oven to 350°. Add eggs, milk, bread, cheese, rosemary, salt and pepper to vegetables. Crumble beef and pork over mixture and mix well.
3. Pat into 2 greased 9x5-in. loaf pans. Combine ketchup, brown sugar and vinegar in a small bowl. Spread over tops.

4. Bake, uncovered, until no pink remains and a thermometer reads 160°, 50-55 minutes. Let stand for 10 minutes before slicing.
Freeze option: Shape meat loaves in plastic wrap-lined loaf pan; cover and freeze until firm. Remove from pan and wrap securely in foil; return to freezer. Freeze up to 3 months. To use, preheat oven to 350°. Unwrap meat loaf and place in pan. Bake, uncovered, 1¼-1½ hours, or until a thermometer inserted in center to read 160°.
1 slice: 286 cal., 14g fat (6g sat. fat), 89mg chol., 765mg sod., 18g carb. (11g sugars, 1g fiber), 21g pro.

PRO TIPS

Secrets to Tender Meat Loaf

• An all-beef loaf can have a coarse texture. Go for a beef-pork mixture to get a finer consistency, as with the All-American Meat Loaf.

• Mix the other loaf ingredients, then crumble the meat on top and lightly mix just until combined. This ensures a tender meat loaf.

Debra's Cavatini

I love this recipe because it makes two hearty casseroles. I add a little something different every time I make it, such as extra garlic, to give it an added boost of flavor.
—*Debra Lynn Butcher, Decatur, IN*

Prep: 45 min. • **Bake:** 35 min.
Makes: 2 casseroles (6 servings each)

- 1 pkg. (16 oz.) penne pasta
- 1 lb. ground beef
- 1 lb. bulk Italian pork sausage
- 1¾ cups sliced fresh mushrooms
- 1 medium onion, chopped
- 1 medium green pepper, chopped
- 2 cans (14½ oz. each) Italian diced tomatoes
- 1 jar (23½ oz.) Italian sausage and garlic spaghetti sauce
- 1 jar (16 oz.) chunky mild salsa
- 1 pkg. (8 oz.) sliced pepperoni, chopped
- 1 cup shredded Swiss cheese, divided
- 4 cups shredded part-skim mozzarella cheese, divided
- 1½ cups shredded Parmesan cheese, divided
- 1 jar (24 oz.) three-cheese spaghetti sauce

1. Cook pasta according to package directions. Meanwhile, in a Dutch oven, cook beef, sausage, sliced mushrooms, chopped onion and green pepper over medium heat until meat is no longer pink; drain.
2. Drain pasta; add to the meat mixture. Stir in tomatoes, sausage and garlic spaghetti sauce, salsa and pepperoni.
3. Preheat oven to 350°. Divide half the pasta mixture between 2 greased 13x9-in. baking dishes. Sprinkle each with ¼ cup shredded Swiss cheese, 1 cup mozzarella cheese and ⅓ cup Parmesan cheese. Spread ¾ cup 3-cheese spaghetti sauce over each. Top with remaining pasta mixture and 3-cheese spaghetti sauce. Sprinkle with remaining cheeses.
4. Cover and bake until bubbly, about 25 minutes. Uncover; bake until the cheese is melted, 10 minutes longer.
Freeze option: Cover unbaked casserole; freeze up to 3 months. To use, thaw in refrigerator overnight. Remove from refrigerator 30 minutes before baking. Preheat oven to 350°. Bake casserole, covered, 45 minutes. Uncover; bake 10 minutes or until cheese is melted.
1 serving: 669 cal., 34g fat (15g sat. fat), 90mg chol., 1825mg sod., 54g carb. (20g sugars, 5g fiber), 37g pro.

Stamp-of-Approval Spaghetti Sauce

My father is pretty opinionated... about food. This recipe received his coveted stamp of approval, and I have yet to hear any disagreement from anyone who has tried it!
—*Melissa Taylor, Higley, AZ*

Prep: 30 min. • **Cook:** 8 hours
Makes: 12 servings (3 qt.)

- 2 lbs. ground beef
- ¾ lb. bulk Italian sausage
- 4 medium onions, finely chopped
- 8 garlic cloves, minced
- 4 cans (14½ oz. each) diced tomatoes, undrained
- 4 cans (6 oz. each) tomato paste
- ½ cup water
- ¼ cup sugar
- ¼ cup Worcestershire sauce
- 1 Tbsp. canola oil
- ¼ cup minced fresh parsley
- 2 Tbsp. minced fresh basil or 2 tsp. dried basil
- 1 Tbsp. minced fresh oregano or 1 tsp. dried oregano
- 4 bay leaves
- 1 tsp. rubbed sage
- ½ tsp. salt
- ½ tsp. dried marjoram
- ½ tsp. pepper
  Hot cooked spaghetti

1. In a Dutch oven, cook the beef, sausage, onions and garlic over medium heat until meat is no longer pink; drain.
2. Transfer to a 5-qt. slow cooker. Stir in the tomatoes, tomato paste, water, sugar, Worcestershire sauce, oil and the seasonings.
3. Cook sauce, covered, on low for 8-10 hours. Discard bay leaves. Serve with spaghetti.
Freeze option: Cool before placing in a freezer container. Cover and freeze up to 3 months. Thaw in refrigerator overnight. Place in a large saucepan; heat through, stirring occasionally.
1 cup: 335 cal., 16g fat (5g sat. fat), 62mg chol., 622mg sod., 27g carb. (16g sugars, 5g fiber), 22g pro.

HACK

Add a Carrot

Carrots add sweetness and take the acidic edge off tomato sauce. When you're cooking up pizza or spaghetti sauce, peel a carrot and let it simmer, whole, in the sauce. It adds a subtle sweetness. Just take out the carrot before using the sauce.

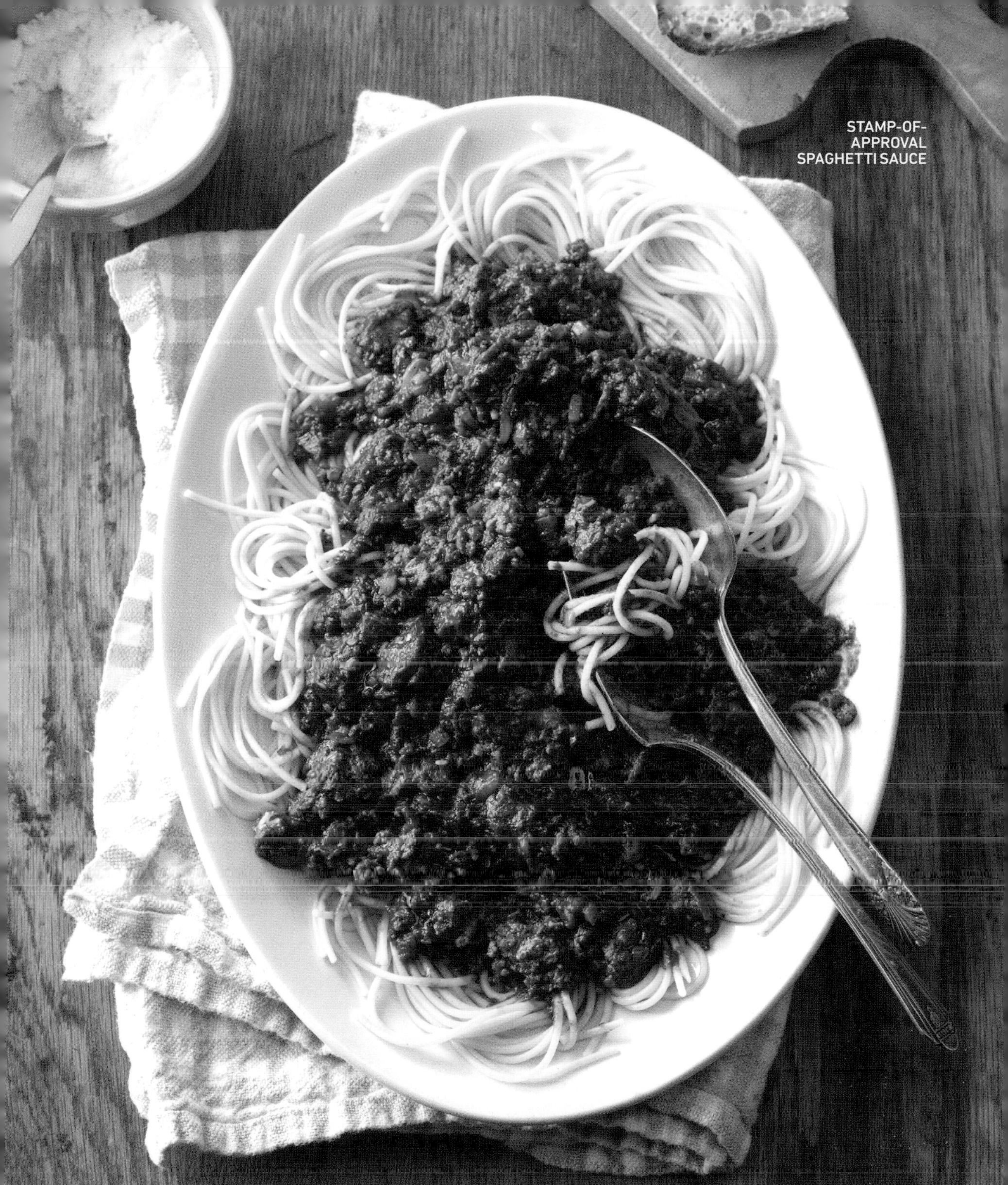

STAMP-OF-APPROVAL SPAGHETTI SAUCE

CAFE MOCHA
COOKIES

Get Portion-Perfect with a Cookie Scoop

Bakers love sturdy ice cream scoops with spring-release handles. They let you easily pop out dough in matching drops. There are many sizes available. A 1-Tbsp. size is useful for most cookie recipes.

Cafe Mocha Cookies

These taste like my favorite coffeehouse drink in cookie form. They're crispy outside but nice and soft in the middle.

—*Angela Spengler, Niceville, FL*

Prep: 20 min. • **Bake:** 10 min./batch
Makes: about 3 dozen

- 6 Tbsp. butter, softened
- ⅓ cup shortening
- ½ cup packed brown sugar
- ⅓ cup sugar
- 1 large egg, room temperature
- 2 Tbsp. hot caramel ice cream topping
- 1 tsp. vanilla extract
- 1½ cups all-purpose flour
- 4 tsp. dark roast instant coffee granules
- ½ tsp. baking soda
- ½ tsp. salt
- 1½ cups (9 oz.) dark chocolate chips

1. Preheat oven to 350°. In a large bowl, cream butter, shortening and sugars until light and fluffy. Beat in egg, ice cream topping and vanilla. In another bowl, whisk flour, coffee granules, baking soda and salt; gradually beat into creamed mixture. Fold in chocolate chips.

2. Drop cookie dough by rounded tablespoonfuls 2 in. apart onto ungreased baking sheets. Bake for 8-10 minutes or until set. Cool on pans for 2 minutes. Remove to wire racks to cool.

Freeze option: Drop dough by rounded tablespoonfuls onto waxed paper-lined baking sheets; freeze until firm. Transfer to airtight container; return to freezer. To use, bake frozen cookies as directed, increasing time by 1-2 minutes.

1 cookie: 123 cal., 7g fat (4g sat. fat), 10mg chol., 76mg sod., 16g carb. (11g sugars, 1g fiber), 1g pro.

MEXICAN CHOCOLATE SUGAR CRISPS

Mexican Chocolate Sugar Crisps

My grandma loved these so much, she would hide them from my grandpa! I think of her every time I make a batch. Like Mexican spice? Try stirring in a little chili powder.

—*Michele Lovio, Thousand Oaks, CA*

Prep: 30 min. • **Bake:** 10 min./batch
Makes: 4½ dozen

- ¾ cup shortening
- 1¼ cups sugar, divided
- 1 large egg, room temperature
- ¼ cup light corn syrup
- 2 oz. unsweetened chocolate, melted and cooled
- 1¾ cups all-purpose flour
- 1½ tsp. ground cinnamon
- 1 tsp. baking soda
- ¼ tsp. salt
- 1 cup (6 oz.) semisweet chocolate chips

1. Preheat oven to 350°. In a large bowl, cream shortening and 1 cup sugar until fluffy. Beat in egg, corn syrup and melted chocolate. In another bowl, whisk flour, cinnamon, baking soda and salt; gradually beat into creamed mixture. Stir in chocolate chips.

2. Shape dough into 1-in. balls; roll in remaining sugar. Place cookies 2 in. apart on ungreased baking sheets (do not flatten). Bake 8-10 minutes or until tops are puffed and cracked. Cool on pans 2 minutes. Remove to wire racks to cool.

Freeze option: Freeze shaped balls of dough on baking sheets until firm. Transfer to airtight containers; return to freezer. To use, bake cookies as directed.

1 cookie: 85 cal., 4g fat (2g sat. fat), 3mg chol., 37mg sod., 11g carb. (8g sugars, 1g fiber), 1g pro.

BANANA SPLIT
SUPREME

Banana Split Supreme

Transform the classic flavor of a banana split into a whole new recipe! This is a cool, creamy treat with no last-minute fuss since you just pull it from the freezer. It always gets praise from our big family.

—Marye Franzen, Gothenburg, NE

- -

Prep: 30 min. + freezing
Makes: 12 servings

- 2 cups confectioners' sugar
- 1 cup evaporated milk
- ¾ cup semisweet chocolate chips
- ¾ cup butter, divided
- 24 Oreo cookies, crushed
- 3 to 4 medium firm bananas, cut into ½-in. slices
- 2 qt. vanilla ice cream, softened, divided
- 1 can (20 oz.) crushed pineapple, drained
- 1 jar (10 oz.) maraschino cherries, drained and halved
- ¾ cup chopped pecans
  Whipped topping, optional

1. In a large saucepan, combine sugar, milk, chocolate chips and ½ cup butter. Bring to a boil over medium heat; cook and stir for 8 minutes. Remove from the heat and cool completely.

2. Meanwhile, melt the remaining butter; toss with cookie crumbs. Press into a greased 13x9-in. pan. Freeze for 15 minutes. Arrange banana slices over crust; spread with 1 qt. of ice cream. Top with 1 cup of chocolate sauce. Freeze for 1 hour. Refrigerate remaining chocolate sauce. Spread remaining ice cream over dessert; top with pineapple, cherries and pecans. Cover and freeze overnight.

3. Remove from the freezer about 10 minutes before serving. Reheat the chocolate sauce. Cut dessert into squares. Serve with whipped topping and chocolate sauce, if desired.

1 piece: 677 cal., 35g fat (18g sat. fat), 76mg chol., 277mg sod., 90g carb. (75g sugars, 4g fiber), 7g pro.

Mint Chip Freeze

I'm a retired home economics teacher and have quite a collection of recipes from my classes. My students really like this refreshing frozen dessert made with ice cream and Oreos.

—Robert Lamb, Daleville, IN

- -

Prep: 30 min. + chilling
Makes: 2 desserts (18 servings each)

- 2 pkg. (15½ oz. each) Oreo cookies, crushed
- ½ cup butter, melted
- 1 can (12 oz.) evaporated milk
- 1 cup sugar
- ½ cup butter, cubed
- 2 oz. unsweetened chocolate, chopped
- 1 gallon mint chocolate chip ice cream, softened
- 1 carton (16 oz.) frozen whipped topping, thawed
  Shaved chocolate

1. In a large bowl, combine the cookie crumbs and butter. Press into two 13x9-in. dishes. Refrigerate for 30 minutes.

2. In a small saucepan, combine the milk, sugar, butter and chocolate. Cook and stir over medium heat until thickened and bubbly, about 12 minutes. Remove from the heat; cool completely.

3. Spread ice cream over each crust. Spoon cooled chocolate sauce over top; evenly spread to cover. Freeze until firm. Spread with whipped topping. Desserts may be frozen for up to 2 months.

4. Remove dessert from freezer 10 minutes before cutting. Garnish with shaved chocolate.

1 piece: 395 cal., 23g fat (13g sat. fat), 39mg chol., 215mg sod., 43g carb. (32g sugars, 1g fiber), 3g pro.

HACK

Quick Crumb Crust

Pulse Oreo cookies in batches in a food processor to quickly make crumbs for your almost-instant desserts.

SLOW-COOKER CHOCOLATE
POTS DE CREME, P. 144

MEAL PREPS
YOU'LL REALLY USE

[Don't let the workweek derail your plans to eat good, healthy, homemade food. Sail on through to Saturday with these smart, fun meal preps.]

MAPLE MUESLI

Maple Muesli

After tasting muesli while on a trip to Switzerland, I began my own muesli experiments at home. Keep things interesting (and avoid mid-morning munchies) by adding different fruits and nuts every day.
—*Maddie Kirk, Springfield, PA*

- -

Prep: 10 min. + chilling
Makes: 6 servings

  2 cups old-fashioned oats
  1 cup fat-free milk
  ¼ cup maple syrup
  2 tsp. vanilla extract
  1 cup vanilla yogurt
  ½ cup chopped walnuts, toasted
     Assorted fresh fruit

1. In a large bowl, combine oats, milk, syrup and vanilla. Refrigerate, covered, overnight.
2. Just before serving, stir in yogurt. Top with walnuts and fruit.

½ cup: 249 cal., 9g fat (1g sat. fat), 3mg chol., 46mg sod., 36g carb. (16g sugars, 3g fiber), 9g pro. **Diabetic exchanges:** 2½ starch, 1 fat.

Overnight Flax Oatmeal

Fans of the healthy benefits of flaxseed will enjoy this hearty oatmeal. It's full of yummy raisins and dried cranberries, too. Any combination of dried fruit will work, so get creative!
—*Susan Smith, Ocean View, NJ*

- -

Prep: 10 min. • **Cook:** 7 hours
Makes: 4 servings

  3 cups water
  1 cup old-fashioned oats
  1 cup raisins
  ½ cup dried cranberries
  ½ cup ground flaxseed
  ½ cup 2% milk
  1 tsp. vanilla extract
  1 tsp. molasses

In a 3-qt. slow cooker, combine all ingredients. Cover and cook on low for 7-8 hours or until liquid is absorbed and oatmeal is tender.

1 cup: 322 cal., 9g fat (1g sat. fat), 2mg chol., 28mg sod., 63g carb. (34g sugars, 8g fiber), 9g pro.

Apple Cinnamon Overnight Oats

Many folks love this oatmeal cold. Not being a big fan of it right out of the fridge, I prefer to heat it up a bit. Add a handful of nuts for crunch, flavor and extra health benefits.
—*Sarah Farmer, Waukesha, WI*

- -

Prep: 5 min. + chilling
Makes: 1 serving

  ½ cup old-fashioned oats
  ½ medium Gala or Honeycrisp apple, chopped
  1 Tbsp. raisins
  1 cup 2% milk
  ¼ tsp. ground cinnamon
     Dash salt
     Toasted, chopped nuts, optional

In a small container or mason jar, combine all ingredients. Seal; refrigerate overnight.

1 serving: 349 cal., 8g fat (4g sat. fat), 20mg chol., 263mg sod., 59g carb. (28g sugars, 7g fiber), 14g pro.

Types of Oats

Our recipes use versatile rolled oats, but steel-cut oats work fine, too. Increase soak or cook time if needed.

Oat Groats

With whole oats, known as groats, only the grain's outer hull has been removed. You can use groats as a substitute for barley or rice, but they are chewy and must be soaked and cooked for a long time.

Steel-Cut Oats

Also called Irish or Scotch oats, these are groats that have been chopped into small pieces but not rolled into flakes. More chewy and nutty than rolled oats, they're popular in muesli and slow-cooked oatmeal.

Rolled Oats

This is the most common type of oats, also known as old-fashioned oats or just oatmeal. Rolled oats are steamed, rolled and then flaked so they cook quickly.

Instant Oats

This speedy breakfast consists of very thin, precooked oat flakes that need only to be mixed with a hot liquid. Instant oats are often sold in packets and blended with other ingredients.

OVERNIGHT
OATMEAL

Overnight Oatmeal

Start this breakfast the night before
so you can get a few extra *zzzs* in the
morning. My husband adds coconut
to his, and I stir in dried fruit.
—*June Thomas, Chesterton, IN*

- -

Prep: 10 min. + chilling
Makes: 1 serving

- ⅓ **cup old-fashioned oats**
- 3 **Tbsp. fat-free milk**
- 3 **Tbsp. reduced-fat plain yogurt**
- 1 **Tbsp. honey**
- ½ **cup assorted fresh fruit**
- 2 **Tbsp. chopped
  walnuts, toasted**

In a small container or mason jar,
combine the oats, milk, yogurt and
honey. Top with fruit and nuts. Seal;
refrigerate overnight.

Note: To toast nuts, bake in a shallow
pan in a 350° oven for 5-10 minutes
or cook in a skillet over low heat until
lightly browned, stirring occasionally.
1 serving: 345 cal., 13g fat (2g sat.
fat), 4mg chol., 53mg sod., 53g carb.
(31g sugars, 5g fiber), 10g pro.

» **Chocolate-Cherry Oats:** Use
  cherry-flavored yogurt; add 1 Tbsp.
  cocoa powder, and top with fresh
  or frozen pitted cherries.
» **Banana Bread Oats:** Replace honey
  with maple syrup. Stir in ½ mashed
  banana and ½ tsp. cinnamon. Top
  with toasted pecans.
» **Carrot Cake Oats:** Add 2 Tbsp.
  grated carrots. Substitute spreadable
  cream cheese for the yogurt.
» **Pina Colada Oats:** Add ½ mashed
  banana, 2 Tbsp. crushed pineapple
  and 1 Tbsp shredded coconut to
  oat mixture.

Overnight Fruit Salad

I first tasted this rich fruit salad at my wedding reception many years ago. The ladies who did the cooking wouldn't share the recipe at the time, but I eventually got it. I've made it for many meals, and our daughters copied the recipe when they married.
—*Eileen Duffeck, Lena, WI*

- -

Prep: 30 min. + chilling
Makes: 16 servings

- 3 **large eggs, beaten**
- ¼ **cup sugar**
- ¼ **cup vinegar**
- 2 **Tbsp. butter**
- 2 **cups green grapes**
- 2 **cups miniature marshmallows**
- 1 **can (20 oz.) pineapple chunks, drained**
- 1 **can (15 oz.) mandarin oranges, drained**
- 2 **medium firm bananas, sliced**
- 2 **cups heavy whipping cream, whipped**
- ½ **cup chopped pecans**

1. In a double boiler over medium heat, cook and stir eggs, sugar and vinegar until mixture is thickened and reaches 160°. Remove from the heat; stir in butter. Cool.

2. In a large serving bowl, combine grapes, marshmallows, pineapple, oranges and bananas; add cooled dressing and stir to coat. Refrigerate for 4 hours or overnight. Just before serving, fold in whipped cream and chopped pecans.

½ cup: 244 cal., 16g fat (8g sat. fat), 84mg chol., 44mg sod., 24g carb. (21g sugars, 1g fiber), 3g pro.

HACK

Wrap plastic around banana stems to slow their ripening.

OVERNIGHT
FRUIT SALAD

Pancake Success

• For the lightest, fluffiest pancakes, mix batter quickly and gently (there may still be a few lumps) after combining your other ingredients.

• Less is more: Resist the urge to flip pancakes more than once. And don't press down with a spatula, which will only create gummy flapjacks.

• If you like the idea of variations but have picky eaters, mix the goodies into softened butter to serve alongside instead. Stir chopped dried fruits, citrus zest, honey or maple syrup into butter before serving. (See p. 130 for ways to freeze your favorite flavored butter.)

CORNMEAL
PANCAKE MIX

Cornmeal Pancake Mix

I like to joke that these pancakes are so light, you have to hold them down! When we have a chance, we'll make them with freshly ground cornmeal bought at local festivals.

—Betty Claycomb, Alverton, PA

- -

Takes: 30 min. • **Makes:** 3 batches (12 pancakes per batch)

    4   cups all-purpose flour
    2   cups cornmeal
    ⅓   cup sugar
    ¼   cup baking powder
    3   tsp. salt
**ADDITIONAL INGREDIENTS
(FOR EACH BATCH)**
    2   large eggs,
        room temperature
  1⅓   cups 2% milk
    ¼   cup canola oil
        Pancake syrup

1. In a large bowl, combine the first 5 ingredients. Divide the mixture among 3 airtight containers. Store up to 6 months.

2. To prepare pancakes, place the contents of 1 pancake mix container in a large bowl. In a small bowl, whisk eggs, milk and oil. Stir into dry ingredients just until moistened.

3. Pour batter by ¼ cupfuls onto a lightly greased hot griddle. Turn when bubbles on top begin to pop; cook until second side is golden brown. Serve with syrup.

2 pancakes: 314 cal., 13g fat (2g sat. fat), 66mg chol., 764mg sod., 42g carb. (7g sugars, 1g fiber), 8g pro.

» **Cranberry-Orange Pancakes:** Stir ¾ cup chopped fresh cranberries and 1 tsp. grated orange zest into prepared batter.

» **Blueberry-Lemon Pancakes:** Stir ¾ cup fresh blueberries and 1 tsp. grated lemon zest into batter.

» **Bacon Pancakes:** Stir 4-6 cooked and crumbled bacon strips into the prepared batter.

Crack an Egg (3 Ways)

On the Counter
- Gently but firmly rap the egg's equator squarely against the countertop.
- Use your thumbs to press inward and separate the shell, then pour the yolk and white into a bowl.

With Two Eggs
- Hold an egg in each hand. Tap the eggs together at their equators.
- One egg will crack. Use your thumbs to press inward and separate the shell.

One-Handed
- Hold the egg in one hand. Position your thumb and index finger above the egg's equator and your middle and ring fingers below it. Sharply crack the egg against the side of a bowl.
- Immediately pull the eggshell apart using your thumb and middle finger and allow the egg to fall out of the shell.

Egg Burritos

Zap one of these frozen burritos in the microwave and you'll stave off hunger all morning. This recipe is my family's favorite combo, but I sometimes use breakfast sausage instead of bacon.
—*Audra Niederman, Aberdeen, SD*

Takes: 25 min. • **Makes:** 10 burritos

- 12   bacon strips, chopped
- 12   large eggs
- ½   tsp. salt
- ¼   tsp. pepper
- 10   flour tortillas (8 in.), warmed
- 1½   cups shredded cheddar cheese
- 4   green onions, thinly sliced

1. In a large cast-iron or other heavy skillet, cook bacon strips until crisp; drain on paper towels. Remove all but 1-2 Tbsp. drippings from pan.
2. Whisk together eggs, salt and pepper. Heat skillet over medium heat; pour in egg mixture. Cook and stir until eggs are thickened and no liquid egg remains; remove from heat.
3. Spoon about ¼ cup egg mixture onto center of each tortilla; sprinkle with cheese, bacon and green onions. Roll into burritos.

Freeze option: Cool eggs before making burritos. Individually wrap burritos in paper towels and foil; freeze in an airtight container. To use, remove foil; place paper towel-wrapped burrito on a microwave-safe plate. Microwave on high until heated through, turning once. Let stand 15 seconds.

1 burrito: 376 cal., 20g fat (8g sat. fat), 251mg chol., 726mg sod., 29g carb. (0 sugars, 2g fiber), 19g pro.

EGG
BURRITOS

LIGHT & FLUFFY
WAFFLES

✳ Light & Fluffy Waffles

These waffles are so tasty, you can almost skip the butter and syrup, but why would you want to?
—*James Schend, Pleasant Prairie, WI*

- -

Prep: 15 min. • **Cook:** 5 min./batch
Makes: 12 waffles

- 2 large eggs, room temperature
- 1½ cups all-purpose flour
- ½ cup cornstarch
- 1 tsp. baking powder
- ½ tsp. baking soda
- ½ tsp. salt
- ½ cup 2% milk
- 5 Tbsp. canola oil
- 2 tsp. vanilla extract
- 1 tsp. white vinegar
- 2 Tbsp. sugar
- ½ cup club soda, chilled
  Optional: butter and maple syrup

1. Separate eggs. Place egg whites in a clean, dry bowl; let stand at room temperature 30 minutes.
2. In another bowl, whisk together next 5 ingredients. In a small bowl, whisk egg yolks, milk, oil, vanilla and vinegar until blended. Beat egg whites until soft peaks form. Gradually add sugar; continue beating until stiff peaks form.
3. Preheat waffle maker. Stir together flour mixture, egg mixture and club soda just until combined. Fold egg whites into batter. Bake waffles according to manufacturer's directions until golden brown. Serve with butter and syrup if desired.
Freeze option: Arrange waffles in a single layer on sheet pans; freeze until firm. Place between waxed paper in an airtight container. Freeze for up to 2 months. Reheat frozen waffles in a toaster or oven.
2 waffles: 312 cal., 14g fat (2g sat. fat), 64mg chol., 421mg sod., 39g carb. (5g sugars, 1g fiber), 6g pro.

✳ Peanut Butter & Jelly Waffles

Don't count out the grown-ups when making these waffles flavored with good old peanut butter and jelly!
—*Helena Georgette Mann, Sacramento, CA*

- -

Takes: 25 min. • **Makes:** 10 waffles

- 1¼ cups all-purpose flour
- 3 Tbsp. sugar
- 1 Tbsp. baking powder
- ¼ tsp. baking soda
- ¼ tsp. ground cinnamon
- 2 large eggs, room temperature, separated
- 1¼ cups whole milk
- ⅓ cup peanut butter
- 3 Tbsp. butter, melted
  Jelly of your choice

1. In a large bowl, combine the flour, sugar, baking powder, baking soda and cinnamon. In another bowl, whisk the egg yolks, milk, peanut butter and butter; stir into dry ingredients just until moistened.
2. In a small bowl, beat egg whites until stiff peaks form; fold into batter. Bake in a preheated waffle iron according to manufacturer's directions until golden brown. Serve with jelly.
Freeze option: Arrange waffles in a single layer on sheet pans. Freeze until firm. Place between sheets of waxed paper in an airtight container. Freeze up to 2 months. Reheat frozen waffles in a toaster or oven.
2 waffles: 370 cal., 20g fat (8g sat. fat), 109mg chol., 184mg sod., 38g carb. (12g sugars, 2g fiber), 12g pro.

PRO TIPS

DIY Frozen Waffles

Place cooled waffles on a cookie sheet and freeze. Stack frozen waffles between sheets of waxed paper in a freezer container.

To reheat just a few waffles, pop them in the toaster for a minute or two. If you're feeding a crew, place waffles on a rack in a sheet pan and bake in a 325° oven for 5 minutes.

Make breakfast envy on the go: Fill a container with ¼ cup frozen blueberries and 1 Tbsp. maple syrup. Add a frozen fully cooked sausage patty. Microwave this in the break room at work, toast your waffles and get ready to wow!

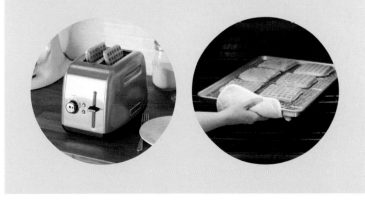

Overnight Pumpkin French Toast Casserole

Recipes that don't tie me to the kitchen—that's what I'm all about. I make this luscious dish the night before a special breakfast or brunch for my guests.
—*Patricia Harmon, Baden, PA*

Prep: 20 min. + chilling
Bake: 65 min. • **Makes:** 12 servings

- 1 loaf (1 lb.) cinnamon-raisin bread
- 1 pkg. (8 oz.) reduced-fat cream cheese, cut into ¾-in. cubes
- 8 large eggs
- 1 can (12 oz.) evaporated milk
- 1 cup canned pumpkin
- ⅔ cup packed brown sugar
- ½ cup fat-free milk
- 2 tsp. ground cinnamon
- ¼ tsp. ground nutmeg
- ¼ tsp. ground ginger
- ⅛ tsp. ground cloves
- ½ tsp. salt
- ½ cup chopped pecans
  Optional: confectioners' sugar and warm maple syrup

1. Cut each slice of bread into quarters. Arrange half the bread in a greased 13x9-in. baking dish; layer with cubed cream cheese and remaining bread, pressing down layers slightly.

2. In a large bowl, whisk the eggs, milks, pumpkin, brown sugar, spices and salt. Pour over top. Refrigerate, covered, overnight.

3. Preheat oven to 350°. Remove casserole from refrigerator while oven heats. Bake, covered, for 40 minutes. Uncover; sprinkle with chopped pecans. Bake, uncovered, for 25-30 minutes or until lightly browned and a knife inserted in the center comes out clean.

4. Let stand 5-10 minutes before serving. If desired, dust with confectioners' sugar and serve with maple syrup.

1 piece: 302 cal., 13g fat (6g sat. fat), 148mg chol., 342mg sod., 36g carb. (20g sugars, 4g fiber), 13g pro.

Overnight Vegetable & Egg Breakfast

My overnight eggs and veggies make a hearty breakfast for those who have to rush out the door...or for those times you want to wake up to a hot meal that's ready to serve!
—*Kimberly Clark-Thiry, Anchor Point, AK*

Prep: 15 min. • **Cook:** 7 hours
Makes: 8 servings

- 4 lbs. potatoes, peeled and thinly sliced (about 8 cups)
- 1 medium green pepper, finely chopped
- 1 pkg. (10 oz.) frozen chopped spinach, thawed and squeezed dry
- 1 cup sliced fresh mushrooms
- 1 medium onion, finely chopped
- 8 large eggs
- 1 cup water
- 1 cup 2% milk
- 1¼ tsp. salt
- ¼ tsp. pepper
- 2 cups shredded cheddar cheese

In a greased 6-qt. slow cooker, layer first 5 ingredients. Whisk the next 5 ingredients; pour over top. Sprinkle with cheese. Cook, covered, on low until potatoes are tender and the eggs are set, 7-9 hours.

1½ cups: 354 cal., 15g fat (7g sat. fat), 217mg chol., 668mg sod., 37g carb. (5g sugars, 4g fiber), 19g pro.

> **PRO TIP**
>
> Dense foods like potatoes take a long time to slow-cook. They are layered in the bottom of the crock, closer to the heat than food placed on top. Always follow layering instructions in recipes.

OVERNIGHT PUMPKIN FRENCH TOAST CASSEROLE

OVERNIGHT
VEGETABLE & EGG
BREAKFAST

❄ Garlic Basil Butter

Instead of serving plain butter alongside an assortment of fresh breads, prepare this herb-laden whipped butter. Place a dollop on hot steak for an immense treat!
—Taste of Home *Test Kitchen*

- -

Takes: 10 min. • **Makes:** ½ cup

½ cup butter, softened
4 tsp. minced fresh basil
1½ tsp. minced fresh parsley
½ tsp. garlic powder

In a small bowl, combine the butter, basil, parsley and garlic powder. Beat on medium-low speed until mixture is combined. Refrigerate up to 1 week or freeze up to several months.

1 Tbsp.: 101 cal., 11g fat (7g sat. fat), 31mg chol., 116mg sod., 0 carb. (0 sugars, 0 fiber), 0 pro.

HOW-TO

Prepare & Freeze Compound Butter

- Place butter on a square of parchment, mounding butter into a rough log shape.

- Fold paper toward you, enclosing the butter. Press butter with a ruler to form a log, holding the edges of paper securely with the other hand. Twist edges to seal. Wrap butter in plastic and freeze. Slice off the desired portions when ready to use, then rewrap the butter and return it to the freezer.

- You can also freeze scoops or rosettes of flavored butter on a parchment-lined baking sheet. Once frozen, arrange the butter portions on layers of paper in a freezer container. Remove the desired number of portions from the freezer when needed.

GARLIC BASIL
BUTTER

Lemon Tarragon Butter

Tarragon, a zesty herb native to central Asia, has been an important ingredient in French cooking since the 16th century. This butter is terrific on grilled fish and chicken, or even on hot cooked asparagus .
—*Michelle Clair, Seattle, WA*

Prep: 5 min. + chilling • **Makes:** ½ cup

½ cup butter, softened
¼ cup fresh tarragon leaves, finely chopped
⅛ tsp. lemon juice
Dash salt
Dash pepper

Beat all ingredients until blended. Shape into a log; wrap in plastic. Refrigerate up to 1 week or freeze up to several months.

1 Tbsp.: 103 cal., 12g fat (7g sat. fat), 31mg chol., 110mg sod., 0 carb. (0 sugars, 0 fiber), 0 pro.

Lime Taco Chicken

—Christine Hair, Odessa, FL

Prep: 10 min. • **Cook:** 3 hours
Makes: 6 servings

- 4   boneless skinless chicken breast halves (6 oz. each)
- 2   cups chicken broth
- 3   Tbsp. lime juice
- 1   Tbsp. chili powder
- 1   tsp. grated lime zest

1. Place chicken breasts in a 3-qt. slow cooker. Combine broth, lime juice and chili powder; pour over chicken. Cook, covered, on low until chicken is tender, about 3 hours.
2. Remove the chicken. When cool enough to handle, shred meat with 2 forks; return to slow cooker. Stir in lime zest.
1 serving: 132 cal., 3g fat (1g sat. fat), 64mg chol., 420mg sod., 2g carb. (1g sugars, 1g fiber), 23g pro. **Diabetic exchanges:** 3 lean meat.

Burrito Bowl *(above)*
Serve over rice with beans, corn, tomatoes, cotija cheese, avocado, cilantro and salsa.

Lettuce Wraps
Scoop up with cool Bibb lettuce and crunch away.

Mexi-gyro
Stuff into a pita with cucumber and sour cream.

1 Chicken Recipe, 3 Tasty Lunches

Pick your favorite flavor of slow-cooked chicken, simmer it up and enjoy the delicious rewards of a quick-prep lunch with these creative options. Each recipe here lists three ideas to get you started!

LIME TACO
CHICKEN

Lemon Chicken with Basil
—*Deborah Posey, Virginia Beach, VA*

Prep: 5 min. • **Cook:** 3 hours
Makes: 4 servings

- 4 boneless skinless chicken breast halves (6 oz. each)
- 2 medium lemons
- 1 bunch fresh basil leaves (¾ oz.)
- 2 cups chicken stock

1. Place chicken breasts in a 3-qt. slow cooker. Finely grate enough zest from lemons to measure 4 tsp. Cut lemons in half; squeeze juice. Add zest and juice to slow cooker.
2. Tear basil leaves directly into slow cooker. Add chicken stock. Cook, covered, on low until meat is tender, 3-4 hours. When cool enough to handle, shred meat with 2 forks.
1 chicken breast half: 200 cal., 4g fat (1g sat. fat), 94mg chol., 337mg sod., 3g carb. (1g sugars, 0 fiber), 37g pro.
Diabetic exchanges: 5 lean meat.

Sandwich (*above*)
Pile onto toast with lettuce and sliced apple.

Pesto Orzo Salad
Mix with cooked orzo, cherry tomatoes and pesto.

Mason Jar Salad
Place salad dressing in a jar, then top with veggies, chicken, lettuce and cheese.

Buffalo Chicken
—*Kim Ciepluch, Kenosha, WI*

Prep: 5 min. • **Cook:** 3 hours
Makes: 6 servings

- ½ cup Buffalo wing sauce
- 2 Tbsp. ranch salad dressing mix
- 4 boneless skinless chicken breast halves (6 oz. each)

1. In a 3-qt. slow cooker, mix wing sauce and dressing mix. Add chicken. Cook, covered, on low until meat is tender, 3-4 hours.
2. When cool enough to handle, shred chicken with 2 forks.
½ cup: 147 cal., 3g fat (1g sat. fat), 63mg chol., 1288mg sod., 6g carb. (0 sugars, 0 fiber), 23g pro.

Buffalo Sticks (*above*)
Stuff into celery, sprinkle with blue cheese and serve with ranch dressing to dip.

Open-Faced Melt
Pile onto an English muffin, top with a slice of sharp cheddar and broil.

Tortilla Pinwheels
Mix chicken with cream cheese and green onions. Spread, roll up and slice.

ROASTED BEETROOT
& GARLIC HUMMUS

PRO TIP

Package the hummus in small grab-and-go containers for quickly adding to the lunch box.

Roasted Beetroot & Garlic Hummus

This beetroot hummus is so tasty, healthy and the prettiest pink snack I've ever seen. This is also a handy recipe to make in large batches and keep in the fridge for lunches and snacks throughout the week.

—*Elizabeth Worndl, Toronto, ON*

- -

Prep: 25 min. • **Bake:** 45 min.
Makes: 4 cups

- 3 **fresh medium beets (about 1 lb.)**
- 1 **whole garlic bulb**
- ½ **tsp. salt, divided**
- ½ **tsp. coarsely ground pepper, divided**
- 1 **tsp. extra virgin olive oil plus ¼ cup olive oil, divided**
- 1 **can (15 oz.) garbanzo beans or chickpeas, rinsed and drained**
- 3 **to 4 Tbsp. lemon juice**
- 2 **Tbsp. tahini**
- ½ **tsp. ground cumin**
- ½ **tsp. cayenne pepper**
- ¼ **cup plain Greek yogurt, optional**
  Minced fresh dill weed or parsley
  Assorted fresh vegetables
  Sliced or torn pita bread

1. Preheat oven to 375°. Pierce beets with a fork; place in a microwave-safe bowl and cover loosely with plastic. Microwave on high for 4 minutes, stirring halfway. Cool slightly. Wrap beets in individual foil packets.
2. Remove papery outer skin from garlic bulb, but do not separate or peel cloves. Cut in half crosswise. Sprinkle halves with ¼ tsp. salt and ¼ tsp. pepper; drizzle with 1 tsp. oil. Wrap in individual foil packets. Roast beets and garlic until cloves are soft, about 45 minutes.
3. Remove from oven; unwrap. Rinse beets with cold water; peel when cool enough to handle. Squeeze garlic from skins. Place beets and garlic in food processor. Add garbanzo beans, lemon juice, tahini, cumin, cayenne pepper and remaining olive oil, salt and pepper. Process until smooth.
4. If desired, pulse 2 Tbsp. Greek yogurt with beet mixture, dolloping remaining yogurt over finished hummus. Sprinkle with dill or parsley. Serve with vegetables and pita bread.

¼ cup: 87 cal., 5g fat (1g sat. fat), 0 chol., 131mg sod., 8g carb. (3g sugars, 2g fiber), 2g pro. **Diabetic exchanges:** ½ starch, 1 fat.

Classic Hummus

We love hummus, and this version is really amazing. If you have a pressure cooker, this is an easy, tasty reason to pull it out! We pair hummus with fresh veggies for a meal or snack.

—*Monica and David Eichler, Lawrence, KS*

- -

Prep: 20 min. + soaking
Cook: 25 min. + chilling
Makes: 2½ cups

- 1 **cup dried chickpeas**
- 1 **medium onion, quartered**
- 1 **bay leaf**
- 4 **cups water**
- ¼ **cup minced fresh parsley**
- ¼ **cup lemon juice**
- ¼ **cup tahini**
- 4 **to 6 garlic cloves, minced**
- 1 **tsp. ground cumin**
- ¾ **tsp. salt**
- ⅛ **tsp. cayenne pepper**
- ¼ **cup olive oil**
  Assorted fresh vegetables

1. Sort chickpeas and rinse in cold water. Place chickpeas in a large bowl; add water to cover by 2 in. Cover and let stand overnight.
2. Drain and rinse soaked chickpeas, discarding liquid. Transfer chickpeas to a stovetop pressure cooker; add the onion, bay leaf and 4 cups water.
3. Close cover securely according to manufacturer's directions. Bring cooker to full pressure over high heat. Reduce heat to medium-high and cook for 12 minutes. (Pressure regulator should maintain a slow, steady rocking motion or release of steam; adjust heat if needed.)
4. Turn off heat; allow pressure to drop on its own. Immediately cool according to the manufacturer's directions until pressure is completely reduced. Drain chickpea mixture, reserving ½ cup cooking liquid. Discard onion and bay leaf.
5. Place chickpeas, parsley, lemon juice, tahini, garlic, cumin, salt and cayenne in a food processor; cover and process until smooth. While processing, gradually add olive oil in a steady stream. Add enough reserved cooking liquid to achieve desired consistency.
6. Cover and refrigerate at least 1 hour. Serve with vegetables.

¼ cup: 139 cal., 10g fat (1g sat. fat), 0 chol., 190mg sod., 14g carb. (1g sugars, 6g fiber), 5g pro. **Diabetic exchanges:** 1½ fat, 1 starch.

Curried Egg Salad

A curry kick gives this delectable egg salad big appeal. We love it when the weather gets warm.

—*Joyce McDowell, West Union, OH*

Takes: 15 min. • **Makes:** 6 servings

- ½ cup mayonnaise
- ½ tsp. ground curry
- ½ tsp. honey
- Dash ground ginger
- 6 hard-boiled large eggs, chopped
- 3 green onions, sliced
- 6 slices whole wheat bread
- Tomato slices and cracked pepper, optional

Mix first 4 ingredients; stir in the eggs and green onions. Spread on bread. If desired, top with tomato and sprinkle with pepper.

1 open-faced sandwich: 273 cal., 20g fat (4g sat. fat), 188mg chol., 284mg sod., 14g carb. (2g sugars, 2g fiber), 10g pro.

Creamy Egg Salad

I love this egg salad's versatility— serve it on a bed of mixed greens, tucked into a sandwich or with your favorite crisp crackers.

—*Cynthia Kolberg, Syracuse, IN*

Takes: 10 min. • **Makes:** 3 cups

- 3 oz. cream cheese, softened
- ¼ cup mayonnaise
- ½ tsp. salt
- ⅛ tsp. pepper
- ¼ cup finely chopped green or sweet red pepper
- ¼ cup finely chopped celery
- ¼ cup sweet pickle relish
- 2 Tbsp. minced fresh parsley
- 8 hard-boiled large eggs, chopped

In a bowl, mix cream cheese, mayonnaise, salt and pepper until smooth. Stir in green pepper, celery, relish and parsley. Fold in eggs. Refrigerate, covered, until serving.

½ cup: 228 cal., 19g fat (6g sat. fat), 264mg chol., 456mg sod., 6g carb. (4g sugars, 0 fiber), 9g pro.

CREAMY EGG SALAD

Hard-Boil Eggs in a Pressure Cooker

• Place trivet insert and 1 cup water in a 6-qt. electric pressure cooker. Set up to 12 eggs on trivet.

• Lock lid; close pressure-release valve. Adjust to pressure-cook on high for 5 minutes (for large eggs). Meanwhile, prepare an ice bath.

• Let pressure release naturally for 5 minutes; quick-release any remaining pressure. Immediately place eggs in ice water to cool. Peel when ready to use.

DIY Ramen Soup

This jarred version of ramen soup is a healthier alternative than most commercial varieties. Play favorites with the veggies to suit your taste.
—*Michelle Clair, Seattle, WA*

- -

Takes: 25 min. • **Makes:** 2 servings

1	pkg. (3 oz.) ramen noodles
1	Tbsp. reduced-sodium chicken base
1	to 2 tsp. Sriracha chili sauce
1	tsp. minced fresh gingerroot
½	cup shredded carrots
½	cup shredded cabbage
2	radishes, halved and sliced
½	cup sliced fresh shiitake mushrooms
1	cup shredded cooked chicken breast
¼	cup fresh cilantro leaves
1	hard-boiled large egg, halved
2	lime wedges
4	cups boiling water

1. Cook ramen according to package directions; cool. In each of two 1-qt. wide-mouth canning jars, divide and layer ingredients in the following order: ramen noodles, chicken base, Sriracha, ginger, carrots, cabbage, radishes, mushrooms, chicken and cilantro. Place egg and lime wedge in 4-oz. glass jars or other airtight containers. Place on top of cilantro in 1-qt. jars. Cover jars; refrigerate until serving.

2. To serve, remove egg and lime. Pour 2 cups boiling water into each 1-qt. glass jar; let stand until warmed through or until chicken base has dissolved. Stir to combine seasonings. Squeeze lime juice over soup and place egg on top.

1 serving: 401 cal., 14g fat (6g sat. fat), 153mg chol., 1092mg sod., 35g carb. (4g sugars, 2g fiber), 31g pro.

DIY RAMEN
SOUP

More Excellent Ways to Upgrade Your Ramen

• Easily dress up cooked ramen by stirring in some peanut butter, chopped green onion or sliced hard-boiled egg.

• If boiling ramen on the stovetop, stir a raw beaten egg into the soup during the last 30 seconds of cooking. Cook and stir until egg is firm. Instant egg drop soup!

• Add snow peas, julienned peppers, sliced mushrooms or other salad-bar fixings to ramen during the last minute of cooking.

PULLED
PORK PARFAIT

Bart's Black Bean Soup

For an unbeatably quick dinner, try
my 10-minute soup!
—*Sharon Ullyot, London, ON*

Takes: 10 min.
Makes: 4 servings (1 qt.)

- 1 **can (15 oz.) black beans,
  rinsed and drained**
- 1½ **cups chicken broth**
- ¾ **cup chunky salsa**
- ½ **cup canned whole
  kernel corn, drained
  Dash hot pepper sauce**
- 2 **tsp. lime juice**
- 1 **cup shredded cheddar cheese**
- 2 **Tbsp. chopped green onions**

In a microwave-safe bowl, combine
the first 5 ingredients. Cover and
microwave on high until heated
through, about 2 minutes. Pour into
4 serving bowls; drizzle each with lime
juice. Sprinkle with cheddar cheese
and green onions.
1 cup: 229 cal., 8g fat (6g sat. fat),
32mg chol., 1004mg sod., 23g carb.
(4g sugars, 5g fiber), 12g pro.

PRO TIPS

Here's how to take this
recipe in a jar:

- After combining the first
  five ingredients, pour
  mixture into jars.

- In separate small jars,
  layer cheddar cheese, green
  onions and a lime wedge
  (omit lime juice).

- Cover jars and refrigerate.
  To serve, pour 1 cup soup
  into a microwave-safe bowl
  and heat through,
  2-3 minutes. Serve with
  cheese, onions and lime.

Pulled Pork Parfait

I tried a version of this meaty parfait
at Miller Park, home of my favorite
baseball team, the Brewers. I take
it up a notch by layering in corn and
creamy mac and cheese, so it truly
is a full barbecue meal you can take
on the go.
—*Rachel Bernard Seis, Milwaukee, WI*

Takes: 15 min. • **Makes:** 4 servings

- 1 **pkg. (16 oz.) refrigerated
  fully cooked barbecued
  shredded pork**
- 1 **cup frozen corn**
- 2 **cups refrigerated
  mashed potatoes**
- 2 **cups prepared macaroni
  and cheese**

1. In each of four 1-pint wide-mouth
canning jars, divide and layer all
ingredients in the following order:
pulled pork, corn, mashed potatoes,
and macaroni and cheese. Cover and
freeze or refrigerate until ready
to serve.
2. When ready to serve, remove lid
and microwave until heated through.
To serve from freezer, partially thaw
in refrigerator overnight before
microwaving.
1 serving: 349 cal., 8g fat (4g sat. fat),
45mg chol., 1116mg sod., 41g carb.
(20g sugars, 1g fiber), 17g pro.

Canning Funnel Makes Meal Preps Easy

Use a canning funnel to quickly, neatly fill jars for your meal preps. To get a tight, spill-free seal, wipe rims with a cloth before putting on the lids.

BART'S BLACK BEAN SOUP

Chilled Turkey Pasta Salad

A Waldorf salad inspired my pasta dish. I use smoked turkey, apples, strawberries and orecchiette. Rotisserie chicken and other fruits would also taste fabulous.

—Sonya Labbe, West Hollywood, CA

Takes: 30 min. • **Makes:** 4 servings

- 2 cups uncooked orecchiette or small tube pasta (about 6 oz.)
- ¼ cup reduced-fat plain yogurt
- 2 Tbsp. mayonnaise
- 2 Tbsp. 2% milk
- 4 tsp. Dijon mustard
- ½ tsp. dried thyme, optional
- 1 medium apple, chopped
- 1 Tbsp. lemon juice
- ½ lb. thick-sliced deli smoked turkey, cut into bite-sized pieces
- 1 cup quartered fresh strawberries
- 1 celery rib, sliced
- ¼ cup toasted chopped walnuts, optional

1. Cook pasta according to package directions. Drain; rinse with cold water and drain well.

2. Meanwhile, in a small bowl, mix yogurt, mayonnaise, milk, mustard and, if desired, thyme until blended. Toss apple with lemon juice.

3. In a large bowl, combine the pasta, apple, turkey, strawberries and celery. Add the dressing; toss gently to coat. Sprinkle with chopped walnuts, if desired. Refrigerate until serving.

1½ cups: 313 cal., 8g fat (1g sat. fat), 24mg chol., 606mg sod., 42g carb. (8g sugars, 3g fiber), 19g pro. **Diabetic exchanges:** 2 starch, 2 lean meat, 1 fat, ½ fruit.

STUFFED CHICKEN ROLLS

Stuffed Chicken Rolls

Just thinking about this dish sparks my appetite. The ham and cheese rolled inside make a tasty surprise. Leftovers reheat great and make a perfect lunch with green salad.
—*Jean Sherwood, Kenneth City, FL*

Prep: 25 min. + chilling • **Cook:** 4 hours
Makes: 6 servings

- 6 boneless skinless chicken breast halves (8 oz. each)
- 6 slices fully cooked ham
- 6 slices Swiss cheese
- ¼ cup all-purpose flour
- ¼ cup grated Parmesan cheese
- ½ tsp. rubbed sage
- ¼ tsp. paprika
- ¼ tsp. pepper
- ¼ cup canola oil
- 1 can (10¾ oz.) condensed cream of chicken soup, undiluted
- ½ cup chicken broth
  Chopped fresh parsley, optional

1. Flatten chicken to ¼-in. thickness; top with ham and cheese. Roll up and tuck in ends; secure with toothpicks.
2. In a shallow bowl, combine the flour, cheese, sage, paprika and pepper; coat chicken on all sides. In a large skillet, brown chicken in oil over medium-high heat.
3. Transfer to a 5-qt. slow cooker. Combine soup and broth; pour over chicken. Cover and cook on low for 4-5 hours or until chicken is tender. Remove toothpicks. Garnish with parsley if desired.

Freeze option: Cool chicken mixture. Freeze in freezer containers. To use, partially thaw in refrigerator overnight. Heat through slowly in a covered skillet, stirring occasionally, until a thermometer inserted in chicken reads 165°.

1 stuffed chicken breast half: 525 cal., 26g fat (10g sat. fat), 167mg chol., 914mg sod., 9g carb. (1g sugars, 1g fiber), 60g pro.

Get Inspired

Fill these chicken rolls with just about anything!

Italian
Prosciutto
Sliced mozzarella
Fresh basil

Mexican
Chorizo
Cilantro
Monterey Jack cheese

French
Mushrooms
Leeks
Boursin garlic and fine herbs cheese

Greek
Kalamata olives
Chopped artichokes
Capers
Feta

Mediterranean
Spinach
Sun-dried tomatoes
Fresh garlic
Goat cheese

American
Bacon
Caramelized onion
Brie

Picnic Berry Shortcakes

These little cakes will be the life of the party! You can make the berry sauce ahead of time and chill it. Assemble the jars a few hours before your picnic or get-together.

—Taste of Home *Test Kitchen*

Prep: 20 min. + chilling
Makes: 4 servings

- 2 Tbsp. sugar
- ½ tsp. cornstarch
- 2 Tbsp. water
- 2 cups sliced fresh strawberries, divided
- ½ tsp. grated lime zest
- 2 individual round sponge cakes
- 2 cups fresh blueberries
  Whipped topping, optional

1. In a small saucepan, mix sugar and cornstarch. Stir in water. Add 1 cup sliced strawberries; mash mixture. Bring to a boil; cook and stir until thickened, 1-2 minutes. Remove from heat; stir in lime zest. Transfer to a small bowl; refrigerate, covered, until chilled.

2. Cut sponge cakes crosswise in half; trim each to fit in bottoms of 4 wide-mouth half-pint canning jars. In a small bowl, mix blueberries and remaining strawberries; spoon over cakes. Top with sauce. If desired, serve with whipped topping.

1 serving: 124 cal., 1g fat (0 sat. fat), 10mg chol., 67mg sod., 29g carb. (21g sugars, 3g fiber), 2g pro. **Diabetic exchanges:** 1 starch, 1 fruit.

Slow-Cooker Chocolate Pots de Creme

Lunch on the go just got a whole lot sweeter. Tuck jars of rich chocolate custard into lunch bags for a midday treat. These desserts in a jar are fun for picnics, too.

—Nick Iverson, Denver, CO

Prep: 20 min.
Cook: 4 hours + chilling
Makes: 8 servings

- 2 cups heavy whipping cream
- 8 oz. bittersweet chocolate, finely chopped
- 1 Tbsp. instant espresso powder
- 4 large egg yolks
- ¼ cup sugar
- ¼ tsp. salt
- 1 Tbsp. vanilla extract
- 8 canning jars (4 oz. each) with lids and bands
- 3 cups hot water
  Optional: whipped cream, grated chocolate and fresh raspberries

1. Place cream, chocolate and espresso in a microwave-safe bowl; microwave on high until chocolate is melted and cream is hot, 4 minutes. Whisk to combine.

2. In a large bowl, whisk egg yolks, sugar and salt until blended but not foamy. Slowly whisk in cream mixture; stir in extract.

3. Pour egg mixture into jars. Center lids on jars and screw on bands until fingertip tight. Add hot water to a 7-qt. slow cooker; place jars in slow cooker. Cook, covered, on low until set, 4 hours. Remove jars from slow cooker; cool on counter 30 minutes. Refrigerate until cold, 2 hours.

4. If desired, top with whipped cream, grated chocolate and raspberries.

1 serving: 424 cal., 34g fat (21g sat. fat), 160mg chol., 94mg sod., 13g carb. (11g sugars, 1g fiber), 5g pro.

HACK

Quickly Hull a Strawberry

Insert a drinking straw into the tip of the berry and push it through the other end.

SLOW-COOKER
CHOCOLATE POTS
DE CREME

Chocolate-Covered Pomegranate Seeds

I dunk pomegranate seeds in chocolate to get these easy little treats. Friends and family love them.

—*Jim Javorsky, Havre de Grace, MD*

- -

Prep: 10 min. + chilling
Makes: 2 dozen (about 1 lb.)

- 1 pkg. (12 oz.) dark chocolate chips
- 1 cup pomegranate seeds, patted dry

1. In a microwave, melt chocolate chips; stir until smooth. Stir in the pomegranate seeds.

2. Drop by tablespoonfuls onto waxed paper-lined baking sheets. Refrigerate until firm, about 1 hour. Store between layers of waxed paper in an airtight container in the refrigerator.

1 piece: 70 cal., 4g fat (3g sat. fat), 0 chol., 5mg sod., 10g carb. (9g sugars, 1g fiber), 1g pro.

No-Bake Peanut Butter Treats

Perfect for road trips, this quick and tasty dessert won't stick to your hands. Keep them in the refrigerator for portable snacks.

—*Sonia Rohda, Waverly, NE*

- -

Takes: 10 min. • **Makes:** 15 treats

- ⅓ cup chunky peanut butter
- ¼ cup honey
- ½ tsp. vanilla extract
- ⅓ cup nonfat dry milk powder
- ⅓ cup quick-cooking oats
- 2 Tbsp. graham cracker crumbs

In a small bowl, combine the peanut butter, honey and vanilla. Stir in the milk powder, oats and graham cracker crumbs. Shape into 1-in. balls. Cover and refrigerate until serving.

1 serving: 70 cal., 3g fat (1g sat. fat), 1mg chol., 46mg sod., 9g carb. (6g sugars, 1g fiber), 3g pro. **Diabetic exchanges:** ½ starch, ½ fat.

Seed a Pomegranate

Here's the simplest way to get to those tart little gems inside a pomegranate.

- Cut the pomegranate in half widthwise.

- Hold it cut side down over a bowl of water, then, using a large spoon, give it a hearty smack on the skin. Keep smacking until all the seed pods—known as arils—fall from the white membrane into the bowl.

- Discard the skin and membrane.

- Drain the water, reserving the arils. Eat the arils whole, seeds and all.

- Each pomegranate yields about 1 cup seeds.

CHOCOLATE-COVERED POMEGRANATE SEEDS

CHERRY-ALMOND TEA MIX

Cherry-Almond Tea Mix

Our family enjoys giving homemade gifts for Christmas, and hot beverage mixes are especially popular. This flavored tea is a favorite.

—*Andrea Horton, Kelso, WA*

- -

Takes: 10 min.
Makes: 40 servings (2½ cups tea mix)

- 2¼ cups iced tea mix with lemon and sugar
- 2 envelopes (0.13 oz. each) unsweetened cherry Kool-Aid mix
- 2 tsp. almond extract

EACH SERVING
- 1 cup boiling or cold water

Place tea mix, Kool-Aid mix and extract in a food processor; pulse until blended. Store in an airtight container in a cool, dry place up to 6 months.

To prepare tea: Place 1 Tbsp. tea mix in a mug. Stir in 1 cup boiling or cold water until blended.

1 cup prepared tea: 41 cal., 0 fat (0 sat. fat), 0 chol., 1mg sod., 10g carb. (10g sugars, 0 fiber), 0 pro.

DIY Hot Cocoa Mix

Because we have long, cold winters in Idaho, hot chocolate is a staple for our family. With this make-ahead mix, a warm cup can be ready in an instant.

—*Tracy Dalin, Gooding, ID*

- -

Prep: 10 min. • **Makes:** 21 servings (7 cups cocoa mix)

- 2¾ cups nonfat dry milk powder
- 2 cups powdered nondairy creamer
- 1 cup confectioners' sugar
- ¾ cup baking cocoa
- 1 pkg. (3.9 oz.) instant chocolate pudding mix
- 1 cup miniature marshmallows, optional
- ½ cup miniature semisweet chocolate chips, optional

EACH SERVING
- ¾ cup hot 2% milk

In a large airtight container, mix first 5 ingredients. If desired, stir in marshmallows and chocolate chips. Store in a cool, dry place up to 6 months.

To prepare cocoa: Place ⅓ cup mix in a mug. Stir in hot milk.

¾ cup prepared hot cocoa: 246 cal., 8g fat (5g sat. fat), 16mg chol., 163mg sod., 35g carb. (25g sugars, 1g fiber), 10g pro.

Drink Your Dessert

Cocoa with marshmallows is a classic. Cocoa that's inspired by a candy bar is just plain dreamy.

Milky Way
Float marshmallows on top and drizzle with caramel sauce.

Almond Joy
Make cocoa with coconut milk, dollop with whipped cream and sprinkle with chopped toasted almonds.

Kit Kat
Use a vanilla sugar wafer as a swizzle stick.

Reese's Pieces
Stir in a spoonful of creamy peanut butter.

Take 5
Stir in peanut butter and caramel sauce, dollop with whipped cream and top with crushed pretzels.

PIGEON RIVER CHICKEN, P. 150;
RADISH, CARROT & CILANTRO SALAD, P. 153;
CRUNCHY RAMEN SALAD, P. 153

ON-THE-GO HACKS

FOR PICNICS, TAILGATES & MORE

[
Get the best goods for game day, reunions
and cookouts. Pack the kid-friendly treats the
whole gang will flip for. Make. Take. Celebrate!
]

SUMMERTIME TEA

Pigeon River Chicken

For a picnic on the Pigeon River, we made chicken marinated in yogurt with just a touch of cayenne. It's delectable warm or cold.
—*Lib Jicha, Waynesville, NC*

Prep: 25 min. + marinating
Cook: 15 min. • **Makes:** 12 servings

- 2 cups plain yogurt
- 2 Tbsp. hot pepper sauce
- 3 tsp. salt
- 2 broiler/fryer chickens (3 to 4 lbs. each), cut up

COATING
- 2 cups all-purpose flour
- 3 Tbsp. paprika
- 4 tsp. cayenne pepper
- 2 tsp. salt
- 2 tsp. pepper
- 1 tsp. dried thyme
   Oil for deep-fat frying

1. In a large bowl, combine yogurt, pepper sauce and 3 tsp. salt. Add chicken; turn to coat. Cover and refrigerate 8 hours or overnight.
2. Drain chicken, discarding marinade. In a shallow bowl, mix the flour and seasonings. Add chicken, a few pieces at a time, and toss to coat; shake off excess. Transfer to a 15x10x1-in. pan; let stand 20 minutes.
3. In a Dutch oven or other deep skillet, heat ½ in. oil over medium heat to 350°. Fry chicken, uncovered, 7-8 minutes per side or until coating is dark golden brown and meat is no longer pink, turning occasionally. Drain on paper towels.
1 serving: 608 cal., 42g fat (7g sat. fat), 109mg chol., 1031mg sod., 19g carb. (2g sugars, 1g fiber), 37g pro.

Summertime Tea

You can't have a summer gathering around here without this sweet tea to cool you down. It's wonderful for sipping while basking by the pool.
—*Angela Lively, Conroe, TX*

Prep: 15 min. + chilling
Makes: 18 servings

- 14 cups water, divided
- 6 black tea bags
- 1½ cups sugar
- ¾ cup thawed orange juice concentrate
- ¾ cup thawed lemonade concentrate
- 1 cup tequila, optional
   Fresh mint leaves and lemon or lime slices, optional

1. In a large saucepan, bring 4 cups water to a boil. Remove from the heat; add tea bags. Cover and steep for 3-5 minutes. Discard tea bags.
2. Stir in the sugar, concentrates and remaining water. Add tequila if desired. Refrigerate until chilled. Garnish with mint leaves and lemon if desired.
¾ cup: 102 cal., 0 fat (0 sat. fat), 0 chol., 1mg sod., 26g carb. (26g sugars, 0 fiber), 0 pro.

PIGEON RIVER CHICKEN

RADISH, CARROT
& CILANTRO SALAD

CRUNCHY
RAMEN SALAD

Crunchy Ramen Salad

For potlucks and picnics, this salad's a knockout. I tote the veggies in a bowl, dressing in a jar and noodles in a bag. Then shake them up together when it's time to eat.

—*LJ Porter, Bauxite, AR*

Takes: 25 min. • **Makes:** 16 servings

- 1 Tbsp. plus ½ cup olive oil, divided
- ½ cup slivered almonds
- ½ cup sunflower kernels
- 2 pkg. (14 oz. each) coleslaw mix
- 12 green onions, chopped (about 1½ cups)
- 1 medium sweet red pepper, chopped
- ⅓ cup cider vinegar
- ¼ cup sugar
- ⅛ tsp. pepper
- 2 pkg. (3 oz. each) chicken ramen noodles

1. In a large skillet, heat 1 Tbsp. oil over medium heat. Add almonds and sunflower kernels; cook until toasted, about 4 minutes. Cool.

2. In a large bowl, combine coleslaw mix, onions and red pepper. In a small bowl, whisk vinegar, sugar, pepper, contents of ramen seasoning packets and remaining oil. Pour over salad; toss to coat. Refrigerate until serving. Break noodles into small pieces. Just before serving, stir in ramen noodles, almonds and sunflower kernels.

¾ cup: 189 cal., 13g fat (2g sat. fat), 0 chol., 250mg sod., 16g carb. (6g sugars, 3g fiber), 4g pro.

Radish, Carrot & Cilantro Salad

Bright carrots and radishes pop in this citrusy salad. My husband likes it with anything from the grill. I like to pile it on tacos.

—*Christina Baldwin, Covington, LA*

Prep: 20 min. + chilling
Makes: 12 servings

- 1½ lbs. radishes, very thinly sliced
- 1½ lbs. carrots, thinly sliced
- 6 green onions, chopped
- ¼ cup coarsely chopped fresh cilantro

DRESSING
- 1 tsp. grated lemon zest
- 1 tsp. grated orange zest
- 3 Tbsp. lemon juice
- 3 Tbsp. orange juice
- 2 Tbsp. extra virgin olive oil
- ½ tsp. salt
- ¼ tsp. pepper

In a large bowl, combine radishes, carrots, onions and cilantro. In a small bowl, whisk dressing ingredients until blended. Pour over salad; toss to coat. Refrigerate, covered, at least 1 hour before serving.

⅔ cup: 51 cal., 2g fat (0 sat. fat), 0 chol., 145mg sod., 7g carb. (4g sugars, 2g fiber), 1g pro. **Diabetic exchanges:** 1 vegetable, ½ fat.

HOW-TO

Zest a Lemon

- Our favorite way is with a rasp, a hand-held grater that makes ready-to-use, superfine zest.

- Using the finest side of a box grater is another technique. Be careful not to grate too far down through the peel, as the pale-colored pith tastes bitter.

- A citrus zester or channel knife makes narrow strips of zest, which you can use whole in drinks or finely minced in recipes.

Cook Bacon in the Oven

- Place a wire rack in a 15x10-in. baking pan. Lightly spritz with cooking spray.

- Place bacon strips in a single layer on rack.

- Bake at 350° to desired crispness, 20-30 minutes. Cooking time depends on the texture you're after; cook longer for extra crispy, shorter if you want the bacon softer. When bacon is done to your liking, remove from oven.

- Use tongs to remove bacon strips from wire rack.

- Pour grease into a heat-safe container.

COBB
SALAD SUB

Cobb Salad Sub

When we need a quick meal to share, we turn Cobb salad into a sandwich masterpiece. Sometimes I substitute tortillas for the bread and make wraps instead.
—*Kimberly Grusendorf, Medina, OH*

Takes: 15 min. • **Makes:** 12 servings

- 1 loaf (1 lb.) unsliced Italian bread
- ½ cup balsamic vinaigrette or dressing of your choice
- 5 oz. fresh baby spinach (about 6 cups)
- 1½ lbs. sliced deli ham
- 4 hard-boiled large eggs, finely chopped
- 8 bacon strips, cooked and crumbled
- ½ cup crumbled Gorgonzola cheese
- 1 cup cherry tomatoes, chopped

Cut loaf of bread in half lengthwise; hollow out top and bottom, leaving a ¾-in. shell (discard removed bread or save for another use). Brush the vinaigrette over bread halves. Layer spinach, ham, eggs, bacon, cheese and tomatoes on bread bottom. Replace top. Cut entire loaf in half lengthwise from top to bottom; cut crosswise 5 times for 12 pieces.

1 slice: 233 cal., 10g fat (3g sat. fat), 97mg chol., 982mg sod., 17g carb. (3g sugars, 1g fiber), 18g pro.

Spinach & Turkey Pinwheels

Need an awesome snack for game day? My kids always love these easy four-ingredient turkey pinwheels. Go ahead and make them the day before—they don't get soggy!
—*Amy Van Hemert, Ottumwa, IA*

- -

Prep: 15 min. • **Makes:** 8 servings

- 1   carton (8 oz.) spreadable garden vegetable cream cheese
- 8   flour tortillas (8 in.)
- 4   cups fresh baby spinach
- 1   lb. sliced deli turkey

Spread cream cheese over tortillas. Layer with spinach and turkey. Roll up tightly; if desired, wrap and refrigerate until serving. Cut rolls crosswise into 1-in. slices.

6 pinwheels: 307 cal., 13g fat (6g sat. fat), 52mg chol., 866mg sod., 31g carb. (1g sugars, 2g fiber), 17g pro.

JUDY'S MACARONI SALAD

Judy's Macaroni Salad

After finding this vintage macaroni salad years ago, I tweaked it a bit and bumped up the pickles. Tuck it inside your picnic basket.

—*Elizabeth Kirchgatter, Maysville, KY*

Prep: 20 min. + chilling
Makes: 12 servings

- 2½ cups uncooked elbow macaroni
- 1½ cups mayonnaise
- ¼ cup sweet pickle juice
- ½ tsp. salt
- ¼ tsp. pepper
- 1 cup shredded cheddar cheese
- 6 hard-boiled large eggs, chopped
- 6 sweet pickles, chopped

1. Cook macaroni according to package directions. Drain macaroni; rinse with cold water and drain well.
2. In a large bowl, combine mayonnaise, pickle juice, salt and pepper. Stir in cheese, eggs and pickles. Add macaroni; toss gently to coat. Refrigerate, covered, at least 2 hours or until chilled.

¾ cup: 347 cal., 28g fat (6g sat. fat), 113mg chol., 413mg sod., 15g carb. (4g sugars, 1g fiber), 8g pro.

HACK

Chop, Chop

Use a grid-style cooling rack to "chop" your hard-boiled eggs. It's faster (and less slippery) than using a knife. Set the rack on top of a bowl and smoosh the peeled egg through.

Easy Peasy Slaw

I get tons of compliments when I bring out this slaw brightened up with peas, peanuts and poppy seed dressing. It's fresh and colorful with a satisfying crunch.
—Sue Ort, Des Moines, IA

- -

Takes: 5 min. • **Makes:** 12 servings

- 4   cups frozen peas (about 16 oz.), thawed
- 1   pkg. (14 oz.) coleslaw mix
- 4   green onions, chopped
- 1   cup poppy seed salad dressing
- 1   cup sweet and crunchy peanuts or honey-roasted peanuts

Place peas, coleslaw mix and green onions in a large bowl. Pour dressing over salad and toss to coat. Stir in peanuts just before serving.

⅔ cup: 202 cal., 12g fat (2g sat. fat), 7mg chol., 178mg sod., 20g carb. (14g sugars, 4g fiber), 4g pro. **Diabetic exchanges:** 2 fat, 1 starch, 1 vegetable.

HACK

Keep a Lid on It

Secure a dish towel, elastic cord or ribbon around the handles of a casserole or Dutch oven, then tie off to secure the lid in place. Now you're ready to transport without risk of a mess.

Fourth of July Bean Casserole

The outstanding barbecue taste of these beans makes them a favorite for cookouts all summer and into the fall. It's a popular dish, even with kids. The beef makes it so much better than plain pork and beans.
—Donna Fancher, Lawrence, IN

- -

Prep: 20 min. • **Bake:** 1 hour
Makes: 12 servings

- ½   lb. bacon strips, diced
- ½   lb. ground beef
- 1   cup chopped onion
- 1   can (28 oz.) pork and beans
- 1   can (16 oz.) kidney beans, rinsed and drained
- 1   can (15¼ oz.) lima beans, rinsed and drained
- ½   cup barbecue sauce
- ½   cup ketchup
- ½   cup sugar
- ½   cup packed brown sugar
- 2   Tbsp. prepared mustard
- 2   Tbsp. molasses
- 1   tsp. salt
- ½   tsp. chili powder

1. In a large skillet over medium heat, cook bacon, beef and onion until meat is no longer pink; drain.
2. Transfer to a greased 2½-qt. baking dish; add all beans and mix well. In a small bowl, combine the remaining ingredients; stir into beef and bean mixture.
3. Cover dish and bake at 350° for 45 minutes. Uncover beans; bake 15 minutes longer.

1 cup: 278 cal., 6g fat (2g sat. fat), 15mg chol., 933mg sod., 47g carb. (26g sugars, 7g fiber), 12g pro.

Layered BLT Dip

When I throw a party for friends, I whip up this addictive layered three-cheese dip. It's always gone within the first 20 minutes.
—Jade Bennett, Kingwood, TX

- -

Takes: 25 min. • **Makes:** 5 cups

- 1   pkg. (8 oz.) cream cheese, softened
- ½   cup mayonnaise
- ¼   cup grated Parmesan cheese
- 1   cup finely chopped lettuce
- 8   bacon strips, cooked and crumbled
- 4   plum tomatoes, chopped
- 4   green onions, chopped
- 1½   cups shredded cheddar cheese
    Toasted French bread baguette slices

In a small bowl, beat cream cheese, mayonnaise and Parmesan cheese until blended; spread into a large shallow dish. Layer with lettuce, bacon, tomatoes, onions and cheddar cheese. Refrigerate until serving. Serve with bread slices.

¼ cup: 137 cal., 13g fat (5g sat. fat), 27mg chol., 204mg sod., 2g carb. (1g sugars, 0 fiber), 4g pro.

LAYERED
BLT DIP

JALAPENO
POPPER BURGERS

Jalapeno Popper Burgers

What do you get when you combine a jalapeno popper and a great burger? This fantastic recipe! It takes all the classic components of a popper and encases them in a juicy patty for a burst of flavor in every bite.

—*Jo Davison, Naples, FL*

- -

Prep: 30 min. • **Grill:** 15 min.
Makes: 4 servings

- 3 jalapeno peppers, halved lengthwise and seeded
- 1 tsp. olive oil
- 6 bacon strips, cooked and crumbled
- 3 oz. cream cheese, softened
- 2 garlic cloves, minced
- 1 tsp. salt
- 1 tsp. lemon-pepper seasoning
- ½ tsp. pepper
- ¼ tsp. paprika
- 2 lbs. ground beef
- 4 slices pepper jack cheese
- 4 hamburger buns, split
- 4 lettuce leaves
- 1 large tomato, sliced
- ¾ cup guacamole

1. Brush jalapenos with oil. Grill, covered, over medium heat for 3-5 minutes or until tender, turning occasionally. When cool enough to handle, finely chop. In a small bowl, combine the bacon, cream cheese and jalapeno until blended.

2. In a large bowl, combine garlic, salt, lemon pepper, pepper and paprika. Crumble beef over mixture and mix well. Shape into 8 thin patties. Spoon bacon mixture onto center of 4 patties; top with remaining patties and press edges firmly to seal.

3. Grill the burgers, covered, over medium heat or broil 4 in. from heat for 6-7 minutes on each side or until a thermometer reads 160° and juices run clear. Top with pepper jack cheese. Cover and cook 1-2 minutes longer or until cheese is melted.

4. Grill buns, cut side down, over medium heat for 30-60 seconds or until toasted. Serve burgers on buns with lettuce, tomato and guacamole.

1 burger: 879 cal., 58g fat (23g sat. fat), 204mg chol., 1715mg sod., 31g carb. (6g sugars, 5g fiber), 59g pro.

HACK

Smart Recipes Let You Travel Light

The on-the-go cook's secret weapon? Prepping foods ahead at home. Stuffed burgers pack in loads of flavor so you don't need to tote along lots of condiments. A little work at home means you're ready to fire up the grill at your destination and pop the burgers on with no mess. The same goes for Chili Coney Dogs. They're easy to keep hot and serve right out of their crock.

Chili Coney Dogs

From the smallest kids to the oldest adults, everyone in our family loves these hot dogs. They're so easy to throw together in the morning or even the night before.

—*Michele Harris, Vicksburg, MI*

- -

Prep: 20 min. • **Cook:** 4 hours
Makes: 8 servings

- 1 lb. lean ground beef (90% lean)
- 1 can (15 oz.) tomato sauce
- ½ cup water
- 2 Tbsp. Worcestershire sauce
- 1 Tbsp. dried minced onion
- ½ tsp. garlic powder
- ½ tsp. ground mustard
- ½ tsp. chili powder
- ½ tsp. pepper
  Dash cayenne pepper
- 8 hot dogs
- 8 hot dog buns, split
  Optional toppings: shredded cheddar cheese, relish and chopped onion

1. In a large skillet, cook beef over medium heat 6-8 minutes or until no longer pink, breaking into crumbles; drain. Stir in tomato sauce, water, Worcestershire sauce, onion and seasonings.

2. Place hot dogs in a 3-qt. slow cooker; top with beef mixture. Cook, covered, on low 4-5 hours or until heated through. Serve on buns with toppings as desired.

1 chili dog: 371 cal., 20g fat (8g sat. fat), 53mg chol., 992mg sod., 26g carb. (5g sugars, 2g fiber), 21g pro.

Herb & Cheese-Stuffed Burgers

Tired of the same old ground beef burgers? This quick-fix alternative, with its creamy cheese filling, will wake up your taste buds.

—*Sherri Cox, Lucasville, OH*

Takes: 30 min. • **Makes:** 4 servings

- ¼ **cup shredded cheddar cheese**
- 2 **Tbsp. cream cheese, softened**
- 2 **Tbsp. minced fresh parsley**
- 3 **tsp. Dijon mustard, divided**
- 2 **green onions, thinly sliced**
- 3 **Tbsp. dry bread crumbs**
- 2 **Tbsp. ketchup**
- ½ **tsp. salt**
- ½ **tsp. dried rosemary, crushed**
- ¼ **tsp. dried sage leaves**
- 1 **lb. lean ground beef (90% lean)**
- 4 **hamburger buns, split**
  Optional toppings: lettuce leaves and tomato slices

1. In a small bowl, mix the cheddar cheese, cream cheese, parsley and 1 tsp. mustard. In another bowl, mix green onions, bread crumbs, ketchup, seasonings and remaining mustard. Add beef; mix lightly but thoroughly.

2. Shape mixture into 8 thin patties. Spoon cheese mixture onto the center of 4 patties; top with remaining patties, pressing edges firmly to seal.

3. Grill the burgers, covered, over medium heat or broil 4 in. from heat until a thermometer reads 160°, 4-5 minutes on each side. Serve on buns with toppings as desired.

1 burger: 383 cal., 16g fat (7g sat. fat), 86mg chol., 861mg sod., 29g carb. (5g sugars, 1g fiber), 29g pro.

PRO TIPS

- Stay loose. The less you handle the patty, the more tender the cooked burger.

- Resist the urge to flatten your burgers with a spatula as they cook. Don't press out precious juices.

- Allow the cooked burgers to stand for a few minutes before serving.

- Combine ripe tomatoes, a bit of basil and fresh mozzarella for a Caprese burger.

- Pack a little heat with fresh jalapeno and pepper jack cheese.

- For a classic Greek pairing, add spinach and feta cheese.

HERB & CHEESE-STUFFED BURGERS

Bacon-Wrapped Corn

After one bite of this grilled corn on the cob, you'll never go back to your old way of preparing it. The incredible flavor of roasted corn combined with bacon and chili powder is sure to please your palate and bring rave reviews at your next barbecue.
—*Lori Bramble, Omaha, NE*

Takes: 30 min. • **Makes:** 8 servings

- 8 **large ears sweet corn, husks removed**
- 8 **bacon strips**
- 2 **Tbsp. chili powder**

1. Wrap each ear of corn with a bacon strip; place on a piece of heavy-duty foil. Sprinkle with chili powder. Wrap securely, twisting foil ends to make handles for turning.

2. Grill corn, covered, over medium heat, turning once, until corn is tender and bacon is cooked, 20-25 minutes.

1 ear of corn: 210 cal., 14g fat (5g sat. fat), 15mg chol., 199mg sod., 18g carb. (5g sugars, 3g fiber), 5g pro.

HACK

Goodbye, Silk

Your produce brush is a handy tool for scrubbing corn silks off the cobs. After shucking the corn, gently brush each ear under running water and the silks will come right off.

BACON-WRAPPED CORN

SLOW-COOKER SRIRACHA CORN

Slow-Cooker Sriracha Corn

A restaurant here advertised Sriracha corn on the cob, but I knew I could make my own. Golden ears cooked up a little sweet, a little smoky and a little hot—perfect, if you ask my three teenage boys!

—*Julie Peterson, Crofton, MD*

Prep: 15 min. • **Cook:** 3 hours
Makes: 8 servings

½ cup butter, softened
2 Tbsp. honey
1 Tbsp. Sriracha chili sauce
1 tsp. smoked paprika
½ tsp. kosher salt
8 small ears sweet corn, husks removed
¼ cup water
   Additional smoked paprika, optional

1. Mix first 5 ingredients. Place each ear of corn on a 12x12-in. piece of heavy-duty foil, spread with 1 Tbsp. butter mixture. Wrap foil around corn, sealing tightly. Place in a 6-qt. slow cooker.
2. Add water; cook, covered, on low until the corn is tender, 3-4 hours. If desired, sprinkle corn with additional paprika before serving.

1 ear of corn: 209 cal., 13g fat (8g sat. fat), 31mg chol., 287mg sod., 24g carb. (11g sugars, 2g fiber), 4g pro.

HACK

Don't want to cook corn on-site or tote it in a slow cooker? Then warm up some microwaveable hot packs (like those used for sore muscles), and pack them in a cooler with hot individually wrapped ears of corn.

CAMPFIRE
DESSERT CONES

Campfire Dessert Cones

Kids love to make these! Set out the ingredients so they can create their own combinations.
—*Bonnie Hawkins, Elkhorn, WI*

Takes: 20 min. • **Makes:** 8 servings

- 8   ice cream sugar cones
- ½   cup milk chocolate M&M's
- ¼   cup miniature marshmallows
- ½   cup salted peanuts
- ½   cup white baking chips

1. Prepare campfire or grill for medium heat. Fill cones with M&M's, marshmallows, peanuts and white chips. Fully wrap each cone with foil, sealing tightly.

2. Place packets over campfire or grill; cook until heated through, 7-10 minutes. Open foil carefully.

1 cone: 217 cal., 11g fat (5g sat. fat), 4mg chol., 78mg sod., 26g carb. (18g sugars, 1g fiber), 5g pro.

Peanut Butter S'mores

I turn to this recipe when I need something fun and easy for dessert.
—*Lily Julow, Lawrenceville, GA*

Takes: 10 min. • **Makes:** 4 servings

- 8   large chocolate chip cookies
- 4   tsp. hot fudge ice cream topping
- 4   large marshmallows
- 4   peanut butter cups

1. Spread the bottoms of 4 cookies with fudge topping.

2. Using a long-handled fork, grill marshmallows 6 in. from medium-hot heat until golden brown, turning occasionally. Carefully place a marshmallow and a peanut butter cup on each fudge-topped cookie; top with remaining cookies.

1 serving: 227 cal., 11g fat (4g sat. fat), 1mg chol., 129mg sod., 30g carb. (19g sugars, 1g fiber), 3g pro.

REESE'S CHOCOLATE SNACK CAKE

Reese's Chocolate Snack Cake

This cake is constantly requested by my family. The yellow and orange toppings make it the perfect dessert for a Halloween party.
—*Eileen Travis, Ukiah, CA*

Prep: 15 min.
Bake: 30 min. + cooling
Makes: 20 servings

- 3⅓   cups all-purpose flour
- ⅔   cup sugar
- ⅔   cup packed brown sugar
- ½   cup baking cocoa
- 2   tsp. baking soda
- 1   tsp. salt
- 2   cups water
- ⅓   cup canola oil
- ⅓   cup unsweetened applesauce
- 2   tsp. white vinegar
- 1   tsp. vanilla extract
- 1   cup Reese's pieces
- ½   cup coarsely chopped salted peanuts

1. Preheat oven to 350°. Coat a 13x9-in. pan with cooking spray.

2. Whisk together first 6 ingredients. In another bowl, whisk together water, oil, applesauce, vinegar and vanilla. Add to flour mixture, stirring just until blended. Transfer batter to prepared pan. Sprinkle with Reese's pieces and peanuts.

3. Bake until a toothpick inserted in center of cake comes out clean, 30-35 minutes. Cool on a wire rack.

1 piece: 240 cal., 8g fat (2g sat. fat), 0 chol., 280mg sod., 38g carb. (19g sugars, 2g fiber), 5g pro.

Italian Steak Sandwich

If you need to feed a hungry crowd, you can't go wrong with steak sandwiches. They're easy to make and rich with the flavors of Italy.
—*Gilda Lester, Millsboro, DE*

- -

Prep: 35 min. + marinating
Grill: 15 min. + chilling
Makes: 8 servings

- ½ cup reduced-sodium teriyaki sauce
- 2 Tbsp. lemon juice
- 2 Tbsp. olive oil
- 2 Tbsp. Worcestershire sauce
- 1 beef flank steak (1 lb.)
- 1 round loaf Italian bread (about 2 lbs.), unsliced
- 4 plum tomatoes, chopped
- 4 green onions, thinly sliced
- ¼ cup Greek olives, coarsely chopped
- ¼ cup sliced pepperoni
- 1 Tbsp. thinly sliced fresh basil leaves
- 2 Tbsp. plus ¼ cup prepared Italian salad dressing, divided
- 2 cups fresh arugula

1. Place first 4 ingredients in a large bowl or shallow dish. Add steak and turn to coat. Refrigerate, covered, 8 hours or overnight.
2. Remove flank steak, discarding marinade. Grill steak, covered, over medium heat or broil 4 in. from heat until meat reaches desired doneness (for medium-rare, a thermometer should read 135°; medium, 140°), 6-8 minutes per side. Cool completely.
3. Cut bread horizontally in half. Hollow out both halves, leaving a ½-in. shell (save removed bread for another use). Cut steak across the grain into thin slices. In a bowl, toss tomatoes with green onions, olives, pepperoni, basil and 2 Tbsp. dressing. In another bowl, toss arugula with remaining dressing.
4. Place half the arugula in bread bottom. Layer with steak, tomato mixture and remaining arugula; replace top. Wrap in foil; refrigerate at least 1 hour. Cut into wedges to serve.
1 wedge: 260 cal., 10g fat (3g sat. fat), 30mg chol., 567mg sod., 24g carb. (4g sugars, 2g fiber), 16g pro. **Diabetic exchanges:** 2 lean meat, 1½ starch, 1 fat.

Pineapple Coleslaw

When I was a child, my mother often served this salad with multicolored marshmallows sprinkled on top, much to my delight. Marshmallows added a touch of sweetness that really complemented this salad's tangy flavor.
—*Betty Follas, Morgan Hill, CA*

- -

Takes: 15 min. • **Makes:** 8 servings

- ¾ cup mayonnaise
- 2 Tbsp. sugar
- 2 Tbsp. cider vinegar
- 1 to 2 Tbsp. 2% milk
- 4 cups shredded cabbage
- ¾ cup pineapple tidbits
  Paprika, optional

1. For coleslaw dressing, mix the first 4 ingredients. Place cabbage and pineapple in a large bowl. Add dressing; toss to coat.
2. Refrigerate until serving. If desired, sprinkle with paprika.
¾ cup: 170 cal., 15g fat (2g sat. fat), 2mg chol., 114mg sod., 9g carb. (6g sugars, 1g fiber), 1g pro.

Orange Gelatin Pretzel Salad

Salty pretzels pair nicely with sweet oranges in this refreshing layered salad. It's a family favorite that's a slam-dunk at potlucks.
—*Peggy Boyd, Northport, AL*

- -

Prep: 20 min. + chilling
Bake: 10 min. + cooling
Makes: 12 servings

- ¾ cup butter, melted
- 1 Tbsp. plus ¾ cup sugar, divided
- 2 cups finely crushed pretzels
- 2 cups boiling water
- 2 pkg. (3 oz. each) orange gelatin
- 2 cans (8 oz. each) crushed pineapple, drained
- 1 can (11 oz.) mandarin oranges, drained
- 1 pkg. (8 oz.) cream cheese, softened
- 2 cups whipped topping
  Optional: additional whipped topping and mandarin oranges

1. Preheat oven to 350°. Mix melted butter and 1 Tbsp. sugar; stir in pretzels. Press onto bottom of an ungreased 13x9-in. baking dish. Bake 10 minutes. Cool on a wire rack.
2. In a large bowl, add boiling water to gelatin; stir 2 minutes to completely dissolve. Stir in fruit. Refrigerate until partially set, about 30 minutes.
3. Meanwhile, in a bowl, beat cream cheese and remaining sugar until smooth. Fold in whipped topping. Spread over crust.
4. Gently spoon gelatin mixture over top. Refrigerate, covered, until firm, 2-4 hours. To serve, cut into squares. If desired, top with additional whipped topping and oranges.
1 serving: 400 cal., 21g fat (13g sat. fat), 50mg chol., 402mg sod., 51g carb. (38g sugars, 1g fiber), 4g pro.

PRO TIP

How Cute Is That?

To make individual servings of Orange Gelatin Pretzel Salad, prepare layers as directed. In each of twelve 9-oz. cups or ½-pint canning jars, layer about 2 Tbsp. of pretzel mixture, 2 Tbsp. of cream cheese mixture and ⅓ cup gelatin mixture. Chill and serve as directed. To take 'em on the road, pop the cups into a muffin tin.

PINEAPPLE COLESLAW

ORANGE GELATIN PRETZEL SALAD

ITALIAN STEAK SANDWICH

Deluxe Walking Nachos

This slow-cooked potluck chili makes an awesome filling for a little bag of walk-around nachos. Cut the bag lengthwise to make it easier to load up your fork.

—Mallory Lynch, Madison, WI

- -

Prep: 20 min. • **Cook:** 6 hours
Makes: 18 servings

- 1 lb. lean ground beef (90% lean)
- 1 large sweet onion, chopped
- 3 garlic cloves, minced
- 2 cans (14½ oz. each) diced tomatoes with mild green chiles
- 2 cans (15 oz. each) pinto beans, rinsed and drained
- 2 cans (15 oz. each) black beans, rinsed and drained
- 2 to 3 Tbsp. chili powder
- 2 tsp. ground cumin
- ½ tsp. salt
- 18 pkg. (1 oz. each) nacho-flavored tortilla chips
- Optional toppings: shredded cheddar cheese, sour cream, chopped tomatoes and pickled jalapeno slices

1. In a large skillet, cook beef, onion and garlic over medium heat until beef is no longer pink, 6-8 minutes, breaking up beef into crumbles; drain.

2. Transfer beef mixture to a 5-qt. slow cooker. Drain 1 can tomatoes, discarding liquid; add to slow cooker. Stir in beans, chili powder, cumin, salt and remaining tomatoes. Cook on low, covered, 6-8 hours to allow the flavors to blend. Mash beans to desired consistency.

3. Just before serving, cut open tortilla chip bags. Divide chili among bags; add toppings as desired.

Freeze option: Freeze cooled chili in a freezer container. To use, partially thaw in refrigerator overnight. Heat through in a saucepan, stirring occasionally and adding a little water if necessary.

1 serving: 282 cal., 10g fat (2g sat. fat), 16mg chol., 482mg sod., 36g carb. (5g sugars, 6g fiber), 12g pro.

HACK

Tailgate Kit

Store all your tailgate needs (such as serveware, games, sunblock and linens) in a plastic bin inside the cooler, so you're ready to go at a moment's notice.

Beer Dip

Ranch dressing mix amps up this irresistible dip packed with shredded cheese and made to go with pretzels. It's one of those snacks that when you start eating it, you just can't stop!
—*Michelle Long, New Castle, CO*

- -

Takes: 5 min. • **Makes:** 3½ cups

- 2 pkg. (8 oz. each) cream cheese, softened
- ⅓ cup beer or nonalcoholic beer
- 1 envelope ranch salad dressing mix
- 2 cups shredded cheddar cheese
  Pretzels

In a large bowl, beat the cream cheese, beer and dressing mix until smooth. Stir in cheddar cheese. Serve with pretzels.

2 Tbsp.: 89 cal., 8g fat (5g sat. fat), 26mg chol., 177mg sod., 1g carb. (0 sugars, 0 fiber), 3g pro.

DELUXE WALKING NACHOS

RASPBERRY ICE
CREAM IN A BAG

HACK

Shake It Up

No freezer needed for this
berry-licious ice cream—
just 15 minutes, plastic
bags and kid power.

Raspberry Ice Cream in a Bag

Making homemade ice cream is fun for the whole family, and the fresh raspberry flavor of this treat makes it a perfect summer activity. Kids can shake the bags until the liquid changes to ice cream and then enjoy the reward!

—Erin Hoffman, Canby, MN

Takes: 15 min. • **Makes:** 1 cup

- 1 cup half-and-half cream
- ½ cup fresh raspberries
- ¼ cup sugar
- 2 Tbsp. evaporated milk
- 1 tsp. vanilla extract
- 4 cups coarsely crushed ice
- ¾ cup salt

1. Using two 1-qt. resealable plastic bags, place 1 bag inside the other. Place the first 5 ingredients inside the inner bag. Seal both bags, pressing out as much air as possible.

2. Place the 2 bags in a gallon-size resealable plastic freezer bag. Add ice and salt. Seal bag, again pressing out as much air as possible.

3. Shake and knead cream mixture until thickened, about 5 minutes. (If desired, wear mittens or wrap bags in a kitchen towel while shaking to protect hands from the cold ice.)
½ cup: 299 cal., 13g fat (9g sat. fat), 65mg chol., 76mg sod., 35g carb. (32g sugars, 2g fiber), 5g pro.

Vanilla Ice Cream

We think that this is the best ice cream recipe ever. With only four ingredients, it just might be the easiest, too. No ice cream maker? No problem.

—Taste of Home *Test Kitchen*

Prep: 5 min.
Process: 20 min. + freezing
Makes: 1¼ qt.

- 2 cups heavy whipping cream
- 2 cups half-and-half cream
- 1 cup sugar
- 2 tsp. vanilla extract

Stir all ingredients until sugar is dissolved completely. Fill cylinder of ice cream maker no more than two-thirds full; freeze according to the manufacturer's directions. (Chill any remaining mixture until ready to freeze.) Serve immediately or freeze.
½ cup: 308 cal., 22g fat (14g sat. fat), 78mg chol., 37mg sod., 23g carb. (23g sugars, 0 fiber), 3g pro.

»**To make strawberry ice cream:** Substitute 2 cups fresh or frozen berries for 1 cup of half-and-half. Puree berries in a blender or food processor; stir into the other ingredients before freezing.

»**To prepare recipe without an ice cream maker:** Place a 13x9-in. dish in freezer until cold. Prepare cream mixture as directed; transfer to prepared dish. Freeze until edges of mixture begin to set, 20-30 minutes. Using a hand mixer, beat mixture until smooth. Freeze, covered, until firm, about 3 hours longer, beating again every 30 minutes.

CAMPFIRE PEACH COBBLER

Cake & Berry Campfire Cobbler

This warm cobbler is one of our favorite ways to end a busy day of fishing, hiking, swimming or rafting. It's yummy with ice cream—and so easy to make!
—June Dress, Meridian, ID

Prep: 10 min. • **Grill:** 30 min.
Makes: 12 servings

- 2 cans (21 oz. each) raspberry pie filling
- 1 pkg. yellow cake mix (regular size)
- 1¼ cups water
- ½ cup canola oil
  Vanilla ice cream, optional

1. Prepare grill or campfire for low heat, using 16-20 charcoal briquettes or large wood chips.
2. Line an ovenproof Dutch oven with heavy-duty aluminum foil; add pie filling. In a large bowl, combine the cake mix, water and oil. Spread over pie filling.
3. Cover the Dutch oven. When briquettes or wood chips are covered with white ash, place Dutch oven directly on top of 8-10 of them. Using long-handled tongs, place remaining briquettes on pan cover.
4. Cook until filling is bubbly and a toothpick inserted in the topping comes out clean, 30-40 minutes. To check for doneness, use the tongs to carefully lift the cover. Serve with ice cream if desired.
1 serving: 342 cal., 12g fat (2g sat. fat), 0 chol., 322mg sod., 57g carb. (34g sugars, 2g fiber), 1g pro.

Campfire Peach Cobbler

Peach cobbler has been a family favorite of ours for 60 years. Fresh cherries and berries are fun, too. Mix and match!
—Jackie Wilson, Wellsville, UT

Prep: 25 min.
Cook: 30 min. + standing
Makes: 8 servings

- 2 cups all-purpose flour
- 1 cup sugar
- 4 tsp. baking powder
- ½ tsp. salt
- 1 cup 2% milk
- ½ cup butter, melted

FILLING
- 2 cans (15¼ oz. each) sliced peaches
- ¼ cup sugar
- ½ tsp. ground cinnamon, optional

1. Prepare campfire or grill for low heat, using 32-40 charcoal briquettes.
2. Line the inside of a 10-in. Dutch oven with heavy-duty foil. In a bowl, whisk together the first 4 ingredients. Add milk and melted butter, stirring just until moistened. Pour batter into prepared pan.
3. Drain peaches, reserving 1 cup syrup. Arrange peaches over batter; sprinkle with sugar and, if desired, cinnamon. Pour reserved syrup over fruit. Place lid on Dutch oven.
4. When briquettes are covered with white ash, place Dutch oven directly on half of the briquettes. Using a long-handled tongs, place remaining briquettes on top of pan lid. Cook 30-40 minutes or until cobbler is set and beginning to brown, using tongs to lift lid carefully when checking. If necessary, cook 5 minutes longer. Remove Dutch oven from heat; let stand, uncovered, about 15 minutes before serving.
1 serving: 455 cal., 12g fat (8g sat. fat), 33mg chol., 505mg sod., 82g carb. (57g sugars, 2g fiber), 4g pro.

Keep Ice Cream Cold on the Road

To keep ice cream firm and scoopable for hours, wrap the pint(s) in plastic bubble wrap, a powerful insulator. If you have an ice cream maker and room in your cooler, pack the wrapped ice cream into the frozen ice cream cylinder.

CAKE & BERRY CAMPFIRE COBBLER

Cold Brew Coffee

Cold brewing reduces the acidity of coffee, which enhances its natural sweetness and complex flavors. Even those who take hot coffee with sugar and cream might find themselves sipping cold brew plain.

—Taste of Home *Test Kitchen*

- -

Makes: 8 servings

1	**cup coarsely ground medium-roast coffee**
1	**cup hot water (205°)**
6	**to 7 cups cold water**
2%	**milk or half-and-half cream, optional**

1. Place the coffee grounds in a clean glass container. Pour hot water over the grounds; let stand 10 minutes. Stir in cold water. Cover and refrigerate for 12-24 hours. (The longer the coffee sits, the stronger the flavor.)
2. Strain the coffee through a fine mesh sieve; discard grounds. Strain the coffee again through a coffee filter; discard grounds. Serve over ice with milk or cream, if desired. Store in the refrigerator for up to 2 weeks.
1 cup: 2 cal., 0 fat (0 sat. fat), 0 chol., 4mg sod., 0 carb. (0 sugars, 0 fiber), 0 pro.

CERVEZA MARGARITAS

FRESH LIME MARGARITAS

Cerveza Margaritas

One sip of this refreshing drink and you'll picture sand, sea and blue skies that stretch for miles. It's like a vacation in a glass, and you can mix it up in moments.
—*Christina Pittman, Parkville, MO*

Takes: 10 min. • **Makes:** 5 servings

- 1 **can (12 oz.) lemon-lime soda, chilled**
- 1 **bottle (12 oz.) beer**
- 1 **can (12 oz.) frozen limeade concentrate, thawed**
- ¾ **cup tequila**
  Lime slices and kosher salt, optional
  Crushed ice

In a pitcher, combine all liquid ingredients. If desired, moisten the rims of 5 margarita or cocktail glasses with lime slices. Sprinkle salt on a plate; dip rims in salt. Serve in prepared glasses over crushed ice with additional lime slices.
1 cup: 272 cal., 0 fat (0 sat. fat), 0 chol., 14mg sod., 44g carb. (39g sugars, 0 fiber), 0 pro.

Fresh Lime Margaritas

This basic margarita recipe is easy to modify to your tastes. Try it frozen or with strawberries.
—Taste of Home *Test Kitchen*

Takes: 15 min. • **Makes:** 4 servings

- ½ **cup tequila**
- ¼ **cup Triple Sec**
- ¼ **cup lime juice**
- ¼ **cup lemon juice**
- 2 **Tbsp. superfine sugar**
- 4 **lime wedges**
- 1 **Tbsp. kosher salt**
- 1⅓ **cups crushed ice**

In a pitcher, combine tequila, Triple Sec, juices and sugar; stir until sugar is dissolved. Moisten rims of 4 margarita

or cocktail glasses with lime wedges. Sprinkle salt on a plate; dip rims in salt. Serve in prepared glasses over crushed ice.
1 serving: 149 cal., 0 fat (0 sat. fat), 0 chol., 2mg sod., 15g carb. (13g sugars, 0 fiber), 0 pro.

Gingerbread Kiss Coffee

Enjoy the flavor of gingerbread on the go with this unique recipe. The mix stores in the refrigerator for several weeks, so it's a breeze to grab and go for spicy-sweet drinks sure to warm you up.
—Taste of Home *Test Kitchen*

Takes: 5 min. • **Makes:** 15 servings (⅔ cup molasses mixture)

- ½ **cup molasses**
- ¼ **cup packed brown sugar**
- 1 **tsp. ground ginger**
- ¾ **tsp. ground cinnamon**
- **EACH SERVING**
- 1 **cup hot brewed coffee**
  Optional: milk, whipped cream and additional ground cinnamon

1. In a small bowl, combine the molasses, brown sugar, ginger and cinnamon.
2. For each serving, place 2 tsp. molasses mixture in a mug. Add 1 cup hot coffee; stir until combined. Serve with milk, whipped cream and cinnamon if desired.
3. Cover and store the remaining molasses mixture in the refrigerator for up to 2 weeks.
1 cup: 48 cal., 0 fat (0 sat. fat), 0 chol., 10mg sod., 12g carb. (10g sugars, 0 fiber), 0 pro.

Red & Blue Berry Lemonade Slush

This delightfully sweet-tart beverage showcases fresh raspberries and blueberries.
—Taste of Home *Test Kitchen*

Prep: 15 min. + freezing
Makes: 8 servings

- 2 **cups lemon juice**
- 1½ **cups fresh raspberries**
- 1½ **cups fresh blueberries**
- 1 **to 1¼ cups sugar**
- 3 **cups cold water**

1. In batches, place lemon juice, raspberries, blueberries and sugar in a blender; cover and process until blended. Strain and discard seeds.
2. Transfer to a 2½-qt. freezer container; stir in water. Freeze for 8 hours or overnight.
3. Just before serving, remove from freezer and let stand 15 minutes or until slushy.
1 cup: 139 cal., 0 fat (0 sat. fat), 0 chol., 1mg sod., 37g carb. (30g sugars, 2g fiber), 1g pro.

HACK

Pack frozen drinks like Lemonade Slush for a trip to the beach. First, the drinks act as an ice pack, then as a beverage once they melt.

HOMEMADE BAGEL
SPREADS, P. 185

GOOD MORNINGS

[Find dozens of wonderful ways to start the day,
everything from better breakfasts on the go
to new somethings for your special mornings.]

Morning Orange Drink

I love to treat overnight guests to this creamy orange frappe. Just blitz a few basic ingredients in your blender and enjoy.

—*Joyce Mummau, Mount Airy, MD*

Takes: 10 min. • **Makes:** 6 servings

- 1 **can (6 oz.) frozen orange juice concentrate**
- 1 **cup cold water**
- 1 **cup whole milk**
- ⅓ **cup sugar**
- 1 **tsp. vanilla extract**
- 10 **ice cubes**

Combine the first 5 ingredients in a blender; process at high speed. Add ice cubes, a few at a time, blending until smooth. Serve immediately.
¾ cup: 115 cal., 1g fat (1g sat. fat), 6mg chol., 21mg sod., 24g carb. (23g sugars, 0 fiber), 2g pro.

Mango Ginger Smoothies

I blend smoothies every morning and change the flavors. My favorite version features mango with a spicy bite of ginger.

—*David Lee, Irvine, CA*

Takes: 5 min. • **Makes:** 4 servings

- 1½ **cups cold water**
- 1 **pkg. (16 oz.) frozen mango chunks**
- 2 **medium ripe bananas, peeled and halved**
- 1 **Tbsp. coconut oil, melted**
- 1 **Tbsp. honey**
- 1 **to 2 tsp. minced fresh gingerroot**

Place all ingredients in a blender; cover and process until smooth. Serve immediately.
1 cup: 172 cal., 4g fat (3g sat. fat), 0 chol., 1mg sod., 37g carb. (29g sugars, 4g fiber), 1g pro.

HACK

Save Those Lids

Parmesan shaker lids fit the tops of wide-mouth mason jars. That makes it easy to take a morning smoothie on the road. You even get a hole for your straw! Check out another use on p. 248.

Lean Green Smoothie

Kids love the bright green color of this frosty and flavorful smoothie. It's fine-tuned to their liking with bananas, creamy yogurt and—they'll never guess!—spinach.

—Madison Mayberry, Ames, IA

- -

Takes: 10 min. • **Makes:** 4 servings

¾	cup fat-free milk
1⅓	cups fat-free vanilla yogurt
1	cup ice cubes
1	cup fresh spinach
1	ripe medium banana
2	Tbsp. lemon juice

In a blender, combine all ingredients; cover and process for 30 seconds or until smooth. Pour into chilled glasses; serve immediately.

1 cup: 99 cal., 0 fat (0 sat. fat), 4mg chol., 24mg sod., 19g carb. (12g sugars, 1g fiber), 5g pro. **Diabetic exchanges:** 1 fat-free milk, ½ fruit.

MANGO GINGER SMOOTHIES

Green Breakfast Smoothie

You'll be surprised by this smoothie's creaminess. It's packed with healthy pears, avocado and spinach.
—Taste of Home *Test Kitchen*

Takes: 10 min. • **Makes:** 3 servings

- ¾ cup unsweetened apple juice
- 1 cup crushed ice
- 2 cups fresh baby spinach
- 1 medium pear, coarsely chopped
- 1 medium ripe avocado, peeled and cubed
- 3 Tbsp. honey

In a blender, combine all ingredients; cover and process for 1 minute or until smooth. Serve immediately.
1 cup: 206 cal., 7g fat (1g sat. fat), 0 chol., 23mg sod., 38g carb. (29g sugars, 6g fiber), 2g pro.

Cran-Blueberry Smoothies

Have a lot to do before your brunch guests arrive? Don't worry! This incredible drink is best when made at the last minute.
—*Lisa Lindsay, Slidell, LA*

Takes: 5 min. • **Makes:** 3 servings

- 1 cup frozen cranberries
- 1 cup fresh or frozen unsweetened blueberries
- 1 medium banana, cut up
- ½ cup 2% milk
- ½ cup vanilla yogurt
- 1 Tbsp. honey

Place all ingredients in a blender; cover and process until smooth. Pour into chilled glasses; serve immediately.
¾ cup: 159 cal., 2g fat (1g sat. fat), 5mg chol., 44mg sod., 35g carb. (26g sugars, 4g fiber), 4g pro. **Diabetic exchanges:** 1 fruit, ½ starch, ½ reduced-fat milk.

Homemade Yogurt

It's affordable and even easier than you'd think.
—Taste of Home *Test Kitchen*

Prep: 5 min. + chilling
Cook: 20 min. + standing
Makes: about 2 qt.

- 2 qt. pasteurized whole milk
- 2 Tbsp. plain yogurt with live active cultures

1. In a Dutch oven, heat milk over medium heat until a thermometer reads 200°, stirring occasionally to prevent scorching. Remove from heat; let stand until a thermometer reads 112°-115°, stirring occasionally. (If desired, place pan in an ice-water bath for faster cooling.)
2. In a small bowl, whisk 1 cup warm milk into yogurt until smooth; return all to pan, stirring gently. Transfer mixture to warm, clean jars, such as 1-qt. canning jars.
3. Cover jars; place in oven. Turn on oven light to keep mixture warm, about 110°. Let stand, undisturbed, 6-24 hours or until yogurt is set, tilting jars gently to check. (Yogurt will become thicker and more tangy as it stands.)
4. Refrigerate, covered, until cold. Store in refrigerator up to 2 weeks.
1 cup: 151 cal., 8g fat (5g sat. fat), 25mg chol., 107mg sod., 12g carb. (12g sugars, 0 fiber), 8g pro. **Diabetic exchanges:** 1 whole milk.

HACK

After pouring off the desired number of smoothies, pop the blender pitcher of leftovers in the fridge. Give 'em a whir on the blender base the next morning, and you have instant breakfast.

HOMEMADE
YOGURT

Bagel with a Veggie Schmear

I got this recipe from my favorite bagel shop in New York City. Now I make it every time I'm craving a quick and healthy meal. I like to add chopped pitted green olives to the schmear.

—*Julie Merriman, Seattle, WA*

- -

Takes: 20 min. • **Makes:** 4 servings

- 4   oz. fat-free cream cheese
- 4   oz. fresh goat cheese
- ½   tsp. grated lime zest
- 1   Tbsp. lime juice
- ⅔   cup finely chopped cucumber
- ¼   cup finely chopped celery
- 3   Tbsp. finely chopped carrot
- 1   radish, finely chopped
- 2   Tbsp. finely chopped red onion
- 2   Tbsp. thinly sliced fresh basil
- 4   whole wheat bagels, split and toasted
- 8   slices tomato
      Coarsely ground pepper, optional

In a bowl, beat the cheeses, lime zest and lime juice until blended. Fold in chopped vegetables and basil. Serve on bagels with tomato slices. If desired, sprinkle with pepper.

2 open-faced sandwiches: 341 cal., 6g fat (3g sat. fat), 22mg chol., 756mg sod., 56g carb. (15g sugars, 10g fiber), 20g pro.

ORANGE MARMALADE

MEDITERRANEAN GOAT CHEESE

INSIDE-OUT "EVERYTHING"

BEER
CHEESE

PECAN
PIE

5 Homemade Bagel Spreads in a Hurry

Whip up a couple of these toppings and pop them in the fridge the day before your brunch party. Then all you have to do is have someone pick up bagels on the way over. Done and done!

Orange Marmalade Combine 1 cup softened cream cheese with ⅓ cup orange marmalade.

Mediterranean Goat Cheese Combine 1 cup softened cream cheese, ⅓ cup goat cheese, ¼ cup chopped olives, ¼ cup chopped roasted red peppers and 2 tsp. grated lemon zest. Season with salt and pepper to taste.

Inside-Out "Everything" Combine 1 cup cream cheese, 1 Tbsp. each poppy seeds and sesame seeds, 2 tsp. each dried minced garlic and dried minced onion, and 1 tsp. Worcestershire sauce. Season with salt and pepper to taste.

Beer Cheese Combine 1 cup softened cream cheese, ½ cup shredded cheddar cheese, 3 Tbsp. beer and ½ envelope ranch dressing mix. Add salt and pepper to taste.

Pecan Pie Combine 1 cup softened cream cheese, ½ cup toasted chopped pecans and ¼ cup caramel sauce.

CARROT
CAKE JAM

Carrot
Jam

Carrot Cake Jam

For a change of pace from berry jams, try this unique option. Spread on a bagel with cream cheese, it tastes almost as good as real carrot cake!

—*Rachelle Stratton, Rock Springs, WY*

- -

Prep: 45 min. • **Process:** 5 min.
Makes: 8 half-pints

- 1 can (20 oz.) unsweetened crushed pineapple, undrained
- 1½ cups shredded carrots
- 1½ cups chopped peeled ripe pears
- 3 Tbsp. lemon juice
- 1 tsp. ground cinnamon
- ¼ tsp. ground cloves
- ¼ tsp. ground nutmeg
- 1 pkg. (1¾ oz.) powdered fruit pectin
- 6½ cups sugar

1. Place first 7 ingredients in a large saucepan; bring to a boil. Reduce heat; simmer, covered, until pears are tender, 15-20 minutes, stirring occasionally. Stir in pectin. Bring to a full rolling boil over high heat, stirring constantly. Stir in sugar; return to a full rolling boil. Boil and stir 1 minute.
2. Remove from heat; skim off foam. Ladle hot mixture into 8 hot sterilized half-pint jars, leaving ¼-in. headspace. Remove air bubbles and adjust headspace, if necessary, by adding hot mixture. Wipe jar rims. Center lids on jars; screw on bands until fingertip tight.
3. Place filled jars into canner with simmering water, ensuring that they are completely covered with water. Bring to a boil; process for 5 minutes. Remove jars and cool.
2 Tbsp. jam: 88 cal., 0 fat (0 sat. fat), 0 chol., 2mg sod., 23g carb. (22g sugars, 0 fiber), 0 pro.

Quince Orange Marmalade

Quince sweetens this marmalade as it simmers and fills the house with its distinctive autumn aroma.

—*Taste of Home Test Kitchen*

- -

Prep: 30 min.
Cook: 1½ hours + chilling
Makes: 3 cups

- 5 cups chopped peeled quince (about 4 medium)
- 1½ cups water
- 1⅓ cups sugar
- 1 cup orange juice
- 1 Tbsp. grated orange zest

1. In a large saucepan, bring all ingredients to a boil. Reduce heat; simmer, uncovered, 1½-1¾ hours or until mixture is reduced to 3 cups, stirring frequently.
2. Cool slightly; carefully mash. Fill all containers to within ½ in. of tops. Wipe top edges of containers. Cool to room temperature. Refrigerate up to 3 weeks or freeze up to 1 year.
2 Tbsp. marmalade: 58 cal., 0 fat (0 sat. fat), 0 chol., 1mg sod., 15g carb. (14g sugars, 0 fiber), 0 pro.
Diabetic exchanges: 1 starch.

HACK

In a pinch for labels? Just reach for the rubber bands. As an added benefit, they make jars easy to open, too.

Bacon Monkey Bread

My daughters made this addictive pull-apart bread when they were in 4-H, and we've shared it for many years. With refrigerated biscuits, it's easy breezy.
—*Virginia Krites, Cridersville, OH*

Prep: 15 min. • **Bake:** 30 min.
Makes: 12 servings

- ½ lb. bacon strips, diced
- ¼ cup grated Parmesan cheese
- ¼ cup chopped onion, optional
- ¼ cup chopped green pepper, optional
- 1 tube (16.3 oz.) large refrigerated flaky biscuits
- ⅓ cup butter, melted

1. Preheat oven to 350°. In a large skillet, cook bacon until crisp; drain. Combine bacon with cheese and, if desired, onion and green pepper. Cut biscuits into quarters; add to bacon mixture. Stir in butter and toss to coat. Transfer to a greased 10-in. tube pan.
2. Bake until browned, about 30 minutes. Cool 10 minutes before inverting onto a serving platter. Refrigerate leftovers.
1 piece: 214 cal., 14g fat (6g sat. fat), 22mg chol., 557mg sod., 17g carb. (4g sugars, 1g fiber), 6g pro.

Egg-Topped Avocado Toasts

We always have avocados on hand, so it's easy to make this quick breakfast toast for my husband and me. It's really tasty!
—*Kallee Krong-Mccreery, Escondido, CA*

Takes: 20 min. • **Makes:** 2 servings

- 2 slices multigrain bread, toasted
- 2 tsp. butter
- ½ medium ripe avocado, peeled and thinly sliced
- 4 thin slices tomato
- 2 thin slices red onion
- 2 large eggs
- ⅛ tsp. seasoned salt
- 2 Tbsp. shredded cheddar cheese
- 2 bacon strips, cooked and crumbled

1. Spread each slice of toasted bread with butter; place on a plate. Top with avocado; mash gently with a fork. Top with tomato and onion.
2. To poach each egg, place ½ cup water in a small microwave-safe bowl or glass measuring cup; break an egg into the water. Microwave, covered, on high 1 minute. Microwave in 10-second intervals until white is set and yolk begins to thicken; let stand 1 minute. Using a slotted spoon, place egg over sandwich.
3. Sprinkle eggs with seasoned salt. Top with cheese and bacon.
1 open-faced sandwich: 313 cal., 21g fat (7g sat. fat), 211mg chol., 492mg sod., 18g carb. (4g sugars, 5g fiber), 15g pro.

PRO TIP

Good Grease

Bacon grease is so tasty, it's worth saving for other dishes. Once slightly cooled, strain grease through cheesecloth or a coffee filter. Cover and refrigerate cooled grease up to 6 months.

Cook your morning eggs and potato dishes in the bacon grease. Want a real taste surprise? Use the bacon fat for popping corn.

EGG-TOPPED
AVOCADO TOASTS

Savory Apple-Chicken Sausage

These easy, healthy sausages make an elegant brunch dish. The versatile recipe can be doubled or tripled for a crowd, and the sausage freezes well either cooked or raw.

—*Angela Buchanan, Longmont, CO*

Takes: 25 min. • **Makes:** 8 patties

- 1 large tart apple, peeled and diced
- 2 tsp. poultry seasoning
- 1 tsp. salt
- ¼ tsp. pepper
- 1 lb. ground chicken

1. In a large bowl, combine the apple, poultry seasoning, salt and pepper. Crumble chicken over mixture and mix well. Shape into eight 3-in. patties.

2. In a large, greased cast-iron or other heavy skillet, cook sausage patties over medium heat until no longer pink, 5-6 minutes on each side. Drain if necessary.

1 sausage patty: 92 cal., 5g fat (1g sat. fat), 38mg chol., 328mg sod., 4g carb. (3g sugars, 1g fiber), 9g pro. **Diabetic exchanges:** 1 medium-fat meat.

PRO TIP

This breakfast sausage is perfect alongside pancakes, souffle or French toast—with less than half the fat and only one-sixth the saturated fat of a serving of pork sausage.

SAVORY APPLE-CHICKEN SAUSAGE

SWEET BROILED
GRAPEFRUIT

Sweet Broiled Grapefruit

I was never a fan of grapefruit until
I had it broiled at a restaurant—it was
so tangy and delicious! I finally got the
recipe and now make it often for my
whole family.
—*Terry Bray, Auburndale, Fl.*

Takes: 15 min. • **Makes:** 2 servings

- 1 large grapefruit
- 2 Tbsp. butter, softened
- 2 Tbsp. sugar
- ½ tsp. ground cinnamon

1. Preheat broiler. Cut grapefruit
crosswise in half; if desired, cut a thin
slice from the bottom of each to level.
Cut around each grapefruit section
to loosen fruit. Top with butter. Mix
sugar and cinnamon; sprinkle over
the fruit.

2. Place on a baking sheet. Broil 4 in.
from heat until sugar is bubbly.
½ grapefruit: 203 cal., 12g fat (7g sat.
fat), 31mg chol., 116mg sod., 26g
carb. (24g sugars, 2g fiber), 1g pro.

HACK

Coffee Can Lid as Fruit Keeper

Instead of wasting plastic
wrap, try this method of
storing a half grapefruit or
cantaloupe in the fridge.
Simply set the fruit cut-side
down on a clean plastic
coffee can lid.

Sliced Basil

Roll a stack of basil leaves into a tight bunch. Slice crosswise into thin strips.

ASPARAGUS & RED PEPPER FRITTATA

Asparagus & Red Pepper Frittata

What tastier way to start a morning? This frittata has asparagus, potatoes, peppers, fresh herbs and a wonderful blend of cheeses.

—*Toni Donahue, Westerville, OH*

Prep: 20 min. • **Cook:** 25 min.
Makes: 6 servings

- 12 **fresh asparagus spears, trimmed**
- ½ **tsp. plus 3 Tbsp. olive oil, divided**
- 10 **large eggs**
- 3 **large egg whites**
- ¾ **cup whole milk**
- ½ **cup shredded Parmesan cheese**
- ¾ **tsp. salt**
- ½ **tsp. pepper**
- 1 **pkg. (20 oz.) refrigerated shredded hash brown potatoes**
- ½ **large sweet red pepper, julienned**
- 3 **fresh basil leaves, thinly sliced**
- ½ **cup shredded pepper jack cheese**

1. Place asparagus on an ungreased baking sheet; drizzle with ½ tsp. oil. Bake at 400° for 10-12 minutes or until tender, stirring once.
2. In a large bowl, whisk eggs, egg whites, milk, Parmesan cheese, salt and pepper; set aside. Heat 2 Tbsp. oil in a 12-in. ovenproof skillet over medium heat. Add potatoes and press down lightly. Cook, uncovered, until bottom is golden brown for 6-7 minutes. Drizzle with remaining oil; turn over.
3. Pour egg mixture over potatoes. Cover and cook for 9-11 minutes or until nearly set. Arrange asparagus and red pepper over top. Sprinkle with basil and pepper jack cheese.
4. Broil 3-4 in. from the heat until eggs are completely, 2-3 minutes.

Let stand for 5 minutes. Cut frittata into wedges.
1 wedge: 371 cal., 21g fat (7g sat. fat), 370mg chol., 692mg sod., 24g carb. (3g sugars, 2g fiber), 22g pro.

Triple-Cheese Florentine Frittata

This upscale ham and cheese frittata recipe contains many of my favorite ingredients and flavors. It's moist, colorful and most of all delicious.

—*Collette Hunt, Chandler, AZ*

Prep: 30 min. • **Broil:** 5 min.
Makes: 4 servings

- 3 **small red potatoes (about 8 oz.), peeled and cut into ¼-in. slices**
- 2 **Tbsp. water**
- 2 **tsp. plus 1 Tbsp. canola oil, divided**
- ½ **cup chopped onion**
- 1 **cup fresh baby spinach**
- 5 **large eggs**
- ¼ **cup white wine or chicken broth**
- ¼ **tsp. dried oregano**
- ¼ **tsp. pepper**
- ⅛ **tsp. salt**
- 1 **cup shredded cheddar cheese**
- ½ **cup cubed fully cooked ham**
- 3 **Tbsp. shredded Swiss cheese**
- ¼ **cup grated Parmesan cheese**

1. Preheat broiler. In a microwave-safe bowl, combine potatoes and water; microwave, covered, on high for 3-5 minutes or until tender. Cool slightly; drain.
2. In a 10-in. ovenproof skillet, heat 2 tsp. oil over medium heat. Add onion; cook and stir 3-4 minutes or until tender. Remove from pan.
3. Add the spinach to same pan; cook and stir 30-45 seconds or until wilted. Drain spinach and squeeze dry; coarsely chop. In a small bowl, whisk eggs, wine, oregano, pepper and salt; stir in cheddar cheese, ham, Swiss

cheese, onion and spinach. Gently stir in potatoes.
4. In a 10-in. ovenproof skillet, heat remaining oil over medium heat. Pour in egg mixture. Cook, covered, until nearly set, 3-5 minutes. Sprinkle with Parmesan cheese.
5. Broil 3-4 in. from heat 2-4 minutes or until eggs are completely set. Let stand 5 minutes. Cut into wedges.
1 wedge: 362 cal., 25g fat (10g sat. fat), 280mg chol., 667mg sod., 10g carb. (2g sugars, 1g fiber), 22g pro.

Save a Rusty Skillet

• Touch up: If a pan has just a small amount of rust, try wiping it away with cooking oil and a paper towel; then pop it in the oven as shown below to dry fully.

• Scour: Get the pan wet, add a little dish soap, then scrub with a piece of steel wool or a tough scrubber. Scrub in small circles, focusing on the rusty parts. Scrub until the original black iron emerges, then rinse.

• Heat: Set the oven to 350°. Place pan, upside-down, on the upper rack for about an hour, letting it heat up with the oven. Turn the oven off; leave the pan inside until it's cool. The oil bakes into the pores of the pan, creating a nonstick finish.

GERMAN APPLE PANCAKE

German Apple Pancake

If you're looking for a pretty dish to make when having guests for brunch, try this. Everyone I've served it to has enjoyed it—except for one time, that is, when my husband tried to make it following my recipe, which I'd written down incorrectly! If you don't leave out the flour as I did, it'll turnout terrific.

—*Judi Van Beek, Lynden, WA*

Prep: 15 min. • **Bake:** 20 min.
Makes: 6 servings

PANCAKE
- 3 large eggs, room temperature
- 1 cup whole milk
- ¾ cup all-purpose flour
- ½ tsp. salt
- ⅛ tsp. ground nutmeg
- 3 Tbsp. butter

TOPPING
- 2 tart baking apples, peeled and sliced
- 3 to 4 Tbsp. butter
- 2 Tbsp. sugar
  Confectioners' sugar

1. Preheat a 10-in. cast-iron skillet in a 425° oven. Meanwhile, in a blender, combine the eggs, milk, flour, salt and nutmeg; cover and process until smooth.

2. Add butter to hot skillet; return to oven until butter bubbles. Pour batter into skillet. Bake, uncovered, for 20 minutes or until pancake puffs and edges are browned and crisp.

3. For topping, in a skillet, combine the apples, butter and sugar; cook and stir over medium heat until apples are tender. Spoon into baked pancake. Sprinkle with confectioners' sugar. Cut and serve immediately.

1 serving: 192 cal., 12g fat (7g sat. fat), 107mg chol., 273mg sod., 18g carb. (8g sugars, 1g fiber), 5g pro.

Cinnamon Flapjacks

Kids will love helping make this fun breakfast treat for mom or dad. Don't forget to serve the homemade syrup on the side.

—Taste of Home *Test Kitchen*

Prep: 15 min. • **Cook:** 5 min./batch
Makes: 4 servings (¾ cup syrup)

- 2 cups complete buttermilk pancake mix
- 1½ cups water
- 1 Tbsp. maple syrup
- 1 Tbsp. butter, melted
- ½ tsp. ground cinnamon

SYRUP
- 1 cup packed brown sugar
- ¼ cup water
- 1 Tbsp. butter
- ½ tsp. vanilla extract

1. In a small bowl, combine the pancake mix, water, syrup, butter and cinnamon. Pour batter into a plastic squirt bottle. Squeeze batter into desired letters and shapes onto a greased hot griddle. When underside is browned, turn pancakes and cook until second side is golden brown.

2. Meanwhile, in small saucepan, combine the brown sugar, water and butter. Bring to a boil. Reduce heat; simmer, uncovered, for 4-5 minutes or until sugar is dissolved. Remove from the heat; stir in vanilla. Serve with flapjacks.

2 flapjacks with 3 Tbsp. syrup: 501 cal., 8g fat (4g sat. fat), 15mg chol., 1032mg sod., 106g carb. (62g sugars, 1g fiber), 5g pro.

Banana-Nut Waffle Cake

I wanted to use waffles in a creative way and came up with an idea of making a cake out of them. Not only did it take much less time than making an ordinary cake, it came out just as delicious and spectacular. Waffles can be made ahead, then wrapped and stored in the fridge until you're ready to assemble this cake.

—Kristina S., Yonkers, NY

Prep: 25 min. • **Cook:** 20 min.
Makes: 6 servings

- ½ cup whole wheat flour
- ½ cup all-purpose flour
- 2 Tbsp. cornstarch
- 1½ tsp. baking powder
- ¼ tsp. salt
- 2 large eggs, room temperature
- ½ cup plus 2 Tbsp. whole milk
- 1 Tbsp. canola oil
- 1 tsp. vanilla extract

BUTTERSCOTCH SYRUP
- ¾ cup sugar
- 2 Tbsp. water
- 1 Tbsp. light corn syrup
- ¼ cup heavy whipping cream
- 1 Tbsp. unsalted butter
- 1 tsp. ground cinnamon
- ½ tsp. vanilla extract
  Dash salt

TOPPINGS
- ½ cup finely chopped walnuts, toasted
- ½ cup finely chopped pecans, toasted
- 2 medium bananas, sliced
- 1 cup sweetened whipped cream

1. Grease and preheat waffle maker. Whisk together first 5 ingredients. In a separate bowl, whisk together eggs, milk, oil and vanilla until blended. Add to dry ingredients and stir just until moistened. Bake 6 waffles according to manufacturer's directions until golden brown.

2. For butterscotch syrup, combine sugar, water and corn syrup in a small heavy saucepan; stir gently to moisten all the sugar. Cook over medium-low heat, gently swirling pan occasionally, until sugar is dissolved. Cover; bring to a boil over medium-high heat. Cook 1 minute. Uncover saucepan; continue to boil and gently swirl pan until syrup turns a medium amber color, 3-4 minutes. Immediately remove from heat, and gradually stir in remaining syrup ingredients. Cool.

3. To assemble, combine walnuts and pecans. Place 1 waffle on a serving plate. Spoon some butterscotch syrup over it; layer with some of each of the following: banana slices, nut mixture and whipped cream. Repeat layers 4 times. Top with remaining waffle and remaining syrup; sprinkle with remaining nut mixture.

1 waffle: 535 cal., 31g fat (11g sat. fat), 104mg chol., 509mg sod., 60g carb. (36g sugars, 4g fiber), 9g pro.

PRO TIP

Use a squeeze bottle to make pancakes in fun shapes such as snowmen, hearts, caterpillars—or your loved one's name.

BANANA-NUT
WAFFLE CAKE

PEAR-BERRY
BREAKFAST TARTS

Pear-Berry Breakfast Tarts

When my kids were small, I could never get pancakes on the table while they were all still hot. Then I got the idea for these breakfast tarts. It's a simple recipe for any busy family.
—*Joan Elbourn, Gardner, MA*

Prep: 45 min. + chilling
Bake: 20 min. • **Makes:** 10 servings

- ½ cup butter, softened
- 1 cup sugar, divided
- 2 large eggs, room temperature
- 2½ cups all-purpose flour
- 2 tsp. baking powder
- 2 cups chopped peeled pears (about 2 large)
- 2 Tbsp. cornstarch
- 2 Tbsp. water
- ½ cup fresh raspberries
- 1 large egg white
- 3 to 5 Tbsp. 2% milk, divided
- 1⅓ cups confectioners' sugar
  Food coloring, optional

1. Cream butter and ½ cup sugar until light and fluffy. Add eggs, 1 at a time, beating well after each addition. In another bowl, whisk flour and baking powder; gradually beat into creamed mixture to form a dough. Divide dough in half; shape into rectangles. Wrap and refrigerate 1 hour.
2. Meanwhile, in a small saucepan over medium heat, combine pears and remaining sugar. Cook and stir until sugar is dissolved and pears are softened, 6-8 minutes. In a small bowl, mix cornstarch and water until smooth; stir into the pear mixture. Return to a boil, stirring constantly; cook and stir 1-2 minutes or until thickened. Remove from heat; cool. Stir in raspberries.
3. Preheat oven to 350°. On a lightly floured surface, roll half the dough into a 15x8-in. rectangle. Cut into ten 4x3-in. rectangles. Transfer to parchment-lined baking sheets; spoon about 2 Tbsp. filling over each pastry to within ¼ in. of edges. Roll the remaining dough into a 15x8-in. rectangle; cut into 10 more 4x3-in. rectangles and place over filling. Press edges with a fork to seal. Whisk egg white and 1 Tbsp. milk; brush over pastries. Bake until golden brown and filling is bubbly, 20-25 minutes.
4. Remove from baking sheets to wire racks to cool. For icing, mix confectioners' sugar and enough of remaining milk to reach desired consistency; tint with food coloring if desired. Spread or drizzle on pastries.
1 tart: 379 cal., 11g fat (6g sat. fat), 62mg chol., 193mg sod., 67g carb. (39g sugars, 2g fiber), 5g pro.

Mini Caramel Rolls

I have the perfect warm treat for pajama-clad mornings—ooey-gooey sweet rolls that are easy to make with refrigerated crescent dough.
—*Kayla Wiegand, Congerville, IL*

Prep: 20 min. • **Bake:** 15 min.
Makes: 12 servings

- ⅓ cup packed brown sugar
- ⅓ cup butter, cubed
- 2 Tbsp. light corn syrup
- 1½ tsp. 2% milk
- 1 tube (8 oz.) refrigerated crescent rolls
- 2 tsp. sugar
- ½ tsp. ground cinnamon

1. Preheat oven to 375°. In a small saucepan, combine brown sugar, butter, corn syrup and milk; cook and stir over medium heat until blended. Pour into a greased 9-in. pie plate.
2. Separate crescent dough into 4 rectangles; press perforations gently to seal. Mix the sugar and cinnamon; sprinkle evenly over rectangles. Roll up jelly-roll style, starting with a long side; pinch seams to seal.
3. Cut each roll into 9 slices; place in prepared dish, cut side down. Bake 15-18 minutes or until golden brown. Cool 1 minute before inverting onto a serving plate.
3 rolls: 155 cal., 9g fat (4g sat. fat), 13mg chol., 189mg sod., 17g carb. (9g sugars, 0 fiber), 1g pro.

CHOCOLATE FUDGE
BROWNIES, P. 214

LEVEL UP: BAKING

[Picture-perfect, luscious, irresistible...uncover
the clever secrets to sweet success.
Get ready to bake like a boss.]

Slow-Cooker Cinnamon Roll

Come home to the heavenly aroma of fresh-baked cinnamon rolls! This better-for-you version tastes just as decadent as a regular cinnamon roll, but it smartly sneaks in some whole grains.

—*Nick Iverson, Denver, CO*

- -

Prep: 15 min. + rising
Cook: 3½ hours • **Makes:** 12 servings

- 1   pkg. (¼ oz.) active dry yeast
- ¾   cup warm water (110° to 115°)
- ½   cup quick-cooking oats
- ½   cup whole wheat flour
- ¼   cup packed brown sugar
- 2   Tbsp. butter, melted
- 1   large egg, room temperature
- 1   tsp. salt
- 1¾ to 2¼ cups all-purpose flour

FILLING
- 3   Tbsp. butter, softened
- ⅓   cup sugar
- 2   tsp. ground cinnamon

ICING
- 1   cup confectioners' sugar
- 2   Tbsp. half-and-half cream
- 4   tsp. butter, softened

1. Dissolve yeast in warm water. Add next 6 ingredients plus 1 cup all-purpose flour. Beat on medium speed until smooth. Stir in enough remaining flour to form a soft dough (dough will be sticky).

2. Turn onto a lightly floured surface; knead until smooth and elastic, 6-8 minutes. Roll into an 18x12-in. rectangle. For filling, spread dough with butter, then combine sugar and cinnamon; sprinkle over dough to within ½ in. of edges.

3. Roll up jelly-roll style, starting with a long side; pinch seam to seal. Cut crosswise in half to form 2 rolls. Place rolls side by side; pinch top ends together to seal. Using a sharp knife, cut rolls lengthwise in half; loosely twist strips around each other. Pinch bottom ends together to seal. Shape into a coil; place on parchment. Transfer to a 6-qt. slow cooker. Let rise until doubled, about 1 hour.

4. Cook, covered, on low until bread is lightly browned, 3½-4 hours. Remove from slow cooker and cool slightly. Beat icing ingredients until smooth. Spread over warm roll.

1 slice: 240 cal., 7g fat (4g sat. fat), 33mg chol., 254mg sod., 41g carb. (20g sugars, 2g fiber), 4g pro.

SLOW-COOKER
CINNAMON ROLL

HACK

Precise Cuts with Cooking Spray

To create nice, clean cuts in cinnamon rolls and other decorative doughs, spray a serrated knife with cooking spray before cutting.

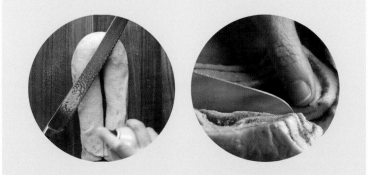

Get Things Settled

Next time you open a new bag of flour, save yourself some mess with this trick. Slap the top of the bag a couple of times before opening it. This settles the flour so it doesn't spray out when you open the bag.

Chocolate Walnut Ring

This is an adaptation of my wife's recipe. It's terrific for a holiday brunch or as a midmorning snack.
—*Peter Halferty, Corpus Christi, TX*

- -

Prep: 55 min. + rising
Bake: 20 min. + cooling
Makes: 20 servings

3	to 3½ cups all-purpose flour
¼	cup sugar
1	pkg. (¼ oz.) active dry yeast
1	tsp. ground cinnamon
½	tsp. salt
½	cup whole milk
¼	cup water
2	Tbsp. butter
2	Tbsp. canola oil
1	large egg
1	large egg yolk

FILLING
½	cup miniature semisweet chocolate chips
½	cup chopped walnuts
3	Tbsp. brown sugar

GLAZE
⅔	cup confectioners' sugar
⅛	tsp. ground cinnamon
¼	tsp. vanilla extract
3	to 4 tsp. whole milk

1. In a large bowl, combine 1 cup flour, sugar, yeast, cinnamon and salt. In a small saucepan, heat milk, water, butter and oil to 120°-130°. Add to the dry ingredients; beat just until moistened. Add egg and yolk; beat until smooth. Stir in enough remaining flour to form a soft dough (dough will be sticky).

2. Turn onto a floured surface; knead until smooth and elastic, 6-8 minutes. Place in a greased bowl, turning once to grease top. Cover and let rise in a warm place until doubled, about 1 hour. Combine filling ingredients in a small bowl; set aside.

3. Punch dough down. Turn onto a lightly floured surface. Roll into an 18x9-in. rectangle; sprinkle with filling to within 1 in. of edges. Roll up tightly jelly-roll style, starting with a long side; seal ends.

4. Place seam side down on a greased baking sheet; pinch ends together to form a ring. With scissors, cut from outside edge two-thirds of the way toward center of ring at 1-in. intervals. Separate strips slightly; twist to allow filling to show. Cover and let rise until doubled, about 40 minutes.

5. Preheat oven to 350°. Bake for 18-22 minutes or until golden brown. Remove to a wire rack and let cool completely. Mix glaze ingredients; drizzle over ring.

1 slice: 175 cal., 7g fat (2g sat. fat), 25mg chol., 79mg sod., 27g carb. (11g sugars, 1g fiber), 4g pro.

CHOCOLATE WALNUT RING

BAKED ELEPHANT EARS

HACK

Even Cuts Every Time

Use a ruler as your guide to make evenly sized pastries and cookies. Either position the ruler next to the roll of dough as you cut or, as shown below with slice-and-bake cookie dough, neatly roll the dough up in a parchment log. Use the ruler and a pencil or food-safe marker to mark the slices. With a knife, lightly score the dough at each mark. Unwrap dough and slice.

Baked Elephant Ears

My mother-in-law handed down this recipe from her mother. They're a special treat—even better, I think, than those at a carnival or festival.
—Delores Baeten, Downers Grove, IL

- -

Prep: 35 min. + chilling
Bake: 10 min. **Makes:** 2 dozen

  1 **pkg. (¼ oz.) active dry yeast**
  ¼ **cup warm water (110° to 115°)**
  2 **cups all-purpose flour**
4½ **tsp. sugar**
  ½ **tsp. salt**
  ⅓ **cup cold butter, cubed**
  ⅓ **cup fat-free milk**
  1 **large egg yolk**
FILLING
  2 **Tbsp. butter, softened**
  ½ **cup sugar**
  2 **tsp. ground cinnamon**

CINNAMON SUGAR
  ½ **cup sugar**
  ¾ **tsp. ground cinnamon**

1. In a small bowl, dissolve yeast in warm water. In a large bowl, mix flour, sugar and salt; cut in butter until crumbly. Stir milk and egg yolk into yeast mixture; add to flour mixture, stirring to form a stiff dough (dough will be sticky). Cover and refrigerate 2 hours.

2. Preheat oven to 375°. Turn dough onto a lightly floured surface; roll dough into an 18x10-in. rectangle. Spread with softened butter to within ¼ in. of edges. Mix the sugar and cinnamon; sprinkle over butter. Roll up jelly-roll style, starting with a long side; pinch seam to seal. Cut crosswise into 24 slices. Cover slices with plastic wrap until ready to flatten.

3. In a small bowl, mix ingredients for the cinnamon sugar. Place a 6-in.-square piece of waxed paper on a work surface; sprinkle with ½ tsp. cinnamon sugar. Top with 1 slice of dough; sprinkle the dough with an additional ½ tsp. cinnamon sugar. Roll dough to a 4-in. circle. Using waxed paper, flip dough onto a baking sheet coated with cooking spray. Repeat with the remaining ingredients, placing slices 2 in. apart. Bake 7-9 minutes or until golden brown. Cool on wire racks.

1 elephant ear: 109 cal., 4g fat (2g sat. fat), 18mg chol., 76mg sod., 18g carb. (9g sugars, 0 fiber), 1g pro. **Diabetic exchanges:** 1 starch, ½ fat.

GLUTEN-FREE
SANDWICH BREAD

BURNT
CUSTARDS

Gluten-Free Sandwich Bread

In my search for a truly satisfying gluten-free bread, this recipe rose to the top. Unlike some types, it's soft and actually has a tender texture.

—*Doris Kinney, Merrimack, NH*

- -

Prep: 20 min. + rising
Bake: 30 min. + cooling
Makes: 1 loaf (16 slices)

1	Tbsp. active dry yeast
2	Tbsp. sugar
1	cup warm fat-free milk (110° to 115°)
2	large eggs
3	Tbsp. canola oil
1	tsp. cider vinegar
2½	cups gluten-free all-purpose baking flour
2½	tsp. xanthan gum
1	tsp. unflavored gelatin
½	tsp. salt

1. Grease a 9x5-in. loaf pan and sprinkle with gluten-free flour; set aside.
2. In a small bowl, dissolve yeast and sugar in warm milk. In a stand mixer with a paddle attachment, combine the eggs, oil, vinegar and yeast mixture. Gradually beat in the flour, xanthan gum, gelatin and salt. Beat on low speed for 1 minute. Beat on medium for 2 minutes. (Dough will be softer than bread dough with gluten.)
3. Transfer to the prepared pan. Smooth the top with a wet spatula. Cover and let rise in a warm place until dough reaches the top of pan, about 25 minutes.
4. Bake at 375° for 20 minutes; cover loosely with foil. Bake 10-15 minutes longer or until golden brown. Remove from pan to a wire rack to cool.
Note: Read all ingredient labels for possible gluten content prior to use. Ingredient formulas can change, and production facilities vary among brands. If you're concerned that your brand may contain gluten, contact the company.
1 slice: 110 cal., 4g fat (0 sat. fat), 27mg chol., 95mg sod., 17g carb. (3g sugars, 2g fiber), 4g pro. **Diabetic exchanges:** 1 starch, ½ fat.

PRO TIP

Dark metal baking pans can help your gluten-free baked goods develop a darker, richer color.

HACK

Reach for the Canning Tongs

It can be tricky to remove ramekins from a hot water bath to cool. The solution: Use jar lifters or canning tongs. Because the edges are rounded and nonslip, they make it easy to lift the ramekins out of hot water without the risk of splashes or burning yourself.

Burnt Custards

I got the recipe for this smooth-as-silk custard from a restaurant years ago. With its broiled topping, it looks pretty in individual cups.

—*Heidi Main, Anchorage, AK*

- -

Prep: 25 min.
Bake: 45 min. + chilling
Makes: 6 servings

- 4   large egg yolks
- ½   cup plus 6 tsp. sugar, divided
- 2   cups heavy whipping cream
- 3   tsp. vanilla extract
       Fresh raspberries, optional

1. In a small bowl, whisk egg yolks and ½ cup sugar. In a small saucepan, heat cream over medium heat until bubbles form around sides of pan. Remove from the heat; stir a small amount of hot cream into egg yolk mixture. Return all to the pan, stirring constantly. Stir in vanilla.

2. Transfer to six 6-oz. broiler-safe ramekins or custard cups. Place cups in a baking pan; add 1 in. of boiling water to pan. Bake, uncovered, at 300° for 30-35 minutes or until the centers are just set (mixture will jiggle). Remove ramekins from water bath; cool for 10 minutes. Cover and refrigerate at least 4 hours.

3. Before serving, let stand at room temperature for 15 minutes. Sprinkle with remaining sugar. Broil 8 in. from the heat for 2-4 minutes or until sugar is caramelized. If desired, garnish with fresh raspberries.

1 serving: 399 cal., 33g fat (19g sat. fat), 250mg chol., 35mg sod., 23g carb. (23g sugars, 0 fiber), 3g pro.

Warm Chocolate Melting Cups

These little cakes have become a favorite of our guests. They are always surprised that such a chocolaty dessert is so light—less than 200 calories apiece!

—*Kissa Vaughn, Troy, TX*

- -

Prep: 20 min. • **Bake:** 20 min.
Makes: 10 servings

- 1¼ cups sugar, divided
- ½   cup baking cocoa
- 2   Tbsp. all-purpose flour
- ⅛   tsp. salt
- ¾   cup water
- ¾   cup plus 1 Tbsp. semisweet chocolate chips
- 1   Tbsp. brewed coffee
- 1   tsp. vanilla extract
- 2   large eggs, room temperature
- 1   large egg white, room temperature
       Sliced fresh strawberries, optional

1. In a small saucepan, combine ¾ cup sugar, cocoa, flour and salt. Gradually stir in water. Bring to a boil; cook and stir for 2 minutes or until thickened. Remove from the heat; stir in the chocolate chips, coffee and vanilla until smooth. Transfer to a large bowl.

2. In another bowl, beat the eggs and egg white until slightly thickened. Gradually add the remaining sugar, beating until thick and lemon-colored. Fold into chocolate mixture.

3. Transfer to ten 4-oz. ramekins coated with cooking spray. Place ramekins in a baking pan; add 1 in. of boiling water to pan. Bake, uncovered, at 350° just until the centers are set, 20-25 minutes. If desired, garnish with strawberries. Serve immediately.

1 dessert: 197 cal., 6g fat (3g sat. fat), 42mg chol., 51mg sod., 37g carb. (33g sugars, 2g fiber), 3g pro.

Caramel Creme Brulee

This dazzling 13x9 recipe is always a crowd-pleaser! A torch works best to get the sugar caramelized while keeping the rest of the custard nice and cool. You may want to use more sugar to create a thicker, more even crust on top.

—Jenna Fleming, Lowville, NY

- -

Prep: 20 min.
Bake: 40 min. + chilling
Makes: 14 servings

- 4½ **cups heavy whipping cream**
- 1½ **cups half-and-half cream**
- 15 **large egg yolks**
- 1⅓ **cups sugar, divided**
- 3 **tsp. caramel extract**
- ¼ **tsp. salt**
- ⅓ **cup packed brown sugar**

1. Preheat oven to 325°. In a large saucepan, heat the creams until bubbles form around sides of pan; remove from heat. In a bowl, whisk egg yolks, 1 cup sugar, extract and salt until blended but not foamy. Slowly stir in hot cream mixture.

2. Place an ungreased broiler-safe 13x9-in. baking dish in a baking pan large enough to hold it without touching the sides. Pour egg mixture into dish. Place pan on oven rack; add very hot water to pan to within 1 in. of top of dish. Bake until center is just set and top appears dull, 40-50 minutes. Immediately remove dish from water bath to a wire rack; cool 1 hour. Refrigerate until cold.

3. Mix brown sugar and remaining sugar. To caramelize topping with a kitchen torch, sprinkle custard evenly with sugar mixture. Hold torch flame about 2 in. above custard surface and rotate it slowly until sugar is evenly caramelized. Serve immediately or refrigerate up to 1 hour.

4. To caramelize topping with a broiler, let custard stand at room temperature 30 minutes. Preheat broiler. Sprinkle custard evenly with sugar mixture. Broil 3-4 in. from heat until sugar is caramelized, 2-3 minutes. Serve immediately or refrigerate up to 1 hour.

Note: This recipe was tested with Watkins caramel extract in a broiler-safe rectangular ceramic Staub baking dish.

½ **cup:** 452 cal., 35g fat (21g sat. fat), 298mg chol., 86mg sod., 28g carb. (27g sugars, 0 fiber), 6g pro.

CARAMEL CREME BRULEE

HACK

Safe Handling

When baking with a water bath, always place the prepared pan on the oven rack, then add hot water. Not only is this safer and easier than trying to carry a filled water bath, it also eliminates the chance of splashing water onto your precious baked goods.

FLOURLESS CHOCOLATE CAKE WITH ROSEMARY GANACHE

Flourless Chocolate Cake with Rosemary Ganache

This rich cake is the essence of moist, dense chocolate—and amazing with silky rosemary-infused silky ganache.
—*Kelly Gardner, Alton, Il*

Prep: 40 min.
Bake: 30 min. + cooling
Makes: 16 servings

- 1   **lb. semisweet chocolate, chopped**
- 1   **cup butter, cubed**
- ¼   **cup dry red wine**
- 8   **large eggs, room temperature**
- ½   **cup sugar**
- 1   **tsp. vanilla extract**
- **GANACHE**
- 9   **oz. bittersweet chocolate, chopped**
- 1   **cup heavy whipping cream**
- 2   **fresh rosemary sprigs**

1. Line the bottom of a greased 9-in. springform pan with parchment; grease the paper. Place pan on a double thickness of heavy-duty foil (about 18 in. square). Securely wrap foil around pan; set aside.

2. In a large heavy saucepan, combine the chocolate, butter and wine over low heat, stirring constantly while melting. Remove from the heat. Cool to room temperature.

3. Meanwhile, in a large bowl, beat the eggs, sugar and vanilla until frothy and doubled in volume, about 5 minutes. Gradually fold eggs into chocolate mixture, one-third at a time, until well blended. Pour into prepared pan. Place springform pan in a large baking pan; add 1 in. of hot water to the larger pan.

4. Bake at 350° for 28-32 minutes or until outer edges are set (center will jiggle). Remove springform pan from water bath. Cool completely on a wire rack.

5. Carefully run a knife around edge of pan to loosen; remove sides of pan. Invert onto a serving platter; remove parchment.

6. Place chocolate in a small bowl. In a small saucepan, bring cream and rosemary just to a boil. Remove from heat; discard rosemary. Pour cream over chocolate; whisk until smooth. Cool slightly, stirring occasionally. Pour over cake. Chill until set.

1 slice: 435 cal., 35g fat (20g sat. fat), 156mg chol., 121mg sod., 31g carb. (26g sugars, 3g fiber), 7g pro.

HACK

Plate Like a Pro

A hot knife is the secret to cutting nice tidy slices of cake and cheesecake. You'll need a sharp knife, some hot water and a towel. Dip the blade in water to heat, then wipe dry and cut. Repeat each time for pretty slices with a clean edge.

CHOCOLATE CHIP
COOKIE DOUGH
CHEESECAKE

Chocolate Chip Cookie Dough Cheesecake

I created this recipe to combine two of my all-time favorites—cheesecake for the grown-up in me and chocolate chip cookie dough for the little girl in me. Sour cream offsets the sweetness and adds a nice tang.

—*Julie Craig, Kewaskum, WI*

Prep: 25 min.
Bake: 45 min. + chilling
Makes: 14 servings

- 1¾ cups crushed chocolate chip cookies or chocolate wafer crumbs
- ¼ cup sugar
- ⅓ cup butter, melted

FILLING
- 3 pkg. (8 oz. each) cream cheese, softened
- 1 cup sugar
- 1 cup sour cream
- ½ tsp. vanilla extract
- 3 large eggs, room temperature, lightly beaten

COOKIE DOUGH
- ¼ cup butter, softened
- ¼ cup sugar
- ¼ cup packed brown sugar
- 1 Tbsp. water
- 1 tsp. vanilla extract
- ½ cup all-purpose flour
- 1½ cups miniature semisweet chocolate chips, divided

1. In a small bowl, combine cookie crumbs and sugar; stir in butter. Press onto the bottom and 1 in. up the sides of a greased 9-in. springform pan. Place pan on a baking sheet; set aside.
2. In a large bowl, beat cream cheese and sugar until smooth. Beat in sour cream and vanilla. Add eggs; beat on low speed just until combined. Pour over crust; set aside.
3. In another bowl, cream butter and sugars until light and fluffy. Add water and vanilla. Gradually add flour and mix well. Stir in 1 cup chocolate chips.

4. Drop dough by teaspoonfuls over filling, gently pushing dough below surface (dough should be completely covered by filling). Place pan on a baking sheet.
5. Bake at 350° for 45-55 minutes or until center is almost set. Cool on a wire rack for 10 minutes. Carefully run a knife around edge of pan to loosen; cool for 1 hour longer. Refrigerate overnight.
6. Remove sides of pan. Sprinkle with remaining chips. Refrigerate leftovers.
1 slice: 551 cal., 36g fat (22g sat. fat), 131mg chol., 328mg sod., 52g carb. (37g sugars, 2g fiber), 8g pro.

Aunt Ruth's Famous Butterscotch Cheesecake

Aunt Ruth was my childhood nanny and often made this cheesecake. It was torture when my sister and I had to wait until the next day since it had to chill overnight. When I visited, she offered me a piece of her wonderful cheesecake. I made sure to leave with a copy of the recipe!

—*Trisha Kruse, Eagle, ID*

Prep: 30 min.
Bake: 65 min. + chilling
Makes: 12 servings

- 1½ cups graham cracker crumbs
- ⅓ cup packed brown sugar
- ⅓ cup butter, melted
- 1 can (14 oz.) sweetened condensed milk
- ¾ cup cold 2% milk
- 1 pkg. (3.4 oz.) instant butterscotch pudding mix
- 3 pkg. (8 oz. each) cream cheese, softened
- 1 tsp. vanilla extract
- 3 large eggs, room temperature, lightly beaten

1. Place a greased 9-in. springform pan on a double thickness of heavy-duty foil (about 18 in. square). Securely wrap foil around pan. In a small bowl, combine cracker crumbs and sugar; stir in butter. Press onto the bottom of prepared pan. Place pan on a baking sheet. Bake at 325° for 10 minutes. Cool on a wire rack.
2. In a small bowl, whisk the milks and pudding mix for 2 minutes. Let stand for 2 minutes or until soft-set.
3. Meanwhile, in a large bowl, beat cream cheese until smooth. Beat in pudding and vanilla. Add eggs; beat on low speed just until combined. Pour over crust. Place springform pan in a large baking pan; add 1 in. of hot water to larger pan.
4. Bake at 325° until center is almost set and top appears dull, 65-75 minutes. Remove springform pan from water bath. Cool on a wire rack 10 minutes. Run a knife around edge of pan to loosen; cool 1 hour longer. Chill overnight.
1 slice: 473 cal., 30g fat (18g sat. fat), 141mg chol., 460mg sod., 42g carb. (34g sugars, 0 fiber), 10g pro.

HACK

Perfectly Baked Each Time

A reliable way to test cheesecake and baked custard for doneness is to gently thump the side of pan or ramekin. If the custard wobbles as one unit (instead of rippling like a stone tossed in a pool), it's ready.

Honey Pecan Triangles

After stirring up batches of these tasty bar cookies for many years, I know to include plenty on cookie trays. They have all the goodness of pecan pie and are so easy to serve to a crowd.

—Debbie Fogel, East Berne, NY

- -

Prep: 20 min.
Bake: 45 min. + cooling
Makes: 4 dozen

- 2 tsp. plus ½ cup butter, softened, divided
- ½ cup packed brown sugar
- 1 large egg yolk, room temperature
- 1½ cups all-purpose flour

TOPPING

- 1 cup packed brown sugar
- ½ cup butter, cubed
- ¼ cup honey
- ½ cup heavy whipping cream
- 4 cups chopped pecans

1. Preheat oven to 350°. Line a 13x9-in. baking pan with foil, letting ends extend up sides; grease foil with 2 tsp. butter.
2. In a large bowl, cream remaining butter and brown sugar until light and fluffy; beat in egg yolk. Gradually beat in flour. Press into prepared pan. Bake until golden brown, about 15 minutes.
3. Meanwhile, in a large saucepan, combine brown sugar, butter and honey. Bring to a boil over medium heat, stirring constantly; cook and stir 3 minutes. Remove from heat; stir in cream and pecans. Pour over crust. Bake until hot and bubbly, about 30 minutes. Cool completely on a wire rack.
4. Lifting with foil, remove from pan. Cut into 24 squares. Cut squares diagonally into triangles.
1 piece: 159 cal., 12g fat (4g sat. fat), 18mg chol., 44mg sod., 13g carb. (9g sugars, 1g fiber), 1g pro.

Peanut Caramel Brownie Bites

With their three irresistible layers, these brownies are my family's absolute favorite.

—Ella Agans, Birch Tree, MO

- -

Prep: 1 hour + chilling
Bake: 20 min. + cooling
Makes: 4 dozen

- ¾ cup butter, cubed and softened
- ⅔ cup sugar
- 2 Tbsp. water
- 1 cup (6 oz.) semisweet chocolate chips
- 2 large eggs, room temperature
- 1 tsp. vanilla extract
- 1 cup all-purpose flour
- ½ tsp. baking powder

CANDY BAR TOPPING

- 1 cup sugar
- ¼ cup butter, cubed
- ¼ cup 2% milk
- 1 cup marshmallow creme
- ½ cup creamy peanut butter, divided
- ½ tsp. vanilla extract
- 2½ cups dry roasted peanuts, divided
- 40 caramels
- 2 Tbsp. water
- 1¼ cups (7½ oz.) semisweet chocolate chips

1. Preheat oven to 350°. Line a 13x9-in. baking pan with foil, letting ends extend up sides; coat foil with cooking spray.
2. Microwave butter, sugar and water on high just until mixture comes to a boil, 3-4 minutes; stir until blended. Stir in chocolate chips until melted. Whisk in eggs, 1 at a time, and vanilla until blended. Stir in flour and baking powder.
3. Spread into prepared pan. Bake until a toothpick inserted in center comes out clean, 18-20 minutes. Cool 30 minutes.
4. For the topping, combine sugar, cubed butter and milk in a large saucepan; bring to a boil, stirring constantly, over medium heat. Boil 5 minutes, stirring frequently. Stir in the marshmallow creme, ¼ cup peanut butter and vanilla; pour over brownies. Sprinkle with 2 cups peanuts.
5. In a small saucepan, combine caramels and water; cook, stirring, over medium-high heat until blended. Pour over peanuts.
6. Microwave chocolate chips on high until softened, about 1 minute. Stir in remaining peanut butter until smooth; pour over caramel layer. Chop remaining peanuts; sprinkle on top. Refrigerate at least 1 hour.
7. Lifting with foil, remove brownies from pan. Cut into bars. Store in an airtight container in the refrigerator.
1 bar: 212 cal., 12g fat (5g sat. fat), 19mg chol., 135mg sod., 24g carb. (19g sugars, 1g fiber), 4g pro.

PRO TIPS

- Spread brownie batter evenly in the pan. If one corner is thinner than another, it will bake faster and be overbaked when the rest of the pan is done.

- Be careful not to overbake—that's the death of a good, moist brownie.

PEANUT CARAMEL
BROWNIE BITES

Easily Lift & Cut Brownies & Bars

• Line a brownie or bar pan with foil or parchment to make the treats easy to remove from the pan after baking.

• Grease the lined pan with shortening or butter, or coat with cooking spray.

• After cooling as directed, lift brownies or bars out of the pan and cut. A bench scraper or bench knife is a handy tool for making quick, even cuts.

Chocolate Fudge Brownies

My children always looked forward to these after-school snacks. They're so fudgy they don't even need icing.

—*Hazel Fritchie, Palestine, IL*

- -

Prep: 15 min.
Bake: 35 min. + cooling
Makes: 16 servings

1	cup butter, cubed
6	oz. unsweetened chocolate, chopped
4	large eggs, room temperature
2	cups sugar
1	tsp. vanilla extract
½	tsp. salt
1	cup all-purpose flour
2	cups chopped walnuts Confectioners' sugar, optional

1. Preheat oven to 350°. In a small saucepan, melt butter and chocolate over low heat. Cool mixture slightly.

2. In a large bowl, beat eggs, sugar, vanilla and salt until blended. Stir in chocolate mixture. Add flour, mixing well. Stir in walnuts.

3. Spread batter into a greased 9-in. square baking pan. Bake for 35-40 minutes or until a toothpick inserted in center comes out with moist crumbs (do not overbake).

4. Cool completely in pan on a wire rack. If desired, dust with confectioners' sugar. Cut into bars.

1 brownie: 410 cal., 28g fat (12g sat. fat), 77mg chol., 186mg sod., 36g carb. (26g sugars, 3g fiber), 6g pro.

CHOCOLATE FUDGE BROWNIES

Build-Your-Own Brownie

Customize your favorite chocolate brownie recipe with these most delectable ideas.

Raspberry Rumble

Mash ¼ cup fresh raspberries and stir into the batter. Add a few berries on top if you have them.

Peanut Butter M&M's

Add Peanut Butter M&M's to the batter, bake, then top with fudge frosting. Finish it off with a sprinkling of chopped M&M's.

S'more & More

Pile on mini marshmallows and toasted pecans during the last 5 minutes of baking. To make Rocky Road brownies, drizzle generously with chocolate sauce.

HACK

Dish Towel Prevents Slipping

- Need an extra hand in the kitchen? Take a cue from professional chefs and place a damp dish towel under your mixing bowl.

- This keeps the bowl from sliding away (or worse) while you are mixing. It lets you have a hand free for adding other ingredients.

- Place a damp towel under your cutting board for the same stability.

Flourless Chocolate Torte

Chocoholics—like me—know that nothing says chocolate like a good flourless torte.
—*Kayla Albrecht, Freeport, IL*

- -

Prep: 20 min.
Bake: 40 min. + cooling
Makes: 12 servings

  5 large eggs, room
     temperature, separated
 12 oz. semisweet
     chocolate, chopped
 ¾   cup butter, cubed
 ¼   tsp. cream of tartar
 ½   cup sugar
     Confectioners' sugar, optional

1. Place egg whites in a large bowl; let stand at room temperature for 30 minutes. Preheat oven to 350°. In the top of a double boiler or a metal bowl over barely simmering water, melt chocolate and butter; stir until smooth. Remove from heat; cool slightly.

2. In another large bowl, beat egg yolks until thick and lemon-colored. Beat in chocolate mixture. With clean beaters, beat egg whites and cream of tartar on medium speed until foamy.

3. Gradually add sugar, 1 Tbsp. at a time, beating on high after each addition until the sugar is dissolved. Continue beating until stiff glossy peaks form. Fold a fourth of the egg whites into chocolate mixture, then fold in remaining whites.

4. Grease a 9-in. springform pan; transfer batter to pan. Bake for 40-45 minutes or until a toothpick inserted in center comes out with moist crumbs (do not overbake). Cool completely on a wire rack.

5. Loosen sides from pan with a knife. Remove rim from pan. If desired, dust with confectioners' sugar.

1 slice: 326 cal., 24g fat (14g sat. fat), 108mg chol., 121mg sod., 15g carb. (14g sugars, 1g fiber), 65g pro.

HACK

Dainty Design

Lay a paper doily on top of a cake and dust it with confectioners' sugar or cocoa. (Place a few tablespoons in a fine mesh sieve and shake it over the cake.) For a more elaborate design, try using several doilies with different patterns and work your way from the outer edge in.

**FLOURLESS
CHOCOLATE TORTE**

THICK SUGAR
COOKIES

Hardworking Lazy Susans

• Use a lazy Susan for your next cookie-decorating extravaganza. It's a handy way to keep icings, sugars and sprinkles all at the ready without lots of mess and reaching.

• A lazy Susan near the stove makes for efficient cooking, keeping your favorite oils, utensils and most-reached-for spices in one tidy area.

Thick Sugar Cookies

Thicker than the norm, this sugar cookie is like one you might find at a good bakery. My children often request these for their birthdays and are always happy to help decorate.
—*Heather Biedler, Martinsburg, WV*

- -

Prep: 25 min. + chilling
Bake: 10 min./batch + cooling
Makes: about 3 dozen

- 1 **cup butter, softened**
- 1 **cup sugar**
- 2 **large eggs, room temperature**
- 3 **large egg yolks, room temperature**
- 1½ **tsp. vanilla extract**
- ¾ **tsp. almond extract**
- 3½ **cups all-purpose flour**
- 1½ **tsp. baking powder**
- ¼ **tsp. salt**

FROSTING
- 4 **cups confectioners' sugar**
- ½ **cup butter, softened**
- ½ **cup shortening**
- 1 **tsp. vanilla extract**
- ½ **tsp. almond extract**
- 2 **to 3 Tbsp. 2% milk**
  Assorted colored nonpareils, optional

1. In a large bowl, cream butter and sugar until light and fluffy. Beat in eggs, egg yolks and extracts. In another bowl, whisk flour, baking powder and salt; gradually beat into creamed mixture. Shape into a disk; wrap and refrigerate 1 hour or until firm enough to roll.
2. Preheat oven to 375°. On a lightly floured surface, roll dough to ½-in. thickness. Cut with a floured 2-in. cookie cutter. Place 1 in. apart on ungreased baking sheets.
3. Bake until the edges begin to brown, 10-12 minutes. Cool on pans 5 minutes. Remove to wire racks to cool completely.
4. For frosting, in a large bowl, beat the confectioners' sugar, butter, shortening, extracts and enough milk to reach desired consistency. Spread over cookies. If desired, sprinkle with nonpareils.

1 frosted cookie: 219 cal., 11g fat (6g sat. fat), 49mg chol., 92mg sod., 28g carb. (18g sugars, 0 fiber), 2g pro.

Lemon Stars

These light little cookies have a crunchy texture and a citrusy zing. Try stars for the Christmas season or bunnies and chicks for Easter.
—*Jacqueline Hill, Norwalk, OH*

- -

Prep: 45 min. + chilling
Bake: 10 min./batch + cooling
Makes: 9 dozen

- ½ **cup butter-flavored shortening**
- 1 **cup sugar**
- 1 **large egg, room temperature**
- 1½ **tsp. lemon extract**
- ½ **cup sour cream**
- 1 **tsp. grated lemon zest**
- 2¾ **cups all-purpose flour**
- ½ **tsp. baking soda**
- ½ **tsp. salt**

FROSTING
- 1½ **cups confectioners' sugar**
- 6 **Tbsp. butter, softened**
- ¾ **tsp. lemon extract**
- 3 **drops yellow food coloring, optional**
- 3 **to 4 Tbsp. 2% milk**
  Yellow colored sugar, optional

1. In a large bowl, cream shortening and sugar until light and fluffy. Beat in egg and extract. Stir in sour cream and zest. Combine the flour, baking soda and salt; gradually add to the creamed mixture and mix well. Divide dough into 3 balls; cover and chill for 3 hours or until easy to handle.
2. Remove 1 portion of dough from the refrigerator at a time. On a lightly floured surface, roll out dough to ¼-in. thickness. Cut with a floured 2-in. star cookie cutter. Place 1 in. apart on ungreased baking sheets.
3. Bake at 375° for 6-8 minutes or until edges are lightly browned. Remove to wire racks to cool.
4. For frosting, in a small bowl, combine the confectioners' sugar, butter, extract, food coloring if desired and enough milk to achieve spreading consistency. Frost cookies; sprinkle with colored sugar if desired.

1 cookie: 43 cal., 2g fat (1g sat. fat), 4mg chol., 23mg sod., 6g carb. (4g sugars, 0 fiber), 0 pro.

HACK

Decorate Cookies Before Baking

Place cutouts on the baking sheet. Place the cutter over each cookie as a frame, and gently top with sprinkles or colored sugar. Bake according to recipe directions.

SOUR CREAM
POUND CAKE

Sour Cream Pound Cake

Because I'm our town's postmaster, I can bake only in my spare time. When I do, I especially enjoy making desserts like this one. It tastes amazing as is or tucked under ice cream and chocolate syrup like a hot fudge sundae!
—*Karen Conrad, East Troy, WI*

Prep: 15 min.
Bake: 1¼ hours + cooling
Makes: 20 servings

1	cup butter, softened
3	cups sugar
6	large eggs, room temperature
3	cups all-purpose flour
¼	tsp. baking soda
¼	tsp. salt
1	cup sour cream
2	tsp. vanilla extract
	Confectioners' sugar, optional

1. In a bowl, cream the butter and sugar until light and fluffy, about 5-7 minutes. Add eggs, 1 at a time, beating well after each addition. Combine flour, baking soda and salt; add to creamed mixture alternately with sour cream and vanilla. Beat on low just until blended. Pour into a greased and floured 10-in. fluted tube pan.

2. Bake at 325° for 1¼-1½ hours or until a toothpick comes out clean. Cool in pan 15 minutes before removing to a wire rack to cool completely. Sprinkle with confectioners' sugar if desired.

1 piece: 311 cal., 13g fat (7g sat. fat), 96mg chol., 163mg sod., 45g carb. (30g sugars, 1g fiber), 4g pro.

Homemade Vanilla Extract

Homemade vanilla is fun to give in decorative bottles with attractive labels. Share it with special friends who like to cook or bake.
—*Becky Jo Smith, Kettle Falls, WA*

Prep: 5 min. + standing
Makes: 2 cups

6	vanilla beans, split lengthwise
2	cups vodka

Place vanilla beans in a tall jar; cover with vodka. Seal jar tightly. Let stand in a cool dark place at least 6 weeks, gently shaking jar once a week.

1 tsp.: 11 cal., 0 fat (0 sat. fat), 0 chol., 0 sod., 0 carb. (0 sugars, 0 fiber), 0 pro.

HACK

Add a Little More Vanilla

One of our favorite tricks is to add an extra splash of vanilla to baked goods such as cookies, muffins, cakes and breads. A little extra vanilla has the most impact on delicately flavored foods like cakes and cookies that don't have a lot of mix-ins like caramel bits, peanut butter chips or mint candies.

Cherry Almond Delights

A tender cream cheese dough is filled with homemade almond paste and a pretty maraschino cherry. This makes an elegant cookie tart.
—*Gilda Lester, Millsboro, DE*

- -

Prep: 35 min. + chilling
Bake: 20 min. + cooling
Makes: about 2 dozen

- ½   cup butter, softened
- 3   oz. cream cheese, softened
- 1   large egg, room temperature
- 1   pkg. (17½ oz.) sugar cookie mix

FILLING
- 1½   cups slivered almonds
- ¾   cup sugar
- 2   large eggs, room temperature
- ¼   cup butter, softened
- 2   tsp. vanilla extract
- 24   maraschino cherries, well-drained
  Confectioners' sugar

1. In a large bowl, beat butter and cream cheese until smooth. Beat in egg. Add cookie mix; mix well (dough will be sticky). Shape dough into a disk; wrap and refrigerate 1 hour or until firm enough to handle.
2. In a food processor, pulse almonds and sugar until almonds are finely chopped. Add eggs; process until mixture forms a paste. Add butter and vanilla; process until blended.
3. Preheat oven to 350°. Shape dough into 1¼-in. balls; press onto bottom and up the sides of 24 greased mini muffin cups.
4. Place 1 Tbsp. filling in each cup. Top each with a cherry. Bake until edges are golden and filling is set, 6-18 minutes or. Cool in muffin pans 10 minutes. Remove to wire racks to cool completely. Dust tops with confectioners' sugar before serving.
1 cookie: 235 cal., 13g fat (5g sat. fat), 42mg chol., 114mg sod., 27g carb. (19g sugars, 1g fiber), 3g pro.

Baki's Old-World Cookies

My uncles have always called these cupcake cookies because of the unique and pretty way they're baked. My maternal grandmother mixed up many a batch.
—*Marilyn Louise Riggenbach, Ravenna, OH*

- -

Prep: 25 min. + chilling
Bake: 20 min./batch • **Makes:** 3 dozen

- 1   cup butter, softened
- 1   cup sugar
- 2   large eggs, room temperature
- 1   cup ground walnuts
- 1½   cups all-purpose flour
- 1½   tsp. ground cinnamon
- 1   tsp. ground cloves
- 2   tsp. vanilla extract
  Confectioners' sugar

1. Preheat oven to 350°. Cream butter and sugar until light and fluffy. Add eggs, 1 at a time, beating well after each addition. Add nuts. In another bowl, sift together flour, cinnamon and cloves; add with vanilla to creamed mixture. Refrigerate, covered, for 1 hour.
2. Fill 36 generously greased muffin cups or individual 3-in. tins about one-third to half full. Press dough around sides, leaving a depression in the center. (If dough is too soft, add flour.)
3. Bake until light brown, about 18 minutes. Cool 2 minutes; tap tins to remove cookies. Dust with confectioners' sugar.
1 cookie: 105 cal., 7g fat (3g sat. fat), 24mg chol., 45mg sod., 10g carb. (6g sugars, 0 fiber), 1g pro.

HACK

Cooling Rack + Counter Space

An ironing board with the cover removed can be pressed into service as an additional cooling rack when you're doing a lot of baking. An added advantage is that it frees up counter space in the kitchen for your baking activities. Just be sure to use pans, paper liners, parchment or some other barrier between baked goods and the rack.

BAKI'S
OLD-WORLD
COOKIES

HACK

Change Up the Pan for Chewy Cookies

If you like cookies with tender edges that are chewy in the center, try baking your favorite cookie recipe in a muffin tin instead of on a baking sheet. The walls of a muffin tin protect the cookies while they bake.

Wyoming Cowboy Cookies

These cookies are very popular here in Wyoming. Mix up a batch for your crew and see why.
—*Patsy Steenbock, Shoshoni, WY*

Prep: 25 min. • **Bake:** 15 min.
Makes: 6 dozen

- 1 cup sweetened shredded coconut
- ¾ cup chopped pecans
- 1 cup butter, softened
- 1½ cups packed brown sugar
- ½ cup sugar
- 2 large eggs, room temperature
- 1½ tsp. vanilla extract
- 2 cups all-purpose flour
- 1 tsp. baking soda
- ½ tsp. salt
- 2 cups old-fashioned oats
- 2 cups (12 oz.) chocolate chips

1. Place coconut and pecans on a 15x10x1-in. baking pan. Bake at 350° for 6-8 minutes or until toasted, stirring every 2 minutes. Set aside to cool.

2. In a large bowl, cream butter and sugars until light and fluffy. Add eggs and vanilla; beat well. Combine the flour, baking soda and salt Add to creamed mixture; beat well. Stir in oats, chocolate chips and toasted coconut and pecans.

3. Drop by rounded teaspoonfuls onto greased baking sheets. Bake at 350° about 12 minutes or until browned. Remove to wire racks to cool.

2 cookies: 211 cal., 11g fat (6g sat. fat), 25mg chol., 134mg sod., 27g carb. (18g sugars, 2g fiber), 2g pro.

HOW-TO

Soften Butter Quickly

Here are two ways to soften butter in a flash. Now you're baking!

- With a rolling pin, roll or pound the butter flat. Whether rolling or pounding, the friction will warm the butter—and the broader surface area will encourage quicker softening.

- Shredding creates a dirty grater, but it's the quickest method. Partially unwrap the butter (use the wrapped half as a handle to keep your hand clean) and shred it using the largest holes of a box grater. The butter will become a fluffy heap, similar in appearance to shredded mozzarella cheese.

RED VELVET WHITE CHIP COOKIES

Red Velvet
White Chip Cookies

These cookies are soft, chewy and taste as good as they sound. The first time I baked them, I took them to an aunt's yard sale. Now they're my go-to for any special event.
—*Samantha Gstalder, Montoursville, PA*

- -

Prep: 25 min.
Bake: 10 min./batch + cooling
Makes: about 3½ dozen

½	cup butter, softened
½	cup sugar
½	cup packed brown sugar
1	large egg, room temperature
1	Tbsp. 2% milk
2	tsp. red food coloring
1	tsp. vanilla extract
1½	cups all-purpose flour
⅓	cup baking cocoa
1	tsp. baking soda
¼	tsp. salt
¾	cup white baking chips

1. Preheat oven to 375°. In a large bowl, cream butter and sugars until light and fluffy. Beat in the egg, milk, food coloring and vanilla. In another bowl, whisk flour, cocoa, baking soda and salt; gradually beat into creamed mixture. Stir in baking chips.
2. Drop dough by tablespoonfuls 2 in. apart onto parchment-lined baking sheets. Bake cookies until set, 6-8 minutes. Cool on pans for 2 minutes. Remove to wire racks to cool.
Freeze option: Freeze cookies in freezer containers. To use, thaw before serving.
1 cookie: 75 cal., 3g fat (2g sat. fat), 11mg chol., 67mg sod., 11g carb. (7g sugars, 0 fiber), 1g pro.

Big & Buttery Chocolate Chip Cookies

Our family's version of the classic chocolate chip cookie is based on a recipe from a bakery in California called Hungry Bear. It's big, thick and chewy—splendid for dunking.

—*Irene Yeh, Mequon, WI*

Prep: 35 min. + chilling
Bake: 10 min./batch
Makes: about 2 dozen

- 1   cup butter, softened
- 1   cup packed brown sugar
- ¾   cup sugar
- 2   large eggs, room temperature
- 1½   tsp. vanilla extract
- 2⅔   cups all-purpose flour
- 1¼   tsp. baking soda
- 1   tsp. salt
- 1   pkg. (12 oz.) semisweet chocolate chips
- 2   cups coarsely chopped walnuts, toasted

1. In a large bowl, beat butter and sugars until blended. Beat in eggs and vanilla. In a small bowl, whisk flour, baking soda and salt; gradually beat into butter mixture. Stir in chocolate chips and walnuts.

2. Shape ¼ cupfuls of dough into balls. Flatten each to ¾-in. thickness (2½-in. diameter), smoothing edges as necessary. Place in an airtight container, separating layers with waxed or parchment; refrigerate, covered, overnight.

3. To bake, place dough portions 2 in. apart on parchment-lined baking sheets; let stand at room temperature 30 minutes before baking. Preheat oven to 400°.

4. Bake until edges are golden brown (centers will be light), 10-12 minutes. Cool on pans 2 minutes. Remove to wire racks to cool.

1 cookie: 311 cal., 19g fat (8g sat. fat), 38mg chol., 229mg sod., 35g carb. (23g sugars, 2g fiber), 4g pro.

HACK

Preserve Freshness with Bread

To keep baked goods soft and moist when storing, add a slice of white bread to the container. It will help preserve moisture in cookies, cakes, muffins and more.

BIG & BUTTERY
CHOCOLATE CHIP
COOKIES

French Macarons

Even decorated simply—a sprinkle of sugar, a drizzle of icing—these stylish beauties will be the showstoppers on any cookie tray.

—*Josh Rink, Milwaukee, WI*

- -

Prep: 1 hour + standing
Bake: 15 min./batch + cooling
Makes: 26 macarons

MACARON SHELL

- 1⅓ **cups almond flour (125 grams)**
- 2¼ **cups confectioners' sugar (225 grams), divided**
- 3 **extra-large egg whites (100 grams), room temperature**
- 2 **Tbsp. superfine sugar (25 grams)**
- ⅛ **tsp. salt**

BUTTERCREAM FILLING

- ¼ **cup unsalted butter, softened**
- 1 **cup confectioners' sugar**
- 2 **Tbsp. heavy whipping cream**
- ½ **tsp. vanilla extract**
- ⅛ **tsp. salt**

1. Place the almond flour and 1½ cups plus 3 Tbsp. (175 grams) confectioners' sugar into the bowl of a food processor; pulse until thoroughly mixed and to ensure almond flour is very fine. Pass the almond flour mixture through a fine mesh sieve; discard any large pieces that remain.

2. Place egg whites in a very clean bowl of a stand mixer fitted with whisk attachment; whisk on medium-low speed until frothy. Slowly add the superfine sugar; whisk until dissolved, 1-2 minutes. Slowly add remaining confectioners' sugar; increase speed to high and whip until meringue is glossy and stiff peaks form, 2-3 minutes.

3. Gently fold one-third of the almond flour mixture into the meringue; gently fold in remaining almond flour in 2 additions. Using side of spatula, smooth batter up the sides of bowl several times to remove air bubbles and ensure there are no lumps; do not overmix. When the spatula is run down the center of the bowl, the line created in the batter should remain visible for a moment, before mixture runs back into itself.

4. Position rack in oven to upper third; preheat oven to 300°. Fit a #7 or #10 round pastry tip inside a pastry bag; gently pour batter into pastry bag. Pipe 1⅜-in. rounds onto parchment about 1-in. apart. Tap tray against counter 2 or 3 times to remove excess air bubbles. Let macarons rest until no longer wet or sticky to the touch, 30-60 minutes. Bake, 1 tray at a time, until cookies rise about ⅛-in. to form "feet," 14-16 minutes, rotating tray halfway through cooking. Remove tray and let macarons cool completely; repeat with remaining trays. Once macarons have cooled completely, remove from parchment.

5. To make filling, cream butter in a stand mixer fitted with whisk attachment; slowly add powdered sugar until incorporated. Add heavy cream, vanilla and salt; mix until smooth. Pour frosting into a pastry bag fitted with a small round tip; pipe buttercream onto half the macarons. Top with remaining macaron shells. Refrigerate, covered, until ready to serve.

1 macaron: 253 cal., 11g fat (3g sat. fat), 13mg chol., 69mg sod., 37g carb. (34g sugars, 1g fiber), 4g pro.

FRENCH MACARONS

Cranberry Flavor

Add red gel food coloring (do not use liquid food coloring) to whipped meringue.

TO DECORATE: Place white candy melts or white chocolate in a microwave-safe bowl and microwave for 30-second intervals, stirring frequently, until melted and smooth. Place in a piping bag fitted with a fine round decorating tip; drizzle over macaron shells. Immediately sprinkle with red, green and white assorted sprinkles.

TO FILL: If desired, add 2-3 drops cranberry flavoring to frosting. Pipe a circle of frosting onto bottoms of half the macaron shells. Place ¼ tsp. canned cranberry sauce in center of each frosting circle. Top with remaining macaron shells.

Peppermint Flavor

Add green gel food coloring (do not use liquid food coloring) to whipped meringue.

TO DECORATE: Top macaron shells with crushed candy canes immediately after removing from oven.

TO FILL: Add ¼-½ tsp. peppermint extract to prepared frosting. Assemble as directed.

HACK

Homemade Piping Guide

To help you pipe perfectly round cookies, trace a round cutter on parchment to create a pattern. Flip the parchment and you're ready to start piping. (Works for piping large meringue shells, too!)

COFFEE-CHOCOLATE
CAKE

HACK

Warm Eggs for Better Baking

Many recipes benefit from room-temperature eggs, and it's an easy thing to do. Just place eggs in hot water while you prep your recipe. They'll be ready when it's time to get cracking.

Coffee-Chocolate Cake

Say happy birthday with this dark, moist cake. The basic buttery frosting has an unmistakable homemade taste. With a few simple variations, you can come up with different colors and flavors.

—Taste of Home *Test Kitchen*

- -

Prep: 25 min.
Bake: 25 min. + cooling
Makes: 12 servings

2 cups sugar
1 cup canola oil
1 cup whole milk
1 cup brewed coffee, room temperature
2 large eggs, room temperature
1 tsp. vanilla extract
2 cups all-purpose flour
¾ cup baking cocoa
2 tsp. baking soda
1 tsp. baking powder
1 tsp. salt

BUTTERCREAM FROSTING
1 cup butter, softened
8 cups confectioners' sugar
2 tsp. vanilla extract
½ to ¾ cup whole milk

1. In a large bowl, beat the sugar, oil, milk, coffee, eggs and vanilla until well blended. Combine the flour, cocoa, baking soda, baking powder and salt; gradually beat into sugar mixture until blended.

2. Pour into 2 greased and floured 9-in. round baking pans. Bake at 325° for 25-30 minutes or until a toothpick inserted in the center comes out clean. Cool in pans for 10 minutes before removing to wire racks to cool completely.

3. For frosting, in a large bowl, beat until fluffy. Beat in confectioners' sugar and vanilla. Add milk until frosting reaches desired consistency. Spread frosting between layers and over top and sides of cake.

1 slice: 859 cal., 36g fat (13g sat. fat), 80mg chol., 621mg sod., 133g carb. (109g sugars, 2g fiber), 5g pro.

HOW-TO

Easily Frost a Layer Cake

- Trim tops of cakes to level if needed.

- Add a light coating of frosting (this is called a crumb coating) and chill. This coating sets and helps trap the crumbs, creating a smooth cake surface that's easy to work with.

- Add a second layer of frosting. To achieve a smooth finish, use a hot offset spatula that you've heated in water and wiped dry.

- To create a less formal design, use the back of a spoon to make swirls.

Sandy's Chocolate Cake

Years ago, I drove 4½ hours to a cake contest, holding my entry on my lap the whole way. But it paid off. One bite and you'll see why this velvety beauty was named the best chocolate cake recipe won first prize.
—*Sandy Johnson, Tioga, PA*

- -

Prep: 30 min.
Bake: 30 min. + cooling
Makes: 16 servings

- 1 cup butter, softened
- 3 cups packed brown sugar
- 4 large eggs, room temperature
- 2 tsp. vanilla extract
- 2⅔ cups all-purpose flour
- ¾ cup baking cocoa
- 3 tsp. baking soda
- ½ tsp. salt
- 1⅓ cups sour cream
- 1⅓ cups boiling water

FROSTING
- ½ cup butter, cubed
- 3 oz. unsweetened chocolate, chopped
- 3 oz. semisweet chocolate, chopped
- 5 cups confectioners' sugar
- 1 cup sour cream
- 2 tsp. vanilla extract

1. Preheat oven to 350°. Grease and flour three 9-in. round baking pans.
2. In a large bowl, cream butter and brown sugar until light and fluffy. Add eggs, 1 at a time, beating well after each addition. Beat in vanilla. In another bowl, whisk flour, cocoa, baking soda and salt; add to creamed mixture alternately with sour cream, beating well after each addition. Stir in water until blended. Transfer to prepared pans. Bake until a toothpick comes out clean, 30-35 minutes. Cool in pans 10 minutes; remove to wire racks to cool completely.
3. For frosting, in a metal bowl over simmering water, melt cubed butter and chopped chocolates; stir until smooth. Cool slightly.
4. In a large bowl, combine the confectioners' sugar, sour cream and vanilla. Add chocolate mixture; beat until smooth. Spread frosting between layers and over top and sides of cake. Refrigerate leftovers.
1 slice: 685 cal., 29g fat (18g sat. fat), 115mg chol., 505mg sod., 102g carb. (81g sugars, 3g fiber), 7g pro.

HACK

Use a Dime to Test Your KitchenAid's Bowl Clearance

If your stand mixer is a bowl-lift model (rather than a tilt-head), here's a little-known trick to help save wear and tear on your machine. Put a dime in the bottom of the bowl and turn your mixer (with the whisk attachment) on low. If the dime scrapes the bottom of the bowl, the clearance is too low. If the dime doesn't move, the clearance is too high. If the dime moves but does not scrape the bowl, the clearance is perfect. Use a screwdriver to adjust the bowl-lift mechanism as needed.

SANDY'S CHOCOLATE CAKE

Chocolate Mint Cake

- Replace vanilla extract with 1-1½ tsp. peppermint extract.

- Place candy canes in a bag and crush with a rolling pin.

- Top the cake with crushed candy, chocolate kisses and chocolate chips.

Creme de Menthe Cupcakes

We use creme de menthe, a liqueur that means mint cream in French, to add a cool touch to these impressive mascarpone-frosted cupcakes.

—*Keri Whitney, Castro Valley, CA*

- -

Prep: 30 min.
Bake: 15 min. + cooling
Makes: about 1 dozen

- ¾ cup butter, softened
- 1 cup sugar
- 2 large eggs, room temperature
- ½ tsp. mint extract
- 1½ cups cake flour
- 1½ tsp. baking powder
- ¼ tsp. salt
- ⅔ cup 2% milk
- 2 Tbsp. white (clear) creme de menthe
  Green paste food coloring

FROSTING
- 1 carton (8 oz.) mascarpone cheese
- ⅓ cup heavy whipping cream
- ¼ cup confectioners' sugar
- 4 tsp. white (clear) creme de menthe
  Green paste food coloring

1. Preheat oven to 350°. Cream the butter and granulated sugar until light and fluffy. Add the eggs, 1 at a time, beating well after each addition. Add mint extract. In another bowl, whisk flour, baking powder and salt; add to creamed mixture alternately with milk and creme de menthe, beating well after each addition. Transfer 2 cups batter to a separate bowl. Mix food coloring paste into remaining batter.

2. Cut a small hole in the tip of a pastry bag; insert a #12 round tip. Spoon the batters alternately into bag. Pipe batter into 12 paper-lined muffin cups until three-fourths full. Bake until a toothpick inserted in the center comes out clean, 15-20 minutes. Cool 10 minutes; remove from pan to a wire rack to cool completely.

3. For frosting, stir the mascarpone and whipping cream together until smooth. Add confectioners' sugar and creme de menthe; stir until blended. Transfer half the frosting to a separate bowl and mix food coloring paste into remaining frosting. Stir each portion vigorously until stiff peaks form (do not overmix).

4. Cut a small hole in the tip of a pastry bag; insert a #12 round tip. Spoon the frostings alternately into the bag. Pipe frosting onto cupcakes. Refrigerate leftovers.

Note: For extra-tall frosting like the ones shown here, double the frosting ingredients.

1 cupcake: 372 cal., 24g fat (14g sat. fat), 95mg chol., 222mg sod., 35g carb. (21g sugars, 0 fiber), 5g pro.

CREME DE MENTHE CUPCAKES

HACK

So-Simple Swirled Look

To achieve this pretty cupcake look (or the Gender Reveal Cupcake design on p. 236), place a pastry bag in a tumbler for easy filling. Alternately spoon colored frostings into the bag. *Voila!*

Gender Reveal Cupcakes

• After baking a batch of cupcakes, use a small serrated knife to cut a hollow into each fluffy top. A grapefruit or paring knife works best.

• Next, pipe the "reveal" icing inside the opening. You'll want to cover the tops with extra icing to conceal. At the party, you can pass around a plate of these surprise cupcakes and tell everyone to take a big bite to reveal.

GENDER REVEAL CUPCAKES

Pink Velvet Cupcakes

My daughter loves all things pink, so this recipe was just right for her birthday. Even my teenage son (not a fan of pink) eats his share, too.
—*Paulette Smith, Winston-Salem, NC*

Prep: 30 min. + chilling
Bake: 25 min. + cooling
Makes: 2 dozen

- 1 cup butter, softened
- 1¼ cups sugar
- ⅛ tsp. pink paste food coloring
- 3 large eggs, room temperature
- 1 tsp. vanilla extract
- 2½ cups all-purpose flour
- 1½ tsp. baking powder
- ¼ tsp. baking soda
- ¼ tsp. salt
- 1 cup buttermilk

WHITE CHOCOLATE GANACHE

- 2 cups white baking chips
- ½ cup heavy whipping cream
- 1 Tbsp. butter
  Pink coarse sugar and sugar pearls

1. In a large bowl, cream the butter, sugar and food coloring until light and fluffy. Add eggs, 1 at a time, beating well after each addition. Beat in vanilla. Combine the flour, baking powder, baking soda and salt; add to creamed mixture alternately with the buttermilk, beating well after each addition.

2. Fill 24 paper-lined muffin cups two-thirds full. Bake at 350° until a toothpick inserted in the center comes out clean, 23-27 minutes. Let cool for 10 minutes before removing from muffin pans to wire racks to cool completely.

3. Place white chips in a small bowl. In a saucepan, bring cream just to a boil. Pour over chips; whisk until smooth. Stir in butter. Transfer to a large bowl. Chill 30 minutes, stirring once.

4. Beat on high speed for 2-3 minutes or until soft peaks form and frosting is light and fluffy. Frost cupcakes. Roll edges of cupcakes with coarse sugar; decorate with sugar pearls. Store in the refrigerator.

Note: Sugar pearls are available from Wilton Industries. Call 800-794-5866 or visit wilton.com.

1 serving: 266 cal., 15g fat (9g sat. fat), 57mg chol., 154mg sod., 29g carb. (20g sugars, 0 fiber), 3g pro.

CREAM-FILLED CUPCAKES

Cream-Filled Cupcakes

These chocolate cupcakes have a fun filling and shiny chocolate frosting that make them extra special. They always disappear in a flash!
—*Kathy Kittell, Lenexa, KS*

Prep: 20 min.
Bake: 15 min. + cooling
Makes: 2 dozen

- 1 pkg. devil's food cake mix (regular size)
- 2 tsp. hot water
- ¼ tsp. salt
- 1 jar (7 oz.) marshmallow creme
- ½ cup shortening
- ⅓ cup confectioners' sugar
- ½ tsp. vanilla extract

GANACHE FROSTING

- 1 cup semisweet chocolate chips
- ¾ cup heavy whipping cream

1. Prepare and bake the cake batter according to package directions, using 24 paper-lined muffin cups. Cool for 5 minutes before removing from pans to wire racks to cool completely.

2. For filling, in a small bowl, combine water and salt until salt is dissolved. Cool. In a small bowl, beat the marshmallow creme, shortening, confectioners' sugar and vanilla until light and fluffy; beat in salt mixture.

3. Cut a small hole in the corner of a pastry bag; insert round pastry tip. Fill the bag with cream filling. Push tip through the top of each cupcake to fill center.

4. Place chocolate chips in a small bowl. In a small saucepan, bring cream just to a boil. Pour over chocolate; whisk until smooth. Cool, stirring occasionally, to room temperature or until ganache reaches a dipping consistency.

5. Dip cupcake tops in ganache; chill for 20 minutes or until set. Store in the refrigerator.

1 cupcake: 262 cal., 15g fat (5g sat. fat), 32mg chol., 223mg sod., 29g carb. (20g sugars, 1g fiber), 2g pro.

Showstopping Winter Cake

- For candied citrus, bring 2¼ cups sugar and 2 cups water to a boil. Add thin tangerine or orange slices; reduce heat to medium. Cook until slices are translucent, about 20 minutes, turning occasionally. Reduce heat; simmer until tender, about 10 minutes, turning occasionally.

- With a slotted spoon or tongs, remove slices to a parchment-lined baking pan or wire rack. Let stand at room temperature overnight to dry.

- For sugared cranberries, in small bowl, stir together 2 Tbsp. water and 1 Tbsp. pasteurized liquid egg whites. Lightly coat 1 pkg. (12 oz.) fresh or frozen cranberries in mixture. Place cranberries on a baking pan and sprinkle with ½ cup coarse sugar and ½ cup superfine sugar until coated. Dry on rack at room temperature for 2 hours.

- To add flair to frosted cake, press the back of a small offset spatula against the frosting and gently drag it in an upward motion. Repeat around the sides of the cake. Top with fruit.

- Gently sprinkle a fine border of decorating sugar along the top edge.

CRANBERRY CAKE WITH TANGERINE FROSTING

Cranberry Cake with Tangerine Frosting

Sugary cranberries and candied citrus dress up to this smartly elegant cake. It's my favorite Christmas dessert for its sheer *wow* factor.

—*Sandy Gaulitz, Spring, TX*

- -

Prep: 30 min.
Bake: 35 min. + cooling
Makes: 16 servings

- ¼ cup butter, softened
- 2 cups sugar
- 2 tsp. vanilla extract
- 4 cups plus 2 Tbsp. cake flour, divided
- 2 Tbsp. baking powder
- 1 tsp. salt
- 2 cups 2% milk
- 4 cups fresh or frozen cranberries

FROSTING
- 2 pkg. (8 oz. each) cream cheese, softened
- ¾ cup butter, softened
- 4 cups confectioners' sugar
- 2 Tbsp. tangerine or orange juice
- ½ tsp. grated tangerine or orange zest
  Optional toppings: sugared cranberries, candied tangerine or orange slices and red sugar

1. Line the bottoms of 2 greased 8-in. square or 9-in. round baking pans with parchment; grease paper. In a large bowl, beat butter and sugar until crumbly, about 2 minutes. Beat in vanilla.

2. In another bowl, mix 4 cups flour, baking powder and salt; add to butter mixture alternately with milk, beating well after each addition. In a large bowl, toss cranberries with remaining flour; fold into batter.

3. Transfer to prepared pans. Bake at 400° for 35-40 minutes or until a toothpick inserted in center comes out clean. Cool for 10 minutes before removing from pans to wire racks; remove parchment. Cool completely.

4. For the frosting, in a large bowl, beat cream cheese and butter until smooth. Gradually beat in the confectioners' sugar, tangerine juice and zest. Spread between cake layers and over top and sides of cake. Refrigerate, covered, until serving.

5. If desired, top with sugared cranberries, candied tangerines and red sugar.

1 slice: 572 cal., 22g fat (13g sat. fat), 62mg chol., 524mg sod., 89g carb. (58g sugars, 2g fiber), 6g pro.

Vanilla Bean Angel Food Cake

Angel food cake is my blank canvas for creating awesome desserts. Serve it with a simple glaze, or pile on fruit, chocolate sauce or nutty sprinkles.
—Leah Rekau, Milwaukee, WI

- -

Prep: 30 min.
Bake: 45 min. + cooling
Makes: 16 servings

- 12 **large egg whites (about 1⅔ cups)**
- 1 **cup cake flour**
- 1½ **cups sugar, divided**
- 1 **vanilla bean (see Note) or 1 tsp. vanilla extract**
- ½ **tsp. cream of tartar**
- ¼ **tsp. salt**
  Vanilla, Citrus or Chocolate Glaze

1. Place egg whites in a large bowl; let stand at room temperature 30 minutes.
2. Preheat oven to 325°. In a small bowl, mix the flour and ¾ cup sugar until blended.

3. Add seeds from vanilla bean (or extract if using), cream of tartar and salt to egg whites. Beat on medium speed until soft peaks form. Gradually add remaining ¾ cup sugar, 1 Tbsp. at a time, beating on high after each addition until sugar is dissolved. Continue beating until soft glossy peaks form. Gradually fold in flour mixture, about ½ cup at a time.
4. Gently transfer to an ungreased 10-in. tube pan. Cut through batter with a knife to remove air pockets. Bake on lowest oven rack until top springs back when lightly touched, 45-55 minutes. Immediately invert pan atop a sturdy bottle; cool completely in pan, about 1½ hours.
5. Run a knife around the sides and center tube of pan. Remove the cake to a serving plate.
Note: To remove the seeds from a vanilla bean, cut bean lengthwise in half with a sharp knife; scrape out the dark, pulpy seeds.
1 slice: 177 cal., 0 fat (0 sat. fat), 0 chol., 80mg sod., 41g carb. (34g sugars, 0 fiber), 3g pro.

Glaze Away
Top your masterpiece with a flavorful icing.

Vanilla Glaze
Mix 2 cups confectioners' sugar, 1 scraped vanilla bean (or 1 tsp. vanilla extract) and 3-4 Tbsp. milk; spread over cake.

Citrus Glaze
Mix 2 cups confectioners' sugar, 1 tsp. grated lemon or lime zest and 3-4 Tbsp. lemon or lime juice; spread over cake.

Chocolate Glaze
In a saucepan, heat ½ cup heavy whipping cream and 1 Tbsp. sugar just to a boil, stirring to dissolve sugar. Remove from heat and add 1 cup 60% cacao bittersweet chocolate baking chips. Whisk until smooth; stir in 2 Tbsp. amaretto. Cool 15 minutes. Pour over the cake; sprinkle with ¼ cup toasted sliced almonds.

HOW-TO

Make a Tunnel Cake

- Insert toothpicks an inch from the top of the cake on all sides as a guide for your knife. Slice off top with serrated knife.

- Cut out a tunnel with a small paring knife, leaving a 1-in. shell on all sides. Use your fingers to pull out the cake.

- Fill tunnel with desired filling (opposite page).

- Replace top and glaze.

CHOCOLATE
FILLING & GLAZE

LEMON FILLING
& CITRUS GLAZE

SHERBET FILLING
& CITRUS GLAZE

Pick a Filling

A surprise center makes your Vanilla Bean Angel Food Cake even more awesome.

Sherbet Filling

Spoon 2½-3 cups raspberry sherbet (or any other sherbet or ice cream) into tunnel, mounding slightly. Replace cake top. Wrap securely and freeze overnight. Glaze before serving.

Lemon Filling

Beat ½ cup heavy whipping cream until it begins to thicken. Add ½ cup mascarpone cheese and 2 Tbsp. confectioners' sugar; beat until soft peaks form. Fold in one-third of a 10-oz. jar of lemon curd. Line tunnel bottom with 1 cup sliced fresh strawberries (patted dry); top with the mascarpone mixture, then the remaining lemon curd. Replace cake top; glaze and refrigerate at least 4 hours. Cover once the glaze sets.

Chocolate Filling

Microwave 1 cup 60% cacao bittersweet chocolate baking chips, ¼ cup heavy whipping cream and 1 Tbsp. amaretto on high 60-90 seconds or until chocolate is melted, stirring every 30 seconds until smooth. Cool to lukewarm (90°), about 25 minutes. Beat ¾ cup heavy whipping cream with 1 Tbsp. sugar until soft peaks form. Fold into lukewarm chocolate; fill tunnel. Replace cake top. Glaze and refrigerate at least 4 hours. Cover once glaze sets.

CLEAN, ORGANIZE & SHOP
LIKE A BOSS

[A kitchen you love to use is one of the best gifts you can give yourself. In this special chapter, be inspired by our top ideas.]

CLEAN [You don't need harsh chemicals or pricey cleaners to get a sparkling kitchen you're proud to use. Just use our easy recipes and follow our favorite hacks.]

Multipurpose Cleaner

1. In a spray bottle, combine 3 cups water, ⅓ cup rubbing alcohol, 1 tsp. clear household ammonia, 1 tsp. liquid dish soap and ½ tsp. lemon juice. Shake well before each use.
2. Spray onto countertops, kitchen appliances and fixtures, and tile or painted surfaces. Wipe down with a clean cloth or damp sponge.

Dish Soap

1. Grate a bar of pure soap, such as Ivory, on the coarse side of a kitchen grater to measure ¼ cup.
2. Place 1½ cups hot water in a pitcher; stir in soap flakes with a fork until dissolved. Cool for 5 minutes, then stir in ¼ cup glycerin (available at drugstores) and ½ tsp. lemon oil.
3. Cool. Use the fork to break up any congealed parts, then pour the liquid into a squirt bottle. Use 2-3 tsp. per sink or dishpan of hot water to hand-wash dishes.

Hardwood Floor Cleaner

1. In a large saucepan, boil 1 qt. water. Remove from heat and add 6 peppermint tea bags. Let steep for 2 hours.
2. Pour tea in a mop pail. Add 1 qt. white vinegar, 2 Tbsp. baby oil and 1 tsp. liquid dish soap (commercial or homemade). Stir to combine.
3. Dip a clean mop into cleaning solution, wring or squeeze it out, and clean house. The tannins in the tea attack dirt without damaging the floor finish.

Window & Glass Cleaner

Mix either 2 Tbsp. ammonia in 2 qts. warm water or 1 cup white vinegar in 1 qt. of water. Place in a spray bottle.

Furniture Polish

Combine equal parts vegetable oil and lemon juice. Mix well; pour into a spray bottle. Spray onto finished wooden surfaces, then polish with a soft cloth. Refrigerate up to 6 months.

Liquid Fabric Softener

Mix 2 cups each baking soda and white vinegar with 1 qt. water. Store in a plastic bottle with a lid. Add ¼ cup softener to laundry's final rinse cycle.

Homemade Dryer Sheets

Prepare liquid fabric softener in a wide container with a lid. Dip a washcloth into mixture; wring out. Add cloth to dryer with a load of damp clothes.

Hack Your Way to a Sparkling Kitchen

These tips from our Test Kitchen will make yours shine in no time!

Fridge Use equal parts white vinegar and water to wash both the interior and exterior, including the door gasket. Mix with baking soda to make a scrub if needed. Use undiluted vinegar to clean dust and grime atop the fridge, and to prevent mildew inside.

Oven Clean oven glass and easier spills with a simple paste made from baking soda and water. Use a scouring pad.

Microwave Heat a bowl of water with a squeeze of lemon juice in the micro for about 3 minutes. The steam allows for a quick and easy clean-up.

Dishwasher Noticing debris on your clean dishes or in your dishwasher? Pour a small bottle of white vinegar into an empty dishwasher. Then run it on the highest heat cycle. It will clean your dishwasher and help eliminate odors, too.

Sink Sanitize your sink after messy jobs. After washing with dish soap, spray the sink with undiluted rubbing alcohol, then wipe down with a paper towel.

Walls Clean painted walls with a mixture of 2 qts. water and ¼ cup chlorine bleach. Gently sponge onto walls to remove frying or cooking residue.

Floors Mop up tile and linoleum floors with a simple mix of ½ cup white vinegar and 1 gallon warm water. For stone and brick floors, use a full cup of vinegar.

Cutting Boards Freshen their appearance and remove odors by sprinkling with salt, then rubbing with a lemon half.

Coffee Maker Fill the clean, empty coffeepot with 2 cups white vinegar and 1 cup water. Run a cycle and discard. Run a cycle of fresh water to remove any vinegar traces.

Blender Fill half full with warm water, then add a few drops of dishwashing liquid. Close the lid, give it a whir, and—voila!—clean blender, ready to rinse and reuse.

Chrome Quickly polish chrome faucets and fixtures with a fabric softener sheet. Rubbing alcohol, white vinegar or the inside of a lemon rind will do a good job, too.

Stainless Remove ugly water spots using a cloth dampened with rubbing alcohol. Polish away other marks with club soda or white vinegar.

Marble Remove food stains with a paste of baking soda mixed with equal parts water and lemon juice. Rub paste in, rinse with water and wipe dry.

Glass Add a gorgeous shine by squeezing a fresh lemon over the surface, then rubbing with a clean cloth. Buff with a microfiber cloth or wad of newspaper.

Reviving Grimy Baking Pans

1. Sprinkle some baking soda on the pan. Follow that with hydrogen peroxide and another sprinkling of baking soda. Let this mixture sit for at least 2 hours.

Note: Because this combination of soda and peroxide could be too harsh for some pans, do a test run before cleaning the entire pan, especially if it is made of a specialized material or has a coating of any kind.

2. Use a sponge to wipe away the homemade cleaner. Hard scrubbing usually isn't required. If stains remain, switch to a nonscratch scrubbing pad, try a second application of baking soda and hydrogen peroxide—or both. A little patience will lead to pans that look like new!

ORGANIZE

[No matter what size your kitchen may be, you can maximize its function and beautify the space with these organizational tricks. A well-organized kitchen is a joy to use!]

Grab and Go
Pull-out shelves let you grab cleaners quickly, while baskets corral sponges, scrubbers and smaller stuff.

Hang It Up
Add inexpensive hooks to the inside of a kitchen cabinet. Use them to store potholders, small tools and more when not in use. This will help you save precious drawer space.

Add a Rod
Self-adhering or magnetic towel rods add valuable real estate for towels. Consider a tension rod under the sink, excellent for hanging spray bottles. This takes advantage of often unused vertical space in a big cupboard.

Think Vertically

Tall cabinets are prone to wasted space up top. Utilize every square inch with the help of dish risers, undershelf baskets for bowls and mugs, and stackable containers for pantry staples. To keep small, frequently used items at your fingertips, give a two-tiered lazy Susan a whirl.

Free Up Cabinet Space Store herbs and spices in a kitchen drawer, where you can easily view the contents at a glance. Tiered racks are available that put your favorite spices on display. How best to organize? That's up to you. Some people like alphabetizing, while others prefer separating herbs and spices.

You'd be surprised how many dishes you can avoid dirtying by weighing your ingredients instead of measuring. Weighing works well for tracking your portions, too. Record the weights of your favorite pots, bowls, etc., and post this information inside a cupboard door.

Repurpose Jars: Mason jars are great for storing dried mixes, bulk spices and baking supplies. Save the lids from Parmesan shakers and you'll have a handy way to sprinkle and measure.

Slide and Seek: Slide-out shelves corral pots, pans and lids, and help you grab hard-to-reach cookware in the back of the cabinet without having to unload the whole thing.

File It: Use organizers designed especially for kitchen cabinets to keep baking sheets, lids and cutting boards neatly stored and easy to grab. Or, like our Test Kitchen, adapt economical, heavy-duty office equipment.

Get Hooked: (*facing page*) A simple pegboard from a home improvement store is easy to install and offers boundless opportunities for hanging go-to kitchen gear (and ingredients, too). The hooks are a cinch to shift whenever you need to adjust for more space.

SHOP

[Save both money and time when you're at the grocery store—and prep work at home—with our favorite shopping pointers. They'll help save your sanity, too.]

1. **Decide when you like to shop best.** Don't like crowds? Avoid shopping on Friday, Saturday or Sunday. The slowest days are Monday and Tuesday.

2. **Keep a running list handy in a prominent place in the kitchen.** As groceries start getting low, jot down what you need. Use the last of the macaroni? Running low on nutmeg? Put it on the list. Another alternative is to keep a list on your cellphone—or snap a picture of the list in case you end up at the store.

3. **Keep a well-stocked pantry** to ease meal planning. With the basics, you'll always have dinner options on hand.

4. **Stock up** on seasonal produce and sale items to Feed Your Freezer (p. 88).

5. **Review your coupon stash or mobile app** before you go shopping. Note any brands you want to buy.

6. **Kids in tow?** Use this trick to minimize lobbying. Include a couple of child-friendly snack and cereal options on your list. In the store, let the children decide which ones they'd like. Because they're participating, they're less likely to beg.

7. **Stick to the list.** Going off-list means spending money you didn't plan to.

8. **On the other hand,** if an item you'll use is on closeout or deeply discounted, load up on it! You can save serious money when you stock up.

9. **Shop the salad bar** to save money, potentially, on items like chicken strips, feta cheese, nuts and baby spinach. These foods are sometimes cheaper per pound here than on store shelves. The salad bar is also helpful for picking up precut veggies you need in small amounts for your recipes.

10. **The bulk section** is handy for buying small amounts of key items, such as spices, seeds, specialty grains and dried fruits.

PRO TIPS

The Well-Stocked Kitchen

Have a quick meal at the ready when you stock up on these foods:

• Quick-cooking meats: Boneless chicken, pork tenderloin, chops, ground meat, sausage, sirloin flank steaks, fish and shrimp.

• Frozen vegetables: Simply pour out the amount needed—no additional preparation is required.

• Pastas and rice mixes: These pantry staples have a long shelf life.

• Condiments: Ketchup, mustard, mayonnaise, salad dressings, salsa, taco sauce, soy sauce, stir-fry sauce and lemon juice add flavor. Personalize to suit your family's tastes.

• Fresh fruits and vegetables: They make for healthy snacks and side dishes. Ready-to-use salad greens are convenient.

• Dried herbs, spices, vinegars and seasoning mixes add lots of flavor and keep for months.

• Pasta sauces, olives, beans, broths, canned tomatoes, and canned tuna and soups are ideal to have on hand for a quick meal—and many of these are common recipe ingredients, too.

EQUIVALENT MEASURES

3 TEASPOONS	= 1 tablespoon		**16 TABLESPOONS**	= 1 cup
4 TABLESPOONS	= ¼ cup		**2 CUPS**	= 1 pint
5⅓ TABLESPOONS	= ⅓ cup		**4 CUPS**	= 1 quart
8 TABLESPOONS	= ½ cup		**4 QUARTS**	= 1 gallon

FOOD EQUIVALENTS

MACARONI	1 cup (3½ ounces) uncooked	= 2½ cups cooked
NOODLES, MEDIUM	3 cups (4 ounces) uncooked	= 4 cups cooked
POPCORN	3 cups (4 ounces) uncooked	= 8 cups popped
RICE, LONG GRAIN	1 cup uncooked	= 3 cups cooked
RICE, QUICK-COOKING	1 cup uncooked	= 2 cups cooked
SPAGHETTI	1 cup uncooked	= 4 cups cooked
BREAD	1 slice	= ¾ cup soft crumbs, ¼ cup fine dry crumbs
GRAHAM CRACKERS	7 squares	= ½ cup finely crushed
BUTTERY ROUND CRACKERS	12 crackers	= ½ cup finely crushed
SALTINE CRACKERS	14 crackers	= ½ cup finely crushed
BANANAS	1 medium	= ⅓ cup mashed
LEMONS	1 medium	= 3 tablespoons juice, 2 teaspoons grated zest
LIMES	1 medium	= 2 tablespoons juice, 1½ teaspoons grated zest
ORANGES	1 medium	= ¼-⅓ cup juice, 4 teaspoons grated zest

CABBAGE	1 head = 5 cups shredded		**GREEN PEPPER**	1 large = 1 cup chopped
CARROTS	1 pound = 3 cups shredded		**MUSHROOMS**	½ pound = 3 cups sliced
CELERY	1 rib = ½ cup chopped		**ONIONS**	1 medium = ½ cup chopped
CORN	1 ear fresh = ⅔ cup kernels		**POTATOES**	3 medium = 2 cups cubed
ALMONDS	1 pound = 3 cups chopped		**PECAN HALVES**	1 pound = 4½ cups chopped
GROUND NUTS	3¾ ounces = 1 cup		**WALNUTS**	1 pound = 3¾ cups chopped

EASY SUBSTITUTIONS

WHEN YOU NEED...		USE...
BAKING POWDER	1 teaspoon	½ teaspoon cream of tartar + ¼ teaspoon baking soda
BUTTERMILK	1 cup	1 tablespoon lemon juice or vinegar + enough milk to measure 1 cup (let stand 5 minutes before using)
CORNSTARCH	1 tablespoon	2 tablespoons all-purpose flour
HONEY	1 cup	1¼ cups sugar + ¼ cup water
HALF-AND-HALF CREAM	1 cup	1 tablespoon melted butter + enough whole milk to measure 1 cup
ONION	1 small, chopped (⅓ cup)	1 teaspoon onion powder or 1 tablespoon dried minced onion
TOMATO JUICE	1 cup	½ cup tomato sauce + ½ cup water
TOMATO SAUCE	2 cups	¾ cup tomato paste + 1 cup water
UNSWEETENED CHOCOLATE	1 square (1 ounce)	3 tablespoons baking cocoa + 1 tablespoon shortening or oil
WHOLE MILK	1 cup	½ cup evaporated milk + ½ cup water

[CATEGORY INDEX]

DESERTS

MAIN DISHES

SALADS

[ALPHABETICAL INDEX]